SATISFACTION

———— • ————

# Satisfaction

The Science of Finding
True Fulfillment

GREGORY BERNS, M.D., Ph.D.

HENRY HOLT AND COMPANY • NEW YORK

Henry Holt and Company, LLC
*Publishers since 1866*
175 Fifth Avenue
New York, New York 10010
www.henryholt.com

Henry Holt® and ■® are registered trademarks
of Henry Holt and Company, LLC.

Library of Congress Cataloging-in-Publication Data
Berns, Gregory.
    Satisfaction : The science of finding true fulfillment /
    Gregory Berns. — 1st ed.
        p.  cm.
    Includes index.
    ISBN-13: 978-0-8050-7600-4
    ISBN-10: 0-8050-7600-X
    1.   Satisfaction.   I. Title.
    BF515 . B47205
    155.9—dc22                        2005040259

Henry Holt books are available for special promotions
and premiums. For details contact: Director, Special Markets.

First Edition 2005

Designed by Victoria Hartman

Printed in the United States of America

1   3   5   7   9   10   8   6   4   2

For Kathleen

# CONTENTS

———•———

What do humans want? Forget about the usual suspects like sex, money, and status. Is there something more basic, a drive that trumps pleasure or pain or happiness—that, if understood, would provide the key to a lifetime of satisfying experiences?

Deep in your brain is a structure that sits at the crossroads of action and reward. Based on a decade of study, I have found that this region, which may hold the key to satisfaction, thrives on challenge and novelty. At first glance, challenge and novelty may seem like things to avoid, but they are the exact ingredients that make for a satisfying experience, and the evidence lies in the one place that matters most—your brain. Only in the past few years has medical technology in the form of magnetic resonance imaging—MRI—provided the hard data that make answers to these questions possible.

First, you must accept that satisfying experiences *are* difficult to achieve. Just compare how you feel after an hour of watching television, which requires no more effort than choosing which channel to view, with the way you feel after working out for an hour. Or look at hobbies, which may be complicated and challenging but which give great amounts of satisfaction. But these are trivial examples compared with the difficulties of work and life. I've watched many students come through my lab, and I've observed how they react to the formidable demands of obtaining a Ph.D. Graduate school, like many pursuits, is a long process without a clearly defined path to the end. Some rise to the challenge, others do not; for those who do, I have seen something deep and lasting emerge from their experience. It is not just satisfaction with a job well done, but the blossoming of a sense of purpose and the stoking of a fire in the belly to conquer more obstacles. The fire, though, is not in the belly. It is in the brain.

Which leads to a second assumption: the essence of a satisfying experience exists within your brain. Knowing where in the brain such a feeling comes from might make satisfaction more obtainable, and this knowledge could point the way toward living a life full of satisfying experiences. Not everyone will accept the primacy of the brain in satisfaction, but the feeling I am talking about—the sense of accomplishment following the completion of a challenging project or task—is just as real as emotions like happiness or sadness or anger. Ample evidence exists that those emotions arise in the brain. And with new data in hand about the biology of satisfaction, it is time for a serious look at where satisfaction comes from and how to get more of it.

Unlike some other emotions, satisfaction doesn't just fall in your lap. You have to create it for yourself, and doing so requires motivation. Until recently, most researchers assumed that some variation of the pleasure principle governed human motivation. Freud coined the phrase "pleasure principle," but the idea that life is composed of the pursuit of pleasure and the avoidance of pain goes back at least two thousand years. The pleasure principle is only one of many commonsense ideas about what humans want.

But it is wrong. Since the 1990s, neuroscientists were getting closer to cracking the riddle of satisfaction, and, so far, the answer differs significantly from that suggested by the pleasure principle.

Much of what is known about motivation has to do with the neurotransmitter dopamine, which, until the mid-1990s, many scientists thought of as the brain's pleasure chemical. While dopamine is released in response to pleasurable activities—like eating, having sex, taking drugs—it is also released in response to unpleasant sensations—like loud noises and electric shocks. Actually, dopamine is released prior to the consummation of both good and bad activities, acting more like a chemical of anticipation than of pleasure. The most parsimonious explanation of dopamine's function suggests that it commits your motor system—your body—to a particular action. If this idea is correct, then satisfaction comes less from the attainment of a goal and more in what you must do to get there.

How do you get more dopamine flowing in your brain? Novelty. A raft of brain imaging experiments has demonstrated that novel events, because they challenge you to act, are highly effective at releasing dopamine. A novel event can be almost anything—seeing a painting for the first time, learning a new word, having a pleasant, or an unpleasant, experience—but the key factor is surprise. Your brain is stimulated by surprise because our world is fundamentally unpredictable. Like it or not, nature has given you a brain attuned to the world as it is. You may not always like novelty, but your brain does. You could almost say that your brain has a mind of its own.

Actually, there are many "minds" in your brain, each with its own set of desires. For instance, there is your mind as you work, your mind when you are at home, and your mind when you are enjoying a fine meal. At any given moment, only one mind is in control of your body, but the simple fact that you can hold competing thoughts in your head at the same time indicates that your other minds constantly vie for control too. When you encounter something novel, dopamine is released, setting off a biochemical cascade in your brain. The process is a little like hitting the reset button on a computer: your other minds, each with their own agenda, might strive to gain the upper hand after the reset. Dopamine is the catalyst for all this action.

Though I do not know how much choice we have in this matter, I have found that seeking out novel experiences keeps dopamine pumping, and I, for one, feel better for it. None of us has many dopamine neurons. From adolescence onward, the amount of dopamine in the brain declines at a steady rate. The evidence is spotty, but a use-it-or-lose-it philosophy probably applies to the brain as much as to the body. But how you use your brain is as important as what you use it for. Perhaps the best way to avoid slipping into the equivalent of a mild case of Parkinson's disease as you age is to keep your dopamine system humming like a well-tuned engine. The most effective way to do so is through novel, challenging experiences. The sense of satisfaction after you've successfully handled unexpected tasks or sought out unfamiliar, physically and emotionally demanding activities is your brain's signal that you're doing what nature designed you to do.

· · · ·

The novelty principle I've just described has been extrapolated from the observation of the way a nugget of neurons atop the brain stem functions. The more I have considered the implications of the principle, the more intrigued I have become by its potential to improve our lives. But this is one theory you can't exactly test in the laboratory.

So I began a quest to understand the experiences that give people satisfaction in novel ways. It is easy to take for granted the pleasure derived from obvious pursuits, like sex, food, and money. Digging below the transience of the pleasures these pursuits offer, I have found that great, even transcendent, experiences can arise if they are juxtaposed with novelty and challenge. But the lessons don't stop there. Less common pursuits, activities that go beyond mere challenges to dip into realms of pain and anguish, also bring satisfaction and, in turn, yield surprising insights into what humans want. You will be introduced to the worlds of brain stimulation, sadomasochism, and ultramarathoning—each of which opened my eyes yet wider to the depths of how people choose to live.

I have employed no formal method in deciding where my search for such experiences should begin or end. Naturally, I chose some activities of inherent interest to me, as I suspect I'm not so different from most people. We all have needs for companionship and for physical and intellectual challenges, and we all possess the desire to transcend our day-to-day existence. It is the way you meet these needs, especially in novel ways, that makes for a satisfying life.

I have also searched for new ways of thinking about the brain, because how the brain works tells us something crucial about being human. Science has increasingly developed its own genre of storytelling, a narrative that can be just as gripping as the plot of a good novel. Despite my preference for hard data, I've come to realize that data alone don't tell the whole story. Most researchers today believe that all the easy problems have been solved, and rare is the experiment that cuts to the heart of an outstanding scientific question. As a result, the techniques that my generation employs have become more and more complex. Most of the time, and perhaps no more so than in neuroscience, experiments fall short of definitiveness—a limitation that most scientists accept as part of their profession. A good story can fill the breach created by the ambiguity of experimental findings. The value of knowing the scientists behind their stories goes beyond the question of who owns bragging rights—understanding the meaning of an experiment often necessitates delving into the personalities behind them. It isn't a coincidence that some of the most interesting results in neuroscience have been discovered by people far more colorful than you might expect to find in a laboratory.

Above all else, I have found that knowing what you want is not merely an academic question. Everyone wants satisfaction. Some have found ways of attaining it; others have not, but in contrast to the image of a man retiring on the beach, a newspaper in one hand and a cold beer in the other, the most fulfilled people I meet don't sit still. For them, satisfaction and purpose have become the same thing.

Ultimately your actions define the arc of your life. To understand what you want, and why you want it, you must have some sense of how your brain is wired for action. Though I set out on this search in order to write this book, I have never forgotten that the stakes for the quest are high. In a world changing as rapidly as ours, the failure to act—to adapt to challenges in the workplace or in relationships—can lead to marginalization and bitterness. Understanding what you really want—your brain's need for novelty—can lead you to see life as more wondrous, and more surprising, than you could have ever imagined.

# SATISFACTION

———•———

# 1

## The Slave in the Brain

Read Montague knows how to get in your face. More often than not, he ends up being right, resulting in the rather predictable tendency to piss people off.

I first met Read in the early 1990s, at the Salk Institute in La Jolla, California. Since it was founded by Jonas Salk in the 1960s, the institute has always attracted the brightest and most creative biologists. Read was not exactly your standard newly minted Ph.D. Raised in Macon, Georgia, he landed at the Salk for a two-year postdoctoral stint in computational neuroscience.

Teatime at Salk was a quaint tradition, but it was also where the real science happened. At precisely three-thirty each afternoon, students and faculty members congregated for informal intellectual jousting. Regulars included the likes of Francis Crick; nonetheless, Read was unfazed. Taking teatime to a new level, he'd spin out differential equations on the chalkboard while explaining to Crick how nitric oxide was released from synapses and thus played a role in learning. On one occasion, Crick said he didn't believe Read's calculations. Read turned around and matter-of-factly said to the Nobel Prize winner, "Then you don't understand differential calculus."

Tea was served around a large circular table, and one afternoon, while Read was boasting about his college track exploits, someone challenged him to jump over the table, which was at least six feet in diameter. Read eyed it, no doubt calculating the various vectors of force and velocity necessary to clear the table, and then accepted the challenge. Fanfare was generated around the event, with innumerable bets placed. The table was moved into the expansive outside plaza of the institute. Almost the size of a football field, the plaza is an icon of modern architecture, with a thin trough of water flowing down its length, only to disappear over a ledge that appears suspended before the Pacific Ocean. The table was placed to one side of the trough, at about the fifty-yard line. A score of spectators dotted the sidelines, and a few hung over the Salk's parapets. Read backed up some twenty feet from the table, but his intended running start was immediately judged as a disqualifier. After a brief discussion among the de facto officials, it was agreed that he would be allowed to rock back and forth before he took off. Jumping up and down a few times, and then running in place for about ten seconds to warm up, Read quickly assumed a crouching posture a foot shy of the table. He then began to shadow his planned push-off with his right leg and left arm. In one fluid motion, he launched himself straight up over the table, pulling his knees to his chest, and then rotated them forward as he came down, his left heel barely clipping the far edge. After stumbling a step or two, he managed to stay on his feet and win the bet.

Read and I stayed in contact over the years. One late fall morning, while sitting at an IHOP in Atlanta, our favorite place to kick around theories, we hit upon the idea of doing a brain imaging experiment. At that time, Read was using computers to model the effects of dopamine on neurons, and I was using brain imaging to study reward and motivation. We were discussing some recent experimental findings about the biological basis of reward in the brain. Without warning, he threw down his pancake, splattering everything in the vicinity of his plate with maple syrup. Rivulets of syrup crept toward the edge of the table while, oblivious to the mess, Read sipped a glass of orange juice and pondered the latest results. Although I didn't know it at the time, we were about to embark on a series of experiments that would turn upside down everything I understood about what humans really want.

## Dopamine and the Striatum

Start with dopamine, which until recently has been thought of as a sort of pleasure chemical in the brain but turns out to do much more. Dopamine, a fairly simple molecule, is synthesized in a tiny group of neurons. Cells that make dopamine number roughly thirty thousand to forty thousand, accounting for less than one-millionth of all the neurons in the brain. But without dopamine, you would be unable to obtain any of the things you consider rewarding.

Dopamine neurons are found in two distinct groups in the brain. One group is clustered above the pituitary gland, the small fig-shaped structure dangling from the underside of the brain that secretes all kinds of hormones controlling various glands, such as the thyroid and adrenals, as well as the hormones that regulate ovulation. The group of dopamine neurons linked to reward is found in the other group, located in the brain stem—a four-inch segment of nervous tissue that is the transition zone between the brain and the spinal cord. The brain stem is a compact area through which a great deal of information flows; the brain stem also houses many small collections of specialized neurons. Dopamine cells are one such collection.

A neurotransmitter like dopamine, however, does nothing without a place to go. Like a key and the lock it opens, neurotransmitters have a special relationship to the receptors on which they act, and the part of the brain with the densest concentration of dopamine receptors is the *striatum*. If you make an upside-down U with your thumb and forefinger, you will have a general idea of the size and shape of the striatum. A pair of these arches straddles either side of the brain stem in just about the geographic center of your skull.

The striatum acts like the Grand Central Terminal of your brain, meaning it receives trains of neuronal information from all over your brain but it cannot accommodate them all at once. Most of this information comes from the frontal lobes, which perform many functions. More than any other part of the brain, the frontal lobes are necessary for the preparation of action, including any form of physical movement, eye movement, speech, reading, and internal thought—in short, everything that you do and everything that you can imagine doing. Because of the funneling of this information through the striatum, as in the real Grand Central Terminal, only a few actions make it through at any given moment. What gets through has a lot to do with dopamine. Dopamine momentarily stabilizes the activity coming through the striatum—in effect, deciding which train continues through the station.[1] In practical terms, dopamine commits your motor system to a particular action, chosen from the hundreds of possibilities rattling around your cortex.

Considering how small a piece of real estate they stake out, dopamine and the striatum wield an enormous amount of control over human behavior. If you lose a chunk of your brain's cortex similar in size to the striatum, you probably would not even notice. But blow out your dopamine system, as happens in Parkinson's disease, or damage your striatum, as in Huntington's disease, and in a matter of minutes you feel the devastation. Without dopamine flowing in the striatum, you will not be able to command your movements with any precision, if at all, even though every other part of your motor system is fine; moreover, your sense of purpose—of being able to identify what you wish to do and how you will do it—will be thoroughly derailed.

There is another word that describes this process of commitment—motivation. When you are motivated, you decide on a course of action; and when you commit to something, you become motivated to see it through. Motivation and commitment are two facets of the same process, with dopamine acting as the catalyst that begins the process. When dopamine dumps into the striatum, it commits the train of action to a particular track. But what causes dopamine to be released in the first place? That was the question Read and I pondered over pancakes and orange juice.

## Under the Scanner

The experiment we were planning, which would take place on the striatum of humans, was based on some decade-old experiments with monkeys. We hoped that our experiment would clarify what the human brain takes as its reward, how this biological process determines what you want, and how you go about getting it.

Wolfram Schultz, a Swiss neuroscientist at the University of Fribourg, had been measuring the activity of striatal neurons in monkeys as he gave them various types of rewards. It was his results that caused Read to drop the pancake. When Schultz's monkeys received a small drop of fruit juice on their tongues (which they apparently enjoyed), their striatal neurons fired in a brief burst of activity. But when Schultz preceded the juice with a neutral cue, like a lightbulb turning on, the striatal neurons stopped firing to the juice and began firing to the light—the earliest event that predicted something pleasant.[2] This was a startling discovery, for there is nothing inherently good about a light, which meant that the striatum did not just signal reward but rather the *expectation* of reward. Mere expectation could be highly motivating to monkeys—and to humans.

"Did you see Schultz's latest result?" Read asked. "Looks pretty solid for confirming the dopamine prediction error model."

"But they're monkeys," I said. "It takes Schultz six months to train a single monkey, and then he writes a paper with what, maybe two monkeys? It takes too long." I cut into my eggs, and the yolks oozed into my toast. "Besides, they're monkeys. We gotta figure this stuff out in humans."

"What do humans find rewarding?" Read asked rhetorically.

"Sex. Food. Money."

"I don't think we should use money," Read said, shaking his head. "It's too abstract."

"We can't do sex in the scanner," I said. "I doubt that my ethics board would approve of it, and our friends in Washington are not too fond of using public money to finance sex research."[3]

Read sopped up the last pool of syrup with a piece of pancake and held the golden chunk between us. "Which leaves food."

I stared at the syrupy morsel on the end of his fork and tried to imagine serving pancakes to someone in an MRI scanner. "Too much artifact. People chewing and swallowing in the scanner? Their heads would be moving all over the place, and we'd never be able to pin down the signal to the striatum."

We sipped our coffee and pondered the dilemma. Read eyed his now empty glass of orange juice and said, "Why don't we use juice?"

"Like Schultz's monkeys?"

Read began to get pumped up. "Yeah. It's perfect. We'll just duplicate the Schultz experiment in humans. Certainly we can deliver some type of juice to people in the scanner."

"I guess we could rig up some tubing and a mouthpiece and pump juice into people's mouths while we scanned them."

Read popped the last piece of pancake into his mouth and said, "Let's do it."

. . .

Shortly after our epiphany, we realized that almost no human data existed about where in the brain fruit juice might be processed. For our first experiment, we decided to squirt a drop of Kool-Aid onto the tongue of each participant, but as a control condition, we would sometimes substitute plain water for the Kool-Aid. The key manipulation in the experiment would be whether the Kool-Aid and water squirts would be delivered predictably—that is, alternating with each other at a fixed interval of time, or whether the Kool-Aid and water would be delivered unpredictably, in random order and random intervals. If human brains reacted the way those in Schultz's monkeys did, then the unpredictable squirts would be most rewarding and would result in the most activation of the striatum.

It is not possible to measure dopamine directly in the human brain—at least not in a live person. Although one can map the locations of receptors for dopamine with positron emission tomography (PET), the technology does not yet exist for measuring actual dopamine release in humans. With PET, you inject a person with a radioactive tracer that binds to certain receptors in the brain, in this case dopamine receptors. A ring of detectors placed around the person's head picks up the radiation as it is emitted from the brain, and a computer determines the source and intensity of the radiation. In this way, PET lets you see the locations and concentration of dopamine receptors in different parts of the brain—but that is all it can show you. With PET, you get a static snapshot of the dopamine system and not, as your brain experiences it, a moment-by-moment picture of the fluctuations in dopamine activity. The next best thing to PET is an indirect method based on magnetic resonance imaging. Using a technique called functional MRI, or fMRI, Read and I could measure changes in blood flow to the brain regions where dopamine is released, and we could see it happening on a timescale of seconds, instead of the minutes or hours that PET requires. By looking at blood flow changes in response to various types of stimuli—Kool-Aid, for instance—we could make educated guesses about what might be happening with dopamine.

•   •   •

Read did not look too happy to enter the MRI machine. MRI scanners are such a specialized piece of medical technology that they require their own room. About the size and weight of a semitrailer cab, the main part of the MRI is a hollow tube surrounded by miles of superconducting wire, chilled to −269 degrees Celsius (−452° F) in a bath of liquid helium. The electrical current running through the wire generates a magnetic field thirty thousand times stronger than Earth's, making the MRI so strong that it can grab metallic objects, like ballpoint pens, and turn them into deadly projectiles. You can forget about any electronic equipment. Not only are electronics affected by the MRI's magnetic field, but the same detectors that pick up signals from inside the brain also pick up any stray electrical fields in the vicinity of the scanner. Entering the scanner room, let alone the scanner, is to set foot into a place of reverence—a temple in which the worshipper must be purged of all metal.

Even though magnetic fields should not be perceivable by any human sense, each time I have gone into the scanner, a heaviness has fallen over me, faintly reminiscent of a recurring childhood nightmare the specifics of which I can never recall except for the sensation of being weighed down. I looked at Read and said, "We never do experiments that we don't try on ourselves first."

He agreed.

"Piece of cake," I said. "I'll go first."

The patient table is about one foot wide and eight feet long and projects out from the inside of the scanner. After I had hoisted myself up to the narrow platform, my assistant, Megan, handed me earplugs to muffle the hundred-decibel noise that would soon emanate from the scanner. I lay down, and she secured a Velcro strap across my forehead to limit any movement. The head coil, which was nothing more than a fancy radio antenna resembling a birdcage with the bottom removed, was snapped in place around my head. Megan placed a baby pacifier in my mouth. Two vinyl tubes poked through the pacifier and rested on the back of my tongue. Laughing at the sight of her boss sucking on a pacifier, Megan asked, "Ready?"

I grunted and gave a thumbs-up.

She pressed a button on the scanner's control panel, and a red laser beam shined onto my forehead. Megan nudged the table into the scanner a few inches, using the laser lines to align my head. She smiled and said, "In you go."

After another button activated the gantry motors, the table slid with a soft whirring into the scanner. I opened my eyes and stared at the inside of the bore, a couple of inches from my nose. Heaviness fell upon me, and I closed my eyes.

From a tiny intercom, I could make out Read's voice above the static. "We're going to give you some test squirts. Wiggle your feet if you're ready."

I wiggled my feet and waited.

A cool liquid flowed across my tongue. I couldn't tell what it was. Lying on my back, with the drops creeping toward the back of my throat, I began to swallow. Water. Another liquid drifted across my tongue. It was sweet. Kool-Aid. I swallowed again, and it felt nice. The heaviness was lifted.

Read's voice again, "Here we go!"

A few mechanical clicks came from somewhere deep in the scanner, like acorns falling on a roof. Without warning, the scanning sequence began. The gattling of what sounded like a machine gun startled me, and I momentarily arched off the table.

Liquids kept dripping onto my tongue. Sometimes water; sometimes Kool-Aid. I lost track of the order in which they were coming, but each time one hit my tongue, the coolness transported me to childhood summers of lemonade stands and left me with a tingling feeling in my belly. I was getting high on Kool-Aid.

And then it was over.

The scanner table slid me out of the metal sarcophagus, and I stared into what now appeared to be Megan's angelic face. Read, hovering behind her, asked me, "How was it?"

"Amazing. It was a rush. I think we've tapped into something very primitive in the brain. Something powerful."

Indeed we had. Just to be sure, we eventually scanned twenty-five volunteers, twice the usual number of subjects in a brain imaging experiment. Their striata lit up like Christmas trees to both the Kool-Aid and the water squirts, but only when they were unpredictable. Curiously, almost no one realized that sometimes the squirts were predictable and at other times they were not. Our findings meant that the human striatum, and by implication the dopamine system, was most responsive to novel, unpredictable rewards.[4]

### What Is Reward?

The results raised a knotty question about the biological nature of reward. Whatever you do, from working at a job to reading a book, you do with some expectation of reward. The reward doesn't need to be tangible, like money; it can be as simple as the feeling of satisfaction from a job well done. I can think of few activities that are undertaken without any expectation of reward. Even things that you know will be unpleasant, like going to the doctor, still have a reward—the knowledge that you are doing something good for your health. But where precisely in the chain of actions that make up your daily activities is the reward for doing them? Put a different way, what is the primary source of your motivation? It's not as if you get to a certain point in time and say, "I am done. I have attained all my rewards." Though you may wish for that, and dream one day that it may occur, that doesn't make it so.

The answer to this question is, I think, to be found in the striatum. No other brain region is better positioned to integrate the planning of actions with potential rewards. Because the striatum is where dopamine converges with information from the cortex, the striatum is *the* key structure in which your motivations get mapped into actions. When, using fMRI, Read and I peered into the striatum, we found a clue as to how this mixing process occurs and, indirectly, a window into the nature of human motivation.

The determination of what exactly dopamine is doing in the striatum has profound implications for understanding reward and motivation. Dopamine is a kind of chemical reward for the brain, especially the striatum, so determining the conditions under which dopamine is released may tell us indirectly how to get satisfaction. If dopamine is released in direct response to pleasurable things, then dopamine *is* the biological basis for Freud's pleasure principle. But if dopamine is released in advance of the reward—as a motivator— then there must be a more expansive definition of reward—one that includes the process of committing to an action as a form of reward itself.[5]

In our experiment, squirts of Kool-Aid and water constituted reward. Our subjects didn't have to *do* anything to get this reward; we determined the flow of fluids through the pacifiers. But our participants did have to do something to consummate the reward.

They had to swallow. Because our experiment was centered on oral stimuli, the act of swallowing became the only possible way to harvest the nominal rewards offered. If the participants hadn't swallowed, the liquids would have dribbled uselessly out of the corners of their mouths, depriving them of the sometimes sweet taste and refreshment they provided. As each drop hit their tongues, they committed their motor systems to the act of spitting it out or swallowing it. The need to commit rendered both the Kool-Aid and the water important to the brain, whether the person liked one or the other.

## The Need for Novelty

Although we found that the striatum responded more to unpredictable rewards than to predictable ones, we didn't know whether this meant that unpredictable squirts were more pleasurable than predictable ones or whether the unpredictability rendered swallowing more important because the subjects couldn't prepare for it. Either way, unpredictability was the key factor. The brain, particularly the striatum, seems to care most about what it can't predict.

Predictability is, I think, what every animal wants; by this I mean predictability in the sense of the skill of being able to foresee, and not in the sense of a quality or description of one's environment. If you can predict what will happen in the future, even if it is just a few seconds away, then you have a substantial advantage over someone who can't make such a prediction. Prediction equals survival. Many aspects of the world we inhabit are predictable. Material objects, like rocks, oceans, and mountains, don't appear and disappear. Even an animal, once it has established the locations of its landmarks, doesn't need to relearn them every day.

But just because the physical attributes of our environment are stable doesn't mean that the world itself is. If you never encountered another person or animal, you could master your environment to a high degree. All you would have to do is learn to anticipate seasonal changes. Indeed, this naturalist way of thinking has been held up by some as a sort of ideal way to live, tracing back to Thoreau and Epicurus.[6] If you suddenly found yourself alone in this world, your life would be pretty simple. Thoreau attempted to live this way, holing up for two years on Walden Pond, but the fact is he spent more time at the pub down the road than he cared to admit. Even Thoreau needed the company of friends.

Although we would like to predict events in the world, our ambitions are more or less thwarted by the fact that we must share the world with other people. How is it, for example, that you can live with another human being for your entire life and still not know what that person is thinking? Because the physical manifestation of thought is so sparse. No matter how well you know another person, you can never be sure of what he or she is going to do. Of course, this makes for an unpredictable, if exciting, existence, for no other animal has a social structure as complex as humans'. I think it is for this reason that our brains have expanded as much as they have—so that we can predict how one another will behave.

If you believe that the world is unpredictable because we live in it with other people, then a straightforward way to counteract such unpredictability is to motivate humans to better their predictions. You see immediately how such a drive could lead to an evolutionary advantage, and, in the social realm, how learning to predict one another's behavior patterns, imperfect as these forecasts might be, could lead to mating with the most fit members of the opposite sex. The stronger the drive to predict, the more an individual will learn about how the world and its inhabitants operate, resulting in reproductive success and the transmission of such a drive to one's offspring.

The drive to predict leads to a single outcome in a fundamentally unpredictable world—the need for novelty. I have come to understand novelty as the one thing that we all want.

. . .

One way to pin down novelty is through its relationship with information. Novel events, when they occur, contain a great deal of information that you don't already know. In the 1940s, Claude Shannon, an engineer at Bell Labs, realized that information could be measured by the degree to which something was surprising. To a first approximation, the information contained in an event is inversely proportional to the probability of that event happening.[7] Novel events, by definition, are uncommon, and therefore informative. Information, however, does not necessarily bring with it meaning. The value of information, as opposed to the quantity, can be measured by the extent to which a piece of information reduces our uncertainty about the world.

Because we enter the world in a state of maximal uncertainty, the behaviors of a newborn are hardwired—including the desire to learn and explore the world. But to survive, and ultimately reproduce, we must somehow internalize those properties of the world that we need to understand. The drive to make better predictions leads naturally to the internalization of information; at the same time, we know that our predictions will never be perfect. We will always have some uncertainty; moreover, we don't want to waste mental resources processing random facts that are of no use to us. How does the brain decide what is important? The striatum plays a key role.

The striatum is where the interaction between the individual and the environment happens. Because of the density of information flowing through it, the elements of this interaction are boiled down into a highly concentrated form, and that is why the striatum is critical to an active life. If, for example, you do something at which you are highly practiced, then you have little opportunity to

encounter something novel or unexpected, so dopamine and satisfaction may be low. But when you do something that takes you
beyond what you have done before, you are in unknown territory
and novel information will flow into your striatum, pumping out
dopamine, which in turn forces you to act on the information. The
release of dopamine in response to novel information is the essence
of a satisfying experience and kick-starts the motivational system.
Beyond the warm feeling of dopamine itself, however, the effect of
novelty that spurs its release changes the brain physically.

When a piece of information makes its way into the brain, it
doesn't just lodge in some memory bank. It alters the brain at a
molecular level, which is amazing if you think about it. How is it
that something as abstract as ink on a piece of paper, or photons
emanating from a television, can move proteins around in the neurons of your brain? Your brain transforms information into a physical manifestation of neuronal firing and merges it with other bits
of information in your head; at the level of DNA, dopamine and
other neurotransmitters cause new proteins to be synthesized.
Although I didn't know it at the time Read and I began our experiment, some types of information are better than others at laying
down tracks in the brain.

## The Quest Begins

Months after the Kool-Aid experiment was published, I met Read
to plan a follow-up experiment on reward. This time the national
mood—not to mention my own—had changed and the uncertainty
of what had now become a post–9/11 world weighed heavily
upon us.

Instead of getting right down to planning a new experiment, we
reminisced about Kool-Aid, which seemed to have happened in a
different life.

"You really didn't want to go in that scanner," I joked.

"Sure I did," he replied. "I just don't like enclosed spaces. Besides, I don't back down from a challenge."

Although we both eventually went under the scanner, we never included our own data in the published results. Because the entire experiment depended on the relative difference between predictable and unpredictable stimuli, and because we designed the sequence of stimuli, there really wasn't anything unpredictable about it to us. We did it more in an effort to debug the experiment and to get some sense of what the subjective experience was like. The latter aspect never makes it into scientific publications, but subjective experience should not be underestimated when interpreting cold, hard data.

"You know," Read said, "your striatum was on fire."

It was true. I had had one of the largest striatal activations of the people we studied. Scientifically, this was meaningless. There is so much variation in fMRI activity from person to person that nobody knows how to interpret individual responses, though it is tempting to ascribe some functional meaning to more striatal activity or less. It is just a hunch, but an individual's striatal activity might tell us something about his desire for novelty-seeking. Eventually we would find evidence for this idea, but that will have to wait for later.

If, as I've argued, humans have this drive to predict how the world works, then novel information of the type brought on by shocking events—like earthquakes or plane crashes—might be expected to induce in people two different effects. One is to hunker down and create a cocoon of predictability. The other is to trigger the desire for *more* information—an exploratory response. If the degree of activity in an individual's striatum determines which response will be sought, stability or novelty, then my fMRI results put me squarely in the novelty-seeking category.

I am not saying that individual preferences for novelty-seeking are hardwired, although there is some genetic evidence to suggest that this may be the case.[8] It is more likely that you have a range of behaviors in response to unexpected information, and that depending upon specific circumstances, you may gravitate toward seeking more novelty from the world or retreating into a more controllable environment. The striatum, however, remains the key. The more a piece of information activates your striatum, the more probable it is that you will act to find out more about it.

In the year since we had started the Kool-Aid experiments, I had changed. Maybe it was 9/11. Maybe it was my two young children. But my striatum was firing on all cylinders, and the need for novelty was beating out a competing drive to build a level 4 biohazard shelter in my basement. It stoked my resolve to figure out what humans want—what motivates people and exactly where in the brain the motivation that results in satisfaction resides.

I am sure that a big part of my resolve was the desire, probably innate, to provide an advantage to my children. I do not discount the evolutionary advantage that a drive for novelty gives. People who seek out information about the world get more goodies (or die trying), and they pass their wisdom on to their children, who, in turn, have an advantage over the kids of their less inquisitive neighbors. Far from curiosity killing the cat, the need for novelty has made us who we are—intelligent, curious, and constantly seeking the next new thing.

# 2

## For the Love of Money

Not long after Read and I finished our Kool-Aid experiment, an interest in the links between brain reward and financial reward developed among both neuroscientists and economists. Money, after all, is a prime motivator of human behavior. Historically, economists have assumed that the way in which people use money says something about their wants and preferences. The further assumption that people behave rationally—that is, consistently—with regard to their wants makes economic forecasts possible. But these assumptions strain credulity. People might behave rationally around money sometimes, but certainly not all the time. You will find, among the few people who believe in the rational human, financial forecasters who use economic models that depend on this assumption. Nevertheless, the marriage of neuroscience and economics has given birth to the field of *neuroeconomics*, which holds out hope for better understanding the brain reward system, which in turn might someday explain a host of economic anomalies, ranging from stock market bubbles to why people play the lottery.[1]

The last time I played the multistate lottery was on a deliciously humid summer day in Atlanta. I had joined a crowd of people in a gas station parking lot. Someone's car stereo thumped out a gut-churning hip-hop bass, and the crowd started grooving to the backbeat. As we inched toward the entrance of the convenience store, I saw a well-dressed man, wearing linen slacks and a knit shirt that clung a little too closely to his chest, pour out of his Lexus and join the festive throng to buy a lottery ticket. Sure, the jackpot had reached $200 million, but what possessed this varied group of people to spend money in the hopes of striking it rich when we each had a greater chance of being hit by lightning?

I asked Lexus man how many tickets he was buying.

"A hundred," he said cheerily.

That was a lot of tickets, even at $1 each. From outward appearances, he didn't seem to be lacking financially; then again, I didn't need the money either, so why should I bother? The answer to this question strikes to the heart of everything good and bad about money.

Because of the ridiculous odds of winning, playing the lottery is a quintessentially irrational activity; why anyone—those who need the dollar they spend on their ticket, and those who do not—would choose to do so says something about what humans find satisfying. Lotteries are a great place to start dissecting what humans want, because they dramatize, in a single event, two of the most potent motivators: risk and money. Risk, because of its relationship with the unknown, is tied to the need for novel information, but money itself is a different story. Understanding what people will do for money, and taking that idea farther by exploring financial motivation as visualized in the brain, casts a new light on the nature of satisfying experiences.

## The Hedonic Treadmill

Because a lottery winner is declared in a single day (as opposed to fortunes that accrue gradually), lotteries are ideal events for testing theories about the immediate effects of money. The most obvious question is whether winning the lottery makes a person happier, or more satisfied, and in what demonstrable way. Of course, many would like to believe that the lottery is some sort of gateway to a better life, even though it has been surprisingly difficult to prove that this is the case.

The first serious study of lottery winners occurred in 1978, when Philip Brickman, a social psychologist at Northwestern University, tried to determine whether winning the lottery made people happier. Brickman, along with his colleagues Dan Coates and Ronnie Janoff-Bulman, tracked down, in the state of Illinois, twenty-two winners of between $50,000 and $1 million. They asked the winners a series of questions designed to assess both their overall happiness and the happiness they obtained from everyday pleasures. For the measure of overall happiness, the lottery winners were asked to rate how happy they were at the moment, how happy they were before winning, and how happy they expected to be in a couple of years. As a measure of everyday pleasures, the winners were asked to rate how much they enjoyed seven different activities: talking with a friend, watching television, eating breakfast, hearing a funny joke, getting a compliment, reading a magazine, and buying clothes.

When Brickman compared the responses of the lottery winners with those of people who hadn't won the lottery, there was no significant difference in their current levels of happiness. The answer was clear. Winning the lottery did not make people happier. Moreover, the lottery winners reported significantly *less* pleasure from their seven daily activities than did their less financially secure neighbors.[2]

These findings alone would have rocked the field of social

psychology, but Brickman's remarkable gift as an observer of human behavior brought him to the brink of another significant insight. In addition to surveying lottery winners, he went on to ask the same questions of people who had experienced an equally surprising, but this time tragic, event. In effect, Brickman was asking, "How would it feel to do the opposite of winning the lottery?" Brickman had in mind men and women who, as the result of an accident, became either quadriplegic or paraplegic. Although the accident victims rated their present happiness somewhat lower than the control subjects, they also rated their future happiness no differently from the way the controls did, nor were the victims and controls any different in the amount of pleasure they experienced from everyday activities.

Both the lottery winners and the accident victims had experienced a sudden change in fortune, yet they both adapted to their circumstances, finding themselves surprisingly close to where they had begun in terms of happiness. It was a startling discovery, for it seemed to prove that happiness is relative, marked only by changes from the recent past. Forget about how much or how little you had; what matters is when something as significant as your finances or physical life is altered. For better or worse, we all seem destined to adapt to whatever life throws at us. Brickman noted, "Even as we contemplate our satisfaction with a given accomplishment, the satisfaction fades, to be replaced finally by a new indifference and a new level of striving."[3] This constant adaptation condemns all of us to live on a *hedonic treadmill*, as Brickman described it, whose revolutions cause us to seek out higher levels of reward just to maintain the same level of subjective pleasure.

In fairness, the data on lotteries are not all negative. Using survey questions of well-being, a British study of financial windfalls, from either winning the lottery or receiving an inheritance, found that, in a statistical sense, 50,000 pounds (about $75,000) increased well-being slightly but significantly. Because each of the windfalls studied occurred within one year of the survey, the authors were unable to make any conclusions about the length of time such improvements in well-being might last. They did venture to say that extrapolating the improvement in well-being from modest windfalls leads to the conclusion that it would take about $2 million to convert the unhappiest person into the happiest.[4] One of the authors used the same approach in the United States, this time contrasting happiness produced by money with that produced by sex. By combining measures of income and well-being with data on the frequency with which Americans have sex, the authors concluded that having sex once a week could raise happiness by about the same amount as $50,000 of additional yearly income.[5]

With different groups coming to different conclusions about the effects of money on well-being, what is the answer? Another study, one that examined the relationship of materialism to well-being, revealed that cultures that place a higher level of importance on money tend to have lower levels of well-being. This inverse relationship also holds true at the individual level—the more materialistic a person is, the less happy he or she is.[6] And therein lies the answer to the paradox of the lottery. At any given income level, it seems that people who play the lottery tend to place more importance on money than those who don't. Because they play the lottery in the first place, the winners are probably more materialistic than nonplayers, and therefore less likely to be happy with the result.

## Havana

Although lotteries are great for measuring the psychological effects of instant wealth, winning remains a rarity, and so we must look elsewhere for general principles about money and well-being. The field of neuroeconomics, which might be expected to take an intelligent crack at these questions, continues to pick up momentum, with growing numbers of economists and neuroscientists seeing the value of the two disciplines. In particular, neuroeconomics has the potential to solve the lurking mental problem of bad judgment.

Modern psychiatry focuses on symptoms, like feeling sad, anxious, or irritable. But those feelings are only a small part of the story of being human, and, as I have learned from economists, what matters more than what you say is what you do. The simple maxim that actions speak louder than words has not penetrated deeply enough into the practice of psychiatry, conducted as it is in grave tones and deep chairs, all the while hyperoccupied with the analysis of mental distress. How many shrinks know what their patients do once they leave the office? With neuroeconomics becoming the hot new field and editors at the major scientific journals clamoring for submissions, I thought it was the right time to introduce the field to some fellow academic psychiatrists. I received that opportunity in Cuba, perhaps the strangest of all places for this subject.

While the government of the United States tightly regulates travel by its citizens to Cuba, there exists a provision in the rules of the U.S. Office of Foreign Assets Control—OFAC—that allows academic professionals to attend conferences in Cuba under a "general license." At least in theory, the provision still exists. Just before OFAC reinterpreted who was eligible to travel to Cuba, fifty psychiatrists and neurobiologists gathered for a three-day conference with our Cuban counterparts at the Hotel Nacional, the fanciest hotel in Havana. The conference was to be an international exchange of ideas on the biology of mental illness, but it turned out to be much more.

· · ·

I stepped off the 737 onto a tarmac worn down by years of Caribbean sun and rain, weeds poking through cracks everywhere. A stocky, dark-skinned woman with a head like a praying mantis welcomed us to Cuba. She escorted our group to a holding area in a bland concrete terminal of 1960s-era Soviet design and then introduced herself as Caridad, our guide. A trio of armed soldiers kept a watchful eye on us as Caridad, who spoke in accented but perfect English, took charge.[7]

An hour passed before everyone's documents were in order; we were soon on our way through the streets of Havana. Caridad pointed out the major cultural sights—the Capitolio and the Plaza de la Revolución, where a large obelisk to José Marti sits opposite a mural of Che Guevara, two of the major figures in Cuban history. We then headed down the Malecón toward our hotel, where our hosts were waiting for us.

The Malecón is a broad waterfront boulevard, arcing for miles in an east-west direction to hug the Straits of Florida in a welcoming embrace. Big-finned cars—Packards, DeSotos, and Bel Airs— chugged along the street, their male drivers sometimes stopping in the middle of traffic to admire a particularly hot Latin beauty. On the other side of the Malecón, palatial town homes leaned against one another, propping one another up and keeping the whole waterfront from collapsing like a chain of dominoes. Parts of Art Deco facades lay as rubble in the street. But even in the midst of the decay, the Malecón was stunning to behold—a monument to the Cuban love of life that, although more visible in decades past, was still very much alive.

I walked into the ballroom of our hotel, but not before paying my respects to the faded black-and-white images adorning the walls of the foyer. Hemingway. Sinatra. Churchill. On one side of the ballroom, the Cuban scientists sat in a stately tableau. On the other, the Americans had arranged themselves in a huddle. The groups were mixing about as well as oil and water, and the reception began to resemble a high school dance. One of my American colleagues gave a conspiratorial nod, motioning me to the bar next to the ballroom. I shook a few hands and slipped away.

He handed me a Cohiba—arguably the best of Cuban cigars.

The last time I had smoked a cigar, my evening had ended hunched over a toilet bowl. Then again, I was in Cuba.

The tobacco smelled fresh, and when I drew on it, a sweet smoke drifted upward, filling the room with traces of mahogany and bergamot. Alas, I did not have time to revel in my newfound pleasure, for soon it was time for dinner. We piled into the bus and headed off toward Habana Vieja—the Old City.

## Happiness and Subjective Well-Being

Caridad stepped off the bus in front of us and escorted me and my American colleagues into El Floridita, one of Hemingway's favorite watering holes in Havana.

"Where is everyone?" I asked Caridad.

"What do you mean? Everyone is here."

"No. The Cubans."

I couldn't read her expression. She was about to respond when a woman without any teeth interrupted us. A six-year-old girl with large eyes was clutching the woman's skirt. Caridad exchanged words with the woman, and they both laughed before the woman went away.

"What was that about?" I asked.

"Oh, nothing. She wanted money, but I gave her a joke instead," Caridad said. "You should go inside. They are seating your friends."

"But what about the others?"

Caridad looked down the street and said, very quietly, "After dinner. Now, go."

"You're not coming?"

"No."

I don't remember much about the meal because my thoughts were elsewhere. Much of what I had seen in our brief trips through the city confirmed my expectations about Cuba: a beautiful and historic port crumbling under the corruption of the Castro regime. Children played in the rubble, oblivious to their poverty, but there was something else—something not captured in the news that filters up to the United States. The people seemed happy. A stroll on the Malecón was nothing like a walk down an American street. Life—living—was palpable. Money, as I have said, makes new experiences easier to obtain, but nobody here had much money to speak of. Even if more people had wealth, the opportunities to spend it were limited. Maybe the equanimity that comes with widespread poverty mitigated the lack of opportunities that goes right along with it, but there are shades of poverty, too, and the question of how Cubans found happiness continued to nag at me.

· · ·

The lottery studies showed that sudden increases in wealth don't make people happier, but the interpretation of these results depends on what you mean by "happy." How do you measure happiness? Most economists have dismissed the question, though a bedrock of economic theory assumes that people make choices to improve their happiness. A few psychologists believe that happiness can be measured by asking people to rate their emotions. Since questions such as these require individuals to examine their feelings, a necessarily subjective process, the results have been dubbed subjective well-being, or subjective happiness, depending on how the questions are asked. The emotions of happiness and well-being differ in subtle ways from the feeling of being satisfied that I was seeking, but they are related in at least one important way. When you feel satisfied, your sense of well-being increases and you are happier. So it is worth exploring how happiness and well-being can be measured.

In the late 1990s, Sonja Lyubomirsky, a psychologist at the University of California, Riverside, developed a four-item questionnaire she called the general happiness scale. For each of the four items, Lyubomirsky had people rate themselves from 1 to 7. For example, the first item stated: *In general, I consider myself: 1—not a very happy person to 7—a very happy person.*[8] The second item asks the individual to appraise her happiness in comparison to her peers', and the third and fourth items ask the person to compare herself to a Pollyannaish and curmudgeonly type, respectively. The total happiness score is calculated as the average of the four items. The average score for adults in the United States is 5.6; the middle of the scale is 4.0. The disparity between the average of the population and the middle of the scale suggests that a majority of Americans consider themselves happier than their peers. But it is a mathematical impossibility for more than half of the populace to be above average.

Maybe Americans really are happier than other people, and perhaps it is against this fictive mass of unhappy foreigners that Americans choose to compare themselves. There is, in fact, some evidence for this, which I will get to shortly. Another, darker possibility is that Americans really aren't happier—but neither are they willing to admit it. Or perhaps the expectation of happiness is so deeply engrained in American culture (look no farther than the Declaration of Independence) that when a question like "How happy are you?" is asked, we hear it as, "How happy should I be?" and, in response, we shade the truth a little.

The general happiness scale is a relatively recent development, while measures of life satisfaction have been used for decades. Ed Diener, a psychologist at the University of Illinois, has been studying subjective well-being for over twenty years, and his satisfaction with life scale (SWLS) is used by many psychologists as a sort of global assessment of one's station in life. In fact, many researchers favor using life satisfaction as a proxy for subjective well-being because the phrasing of the questions in the satisfaction scale forces a global appraisal of the respondent's life. The first item in Diener's SWLS states: *In most ways, my life is close to ideal: 1—strongly disagree to 7—strongly agree.* The fifth item states: *If I could live my life over, I would change nothing: 1—strongly disagree to 7—strongly agree.*[9] Note that these questions are written to evoke a quality of introspection different from the happiness scale questions. Happiness is a more transient emotion than satisfaction, so the questions that ask people whether they are happy will be more subject to daily fluctuations of mood than the ones that ask about life satisfaction.[10]

Even though the SWLS asks the individual to step out of his skin and appraise his life from an objective perspective, I am not sure that it is entirely possible to do so. The types of question posed by psychological tests are fundamentally limited by what a respondent is willing to reveal—to the one asking the questions and to himself. While psychologists tend to be sanguine about these issues, acknowledging that there is no other way for them to receive the information, most economists dismiss the same questions as too subjective.

At the heart of the matter is whether we have access to our feelings. I think we do, but are we always honest about them? We know what happiness is, and we know what satisfaction is, and, as I have suggested, we know what a satisfying experience is. Given the limitations of what we are willing to admit about ourselves, the SWLS and its kin are about as well as we can do by asking questions. From neuroeconomics and brain imaging may come a methodology that will shed light on the nature of these emotions. But since I wasn't going to be doing any scans on Cubans in the near future, the only way I was going to find out about the mystery of satisfaction in Cuba was to ask a few questions of Caridad.

## Money and Happiness

After finishing our meal, I caught up with Caridad as we walked down Monserrate, a street built on top of the remnants of the city wall that once had surrounded Old Havana. My colleagues, flush with mojitos, provided acoustic coverage for whoever might be listening. I had no doubt that our group's whereabouts were closely monitored. Avoiding uncontrolled encounters with the locals seemed to be a primary goal of our hosts.

Wearying of my persistence, Caridad finally said, "What is it that you want to know?"

"Why didn't our hosts come to dinner with us?"

Caridad looked at me, sizing up my intentions. She sighed and said, "Because they can't."

"Why not?"

"Cubans are not allowed in many of the tourist places. Were it not for your conference, we would not be allowed in your hotel. Same with the restaurant."

"Does that bother you?"

Caridad just shrugged.

"Are you happy?" I asked.

She laughed, genuinely, but with a hint of bitterness. "Of course. I am happy."

I nodded.

We passed a shrunken woman who held out a tin can with a cadaverous hand. Caridad nodded at the woman and said, "But I am not happy with *this*." She continued, "Everyone who comes here wants to know what will happen when *he* dies."

She wouldn't even speak Castro's name.

"I will tell you. Nothing."

"Nothing?"

"Cubans are a proud people," she said. "Just because things are bad doesn't mean we want your way of life. And those who left for America will not find a very nice welcome when they try to return."

Reading between the lines, I hoped she was implying that a vibrant political debate—and not a military coup—would take place upon Castro's death, but I wasn't so sure. Although no one would admit this, Cuba was already inching toward a free market, at least a free black market, with three different currencies in circulation—U.S. dollars, Cuban pesos, and convertible pesos— a kind of fake money that, until 2004, was strictly for tourists. Until 1993, it had been illegal for Cubans to hold U.S. dollars, but after that ban was lifted, the dollar went from being unofficial to official currency. Because of the U.S. embargo, you cannot use credit cards issued by U.S. banks, but cash is accepted everywhere. U.S. cash eventually flows into the state-run banks, where it is redistributed to provide for the needs of the populace, but there is still a sizable amount under Cuban mattresses. It isn't an exaggeration to say that U.S. currency forms the basis of the Cuban economy. Cuban currencies are not traded on foreign exchanges, so when Castro needed more dollars in 2004, he declared that dollars held by Cubans would automatically be converted to pesos and charged a conversion fee of 10 percent.

"How much money do you make?" I asked.

Caridad glared at me, weighing how to respond. "You know," she said.

"No, I don't."

"What difference does it make?"

It could make a lot of difference, as the surveys relating wealth to subjective well-being have shown. But I had pushed her too hard and, immediately regretting my rudeness, just shrugged.

Caridad sighed. "I make more money than my sister," she said. "And my sister is a doctor."

"How can that be?"

"I am lucky to have a job with tourists. I make good money in tips. And then I am able to help out my family."

Marxism has a price, after all, so I asked, "Do you own anything? Does anybody own anything?"

Caridad laughed again and said, "I own the shoes on my feet."

A private person, she revealed nothing more about her personal life, nor did I pry further, but Caridad's evasion of my question said enough. I never did learn how much money she made, just that a tourist guide makes more than a doctor. I was less interested in the value Cuban society placed on various professions and more interested that, even here, money served as a means to gauge one's social status.

This should come as no surprise, for the effects of money go beyond mere purchasing power. In 1995, Ed Diener compared data collected on surveys of well-being in fifty-five countries, from the Third World to industrialized nations, including Cuba. Diener wanted to know which characteristics of nations—social, economic, political—correlated with well-being. The nation with the highest subjective well-being was Iceland, and the lowest the Dominican Republic. The United States came in seventh, and Cuba was smack in the middle, at twenty-seventh. Diener looked at, among other factors, per capita income, purchasing power, cultural individualism (versus collectivism), and even a measure of social comparison (the wealth or poverty of a country compared with its neighbors).[11]

Across the board, higher income correlated with higher subjective well-being; income also correlated with more individualism, better human rights, and social equality. These four factors, in fact, accounted for almost 75 percent of the variation in well-being among the nations. While higher income leads to improvements in well-being, they do not necessarily come from what money can buy. Improvements in well-being come just as much from societal factors that correlate with higher incomes, like human rights and democratic political systems. Seen in this light, Cuba, which ranks low on income, civil rights, and individualism, appears to be even more of an anomaly.

Nationwide surveys are, of course, just one crude measure of the relationship between societal factors and well-being. To understand how Caridad could be happy with little money in a totalitarian regime requires one more piece of information. A variation of the nationwide survey can single out the effects of income within a single country. By keeping societal factors constant, you can see the effect income has on well-being. A dozen studies in the last decade have done this, and the answer is remarkably consistent. Once basic needs are met—food and shelter—income correlates only weakly with well-being, accounting for 1–5 percent of the variations in it.[12] Although she was poor by American standards, Caridad's basic needs were being met by the government, which, in theory, provides all Cubans with food, shelter, medical care, and education. In practice, however, almost everyone works jobs other than their official ones—jobs that earn U.S. dollars and that let people purchase things that the state doesn't provide. Even so, Caridad, like everyone else, had very little cash. When your ability to survive is ensured, even at a nominal level, the fact that you earn little becomes less of a factor, and why you do what you do becomes more important. Caridad's happiness seemed to flow from what she was doing. Given the constraints of living in Cuba, she might have had one of the best jobs, for it brought her in contact with new people every week—perhaps the best way to sate the human need for novelty.

## Value and Utility

The lottery studies and the survey data on happiness and well-being point to the same conclusion: money makes people a little happier but not as much as you might expect. Whatever pleasures can be derived from money seem to come from something other than the material items on which it can be spent. Money might make satisfying experiences easier to obtain, but what I saw in Cuba suggests that money is not necessary for a satisfying experience. Caridad took great pleasure in showing Havana to foreigners like me. If money is not all it's cracked up to be, then why do people make such a big deal out of it? Some have argued that money is primarily a status symbol, and what you spend it on advertises your wealth.[13] Status is important, but I think there is something more fundamental about money and how it feeds the brain's need for novelty.

To understand the relationship of money and novelty, we should know something about the science of economics. Economics represents one framework in which to analyze the satisfaction that money does, or does not, provide—and it is different from the psychological one. As I noted earlier, economists don't talk about happiness or satisfaction directly; instead, they refer to *utility*. The English philosopher Jeremy Bentham stated the principle of utility:

> By utility is meant that property in any object, whereby it tends to produce benefit, advantage, pleasure, good, or happiness . . . or to prevent the happening of mischief, pain, evil, or unhappiness.[14]

Economics as a science began with the realization that there is a difference between value and utility. Returning to the lottery: the odds of winning are about 100 million to one. A big jackpot is typically $200 million of annuitized value, the lump sum payout being about half that, or $100 million. You can calculate the value of a single lottery ticket simply: multiply the probability of winning by the amount that could be won. This is called the *expected value*, and in this example, it is $1.[15] Since the cost of a ticket is also $1, the whole transaction, on average, is a wash. Most of the time, however, the jackpot is considerably less, even though the odds of winning remain the same. As a result, the expected value of a lottery ticket is far less than $1, which raises this question: Why would anyone pay to lose money?

Daniel Bernoulli, an eighteenth-century Swiss mathematician, considered that precise question in a seminal paper in 1738.

Bernoulli realized that people do not make decisions based on expected value but rather on utility—the benefit one hopes to obtain. Whereas value depends on price, utility is subjective, and is defined by the individual consumer.[16] There is only one problem: utility cannot be measured directly. Bentham's definition of utility is just one instance of an obvious fact—it is not at all clear how to go about quantifying pleasure or happiness, although everyone knows what you mean when you talk about either of them. Perhaps it is not surprising, then, that Bernoulli's idea was largely ignored until the twentieth century.

Today, economists use utility as a way to rank people's preferences. If you like bananas better than oranges, for example, then bananas are said to have a higher utility to you than oranges. The idea seems circular, because utility is just a way to describe the choices that people make, and a person's choices, by definition, determine their utility. It would be a mistake, in this example, to assume that bananas give you more pleasure than oranges. There could be any number of reasons why, at a particular moment, you choose bananas over oranges. Even in this limited form, utility provides a consistent framework for economists to understand how people make purchasing decisions. As I will explain, utility is linked to the brain's need for novelty.

Earlier, I mentioned that part of the appeal of lotteries arose from the element of risk. In the 1940s, two mathematicians, Oskar Morgenstern and John von Neumann, gave utility theory a shot in the arm by showing how risk entered into human decisions, especially events like lotteries. Although Morgenstern and von Neumann didn't think that utility was a real emotion, they hypothesized that the imperative to maximize utility was at hand in decision making. In a monograph packed with equations foreign to most economists of the time, they showed that by assuming people were trying to maximize the utility they *expected* to obtain, you could understand their decisions—specifically, the two mathematicians explained, those involving risk.[17]

What is risk? Risk is any decision in which there is a possibility of failure. Buying a lottery ticket represents one kind of risk. If you can quantify the probability of success or failure, as I did with the lottery, then you are dealing with objective risk. If you can't quantify it, then it is subjective risk.[18] Bernoulli talked about objective risk when he described utility theory, which is the type of risk upon which Morgenstern and von Neumann built their framework of decision making.

The notion of risk may not seem relevant to the experiences money can buy, but, in fact, risk and money always go together. In many ways, money reduces risk. When we think of what money can be used for, we tend to consider purchases as either necessities or luxuries. Consider this dilemma: *You would really like that $500 pair of shoes, but you need to pay the rent.* You might buy the shoes, assuming that you could come up with the rent money later, but that would entail a certain amount of risk. The downside, eviction, could be nasty. It is a fact of life that you face decisions of this kind every day. Some people buy the shoes; others are more prudent. Now, my intention is not to judge the wisdom of one decision over another. You could be hit by a car tomorrow, in which case you would have been better off, for the next twenty-four hours, with some bling on your feet. Whatever the logic, you see that risk is always part of decision making—whether it be the odds of coming up with rent money, getting evicted, or the likelihood of being run over by a car.

For a small group of people, considering whether to buy or not to buy shoes is difficult. A person living in poverty, barely able to eat, would be unlikely to consider such a purchase. Nor would a wealthy person, who, if she liked the shoes, would just buy them. Only the people in the middle struggle with these decisions. Of course, the poor person is faced with certain kinds of decisions, which are arguably harder to make. And the rich suffer angst over how best to spend, invest, or give away their money. But notice how different each of their dilemmas is. The poor person's decisions are related to basic needs. The middle-class person's decisions, while not requiring that necessities be given up, can also produce anxiety. And the decisions of a wealthy person tend to revolve directly around money, not the things that it buys.

## Buying Possibilities

If money does not buy you the right to avoid decisions, it does something even better—it buys you possibilities. The higher up the income ladder you go, the more things become possible. The world begins to open up. At the same time, financial decisions become increasingly abstract; they relate less and less to the goods you buy, until, at the top, you are making decisions about money itself.

Part of the problem with money, at least in terms of satisfaction, is that, by itself, it can't do anything. A ten-dollar bill, after all, is just a piece of paper backed by the promise of the U.S. government to make good on its debts. But ten dollars will get you a pancake breakfast like the one I ate with Read, or a first-run movie (as long as you don't see it in Manhattan, or buy popcorn), or a used book. Depending on your point of view, ten dollars can yield thirty minutes of satisfaction at the breakfast table, two hours of escapism at a movie, or twenty hours of bliss with a good book. Conventional economic wisdom would suggest that money is only as good as what you can turn it into. But the matter goes deeper than that, and it has to do with the brain's need for novelty.

The brain wants novelty, and although money is not the only means of satisfying this desire, money makes it easier to get. Many of the experiences people seek most avidly cost money—like an exotic vacation or a meal at a five-star restaurant—and there may even be an added value to money that goes beyond its ability to deliver raw transactional value. I call this fantasy value, and it is a big factor in why people play the lottery. By serving as a sort of placeholder for potential purchases, money becomes an intermediary step on the road to satisfying experiences. Show me a ten-dollar bill, and I see pancakes, movies, and novels all at once, and there is a certain amount of pleasure in dwelling in this state of possibility. This is perfectly fine as long as you don't lose sight of the goal, a satisfying experience. But experience being nebulous and money concrete, money becomes the easier target at which to aim. What you can count, you know you've hit.

Consider what you can buy for five cents: a piece of bubble gum—if that. Now consider what you can buy with $5: a cheap lunch, an expensive coffee, some socks, a couple of gallons of gas. And for $500, you can make the five-dollar purchases a hundred times over; you can also become the owner of a computer, a television, some nice clothes for your children, a one-way flight to almost anywhere in the world—the list goes on. While these three monetary values differ by a factor of one hundred, the possibilities of what you can do with each amount grow exponentially. Five hundred dollars will buy a thousand, if not a million, more things than five dollars—much more than a hundredfold increase. The buying of possibilities, and not the actual goods purchased, is what accounts for the allure of money. When you increase the number of options available to you, risk actually decreases. Financial managers call this diversification, and our brains seem to have a built-in bias to it. People prefer more choices.[19]

The options that money gives you are really options for acquiring more information about the world. As I have said before, novelty is what the brain really wants, and money is the most efficient means to that end. Even if you don't spend it, just having money represents the possibility of experiencing things you wouldn't otherwise have, which in turn allows you to consider your options.[20] I was about to learn, however, that although money buys possibilities, it is not the only way to achieve this type of freedom.

I picked the dollar amounts in the previous example for a simple reason. Most of the things that a person can buy cost less than $500. Think of all the things (including nonmaterial uses of money—what economists call services) that cost less than $500. Now think of all the things that cost more. The first list is bigger. If we carry this to the extreme, we'd find that the list of the things that cost more than $100 million is exceedingly small.

The utility of money is rooted in the number of its possible uses, but increasing the amount of money is a fool's game. Since most of the purchases you would want to make are relatively modest in price, increasing your supply of money is good only to a point. If you can afford a computer or a television, both of which can be had for about $500, then you have already achieved the peak of purchasing power.

Bernoulli knew that money had diminishing utility, but he never explained why.[21] In the 1970s, Daniel Kahneman and Amos Tversky, both psychologists, showed that Bernoulli had missed a crucial aspect of the way people think about money. You view money not in terms of absolute wealth, they argued, but as gains and losses from your status quo. Moreover, people consider the pain of losing money to be worse than the pleasure of an equivalent gain. Kahneman and Tversky called this idea prospect theory, and it was based largely on observations of the kinds of lotteries people are willing to play.[22]

Why should losses loom larger than gains? The reason, I think, comes from the way the prices of all the goods and services in the world are distributed. Once you have enough money to buy, potentially, anything under $500, then increasing that amount also increases the number of possibilities—but at a diminishing rate.

Conversely, if you lose the same amount of money, you close off a greater number of possibilities than you would have acquired had you gained the equivalent amount. Imagine how it feels to lose $500—say, the cost of a minor auto accident or an unexpected tax bill. You'll probably think about the things you can no longer buy with the money (like a TV or a computer). Such thoughts explain why people are more averse to risk the wealthier they become. The wealthy live with greater possibilities of loss than of gain.

Economists hate this idea. Standard economic theory depends on the ability of consumers to establish preferences in terms of expected utility and not, as I just explained, by simply counting what they might buy with their money. But I can't be the only person who has a hard time gauging how much utility I will get from a high-definition television compared to a plane ticket to Hawaii (the two cost about the same).

Contrary to what most economists think, there is some evidence that people do, indeed, value having options. In an ingenious study, George Loewenstein, a psychologist at Carnegie Mellon University in Pittsburgh, examined the choices of Halloween trick-or-treaters. On Halloween 1993, kids coming to his house in Pittsburgh were offered a pile of candy bars and told they could pick two. All the kids picked two different candy bars. Now, everyone has a favorite candy—be it Snickers, Milky Way, or Three Musketeers—so if people wanted to maximize the expected utility of their future consumption, they would pick two of the favorite bar. This behavior is not limited to children, either; college students acted the same way.[23]

If it is the accrual of possibilities, and not just of material goods, that explains why people apparently wish to have more money, the notion also explains why spending money is not as satisfying as you might hope. The act of buying something closes off any number of other possibilities. You lose potential information during the act of a purchase, which psychologists call regret. You make decisions with one eye on the desired outcome and the other on possible out-comes (often referred to as "counterfactuals").[24] Thus the choices you make come, in part, from the desire to avoid regret. Buyer's remorse—the sinking feeling that you shouldn't have made a major purchase—occurs because you must also consider the other things you could have bought with that money.

The logic of this argument leads to two surprising conclusions. First, if you have enough money for basic needs, with some cash left over for modest discretionary purchases, then acquiring more money will lead to fewer, not more, possibilities on a per dollar basis. Second, once you earn enough to have discretionary money, you shouldn't spend it. Having options is a good thing, and there-fore losing options—when you spend money—is a bad thing.

If economists hate the suggestion that people don't, in fact, compute expected utility but rather count potential purchases, then what I have just said will strike them as daft. Economists will point to the fact that people struggle to increase their income so that they can spend their earnings on bigger and fancier items. The question on my mind, though, is not what most people do with money but why money doesn't lead to lasting improvements in well-being for most people. The answer lies in what you do to get the money.

## Money and the Brain

The next morning in Cuba, I was to give a thirty-minute lecture to my colleagues on brain imaging. The Cubans, of course, knew about fMRI, but they lacked the facilities to do it. For this reason, instead of my speaking about the technical details of fMRI, we dis-cussed some recent research that a graduate student in my lab had been doing on the importance of money to the brain.

Money is the standard reward used in and outside human

psychology experiments. The fMRI experiments my researchers conduct pay people for their time. A hodgepodge of rules about volunteer payment has accumulated over the years. Thirty years ago, people volunteered just to have a role in the advancement of science, but today, people are busy, perhaps jaded, and therefore must be offered an incentive. How much money to pay people? The ethical code that has evolved around human experimentation states that the amount of money individuals are paid should be limited to remuneration for their time and should not be so much that some people feel compelled to volunteer, which would unfairly expose low-income individuals to the risks of an experiment. These regulations make studying the effects of money rather difficult. Although exceptions are made, most fMRI experiments pay about $20 to $50—decent money for an hour or two of time, but often not enough to motivate people in the vicinity of college campuses.

Even using modest sums of money, an expanding number of fMRI experiments have succeeded in pointing to the striatum as a key structure in how the brain processes money. Money is easy to give to a person in the scanner. All you have to do is signal that a certain amount has been placed in a virtual piggy bank. While not exactly an instant reward, because the individual doesn't have the money in hand, it comes pretty close.

In 2001, Brian Knutson, a neuroscientist then at the National Institutes of Health and later at Stanford University, showed subjects being scanned with fMRI a symbol on a computer screen. The symbols were simple: circles indicated potential monetary rewards, squares indicated potential losses, and triangles indicated no money. Horizontal lines were included in each shape, indicating the amount of money that could be gained or lost. The more lines, the more money at stake. The shapes appeared only for a quarter of a second. After they disappeared, the subjects had to wait for another shape to be displayed on the computer and then press a button in a specified period of time. Subjects who pressed the button quickly enough received the money (or avoided losing money if the cue was a square).

The study focused on what happened in the brain during the waiting period between the trial's initial cue and the subsequent appearance of the target. Knutson found that the lowest portion of the striatum—the nucleus accumbens—responded strongly to the anticipation of a monetary reward; apparently this region is involved in processing the expectation of potential gain. Another region of the striatum, about a centimeter above the nucleus accumbens, responded to the anticipation of both potential gains and potential losses.[25] Which parts of the striatum distinguish between potential gains and losses has become a heated debate. Many scientists believe that the lowermost part—the nucleus accumbens—responds only to positive expectations. If this is true, the accumbens would be a pleasure center of the brain, but that is not the case.

The accumbens does respond to pleasurable events and even responds to events that predict future pleasure—cues that are important when considering the role that behavior plays in the expectation of money. In the study Read and I conducted, the Kool-Aid was pleasurable, but it also signaled that there was something to do: swallow. Separating these two components of reward—pleasure and action—is not easy, and the latter element sometimes is forgotten in favor of the sexier, emotional side of reward.

In the real world, action and reward go together. Goodies don't just fall in your lap; you have to go out and find them. Neuroscientists have not failed to notice the close relationship between action and reward; it's just that few have chosen to pursue it. Part of the reason stems from the dominance that classical learning theory has maintained over psychology for the last seventy years. Because learning theorists have focused their attention on stimulus-response relationships, like the ringing of a bell causing salivation in Pavlov's dogs, the study of reward has been restricted to what can be controlled in the laboratory. Seventy years ago, classical learning theory opened up the systematic study of not just learning but also motivation; recently, however, some scientists have questioned the relevance of classical learning theory to the way that animals and humans actually take in information about the real world—a world in which stimuli and rewards are not always clear.

An alternative theory of reward suggests that dopamine is released into the striatum whenever a stimulus in the environment—good or bad—causes an animal to change what it is doing. This view of reward differs radically from the reward-equals-pleasure theory.[26] True, things that release dopamine in the brain—like food and sex—are often pleasurable, which suggests that dopamine acts as a pleasure chemical. But even that explanation is simplistic. Just because pleasurable things release dopamine doesn't mean that those are the only things that release dopamine. Unexpected sounds and electric shocks also release dopamine, and to those can be added a catalog of nonpleasurable events that have caused several neuroscientists to rethink the nature of reward.

## Working for Your Money

Thinking about money this way can give you a brain cramp. Does money motivate you because you know that it will buy you pleasure? Or does money's utility come from its symbolic importance—as proxy for the number of things that can be done with it? I think it is the latter, because if you lay a hundred dollars in front of me, I will not get pleasure out of it. I could turn the money into pleasure by spending it on a nice meal, but I could also turn it into displeasure by paying my tax bill. What these two examples share is that money is important because of its potential.

Because money is an abstract reward and can represent any number of potential uses, I had stayed away from studying it in the scanner. At least until Cary Zink, a graduate student in my lab, took up the challenge.

Cary designed an ingeniously simple fMRI experiment on the importance of money. If the utility of money comes from its dollar value, then whether or not you worked to earn the money should not make a difference. Ten dollars is ten dollars, whether the amount reflects an hour on the job or a winning lottery ticket. If the source of money has no bearing on how it is used or enjoyed, then the response in the striatum when a person is "handed" a sum of money should be independent of how it came to be acquired.

In Cary's experiment, volunteers were shown a series of shapes on a computer screen. Whenever a triangle appeared, they had to press a button on a keypad—a task used only to keep the subject's attention focused on the screen. Every so often, a dollar bill would appear in the middle of the screen, indicating that money was about to be placed in the subject's "bank." In one experiment, the money went into the bank automatically, while in another the person had to press a button to move it physically into a bank. As nominal a task as it was, pressing the button constituted work, and that work made a big difference in terms of the striatal response to receiving money. Actively working to receive a monetary reward resulted in more striatal activity than getting money passively.[27]

Even a trivial button press registered a bigger hit on the striatum than a freebie. Anything you can do to get even a little more activity out of the striatum is a good thing. Is it surprising that nothing tastes as sweet as the fruits of one's labor? This suggests that reward, at least as far as our brains are concerned, is in the action and not in the payoff. Of course, taking pleasure in our efforts has deep roots in the American work ethic,[28] but understanding that the pleasure money confers is significantly increased by the work done to earn it turns upside down a basic tenet of economics—that work is a negative and money is a positive.[29] I think it is the other way around. The brain does not want to be idle, and work is one of the best ways to keep the mind and body busy. Given a choice, even rats prefer to work for their food than to get it for free.[30]

• • •

The taciturn expressions on the faces of my Cuban audience worried me. In theory, Marxist-Leninist Communism should be aligned to the way of thinking about work that I had just outlined— so much so that it might explain Cuba's anomalously high score on Diener's international survey of well-being. But I sure didn't get that sense from my audience. None of the Cuban contingent asked any questions. I feared they disagreed with the findings but were too polite to tell me so.

That evening, I saw Caridad for the last time.

"How did your speech go?" she asked.

I described the reactions of her countrymen.

"Don't worry about it. Most of them are members of the party. They won't say anything in public anyway." She handed me a piece of paper and said, "If you want to see somebody who enjoys their work, go see these men."

It was a flyer for the Buena Vista Social Club.

Taking their name from a jazz club in Havana long since demol-ished, the Buena Vista Social Club could be described as the hardest-working band in Cuba. Ibrahim Ferrer, at age seventy-seven, still has a voice so clean and so true that he puts vocalists a third his age to shame, and Compay Segundo, age ninety-seven, can harmonize and syncopate to Ferrer like no one else. These statesmen of Afro-Cuban jazz were unknown outside Cuba until 1996, when the American musician Ry Cooder recorded them, after which they burst upon the world. By 2000, Ferrer had received the Latin Grammy for best new vocalist.[31]

"They are playing tonight in your hotel," Caridad said. "I suggest you go."

"Thank you. I will."

I wanted to say something more, but there wasn't anything more to say. I was grateful for her honesty. Caridad kissed me on each cheek and said, "Adios."

She was right about the Buena Vista Social Club. The group opened with the classic "Chan Chan"—a fragmented story of Juanita and Chan Chan—two lovers whose passion cannot be stanched. The contrast of the two of them working the sugar-cane fields, then walking on fine-sand beaches, is poignant, and the song goes on in this vein, explaining how, although exhausted from their labors, they somehow find energy to make love among the cane leaves.

High on another Cohiba and caught up in the music, I drifted away into one of those once-in-a-lifetime experiences that must be acknowledged as they are happening. With sadness I realized that I might never get a chance to return to Cuba and certainly would never see these masters of Cuban jazz in their own country again.

The Buena Vista Social Club played music because the group loved it, and they loved making other people love it—the best description I can imagine for work being its own reward. I had no doubt that the lives the singers led had been, and may then have been, harder than mine. Most of the $20 cover charge collected from the hundred or so people in the club that night didn't go to them. It went directly into the government's coffers.

After the show, Compay was standing by the side of the stage, watching the patrons—mostly Europeans, Mexicans, and South Americans—leave, eager to get back to their rooms. I went up to him and shook his right hand. With a firm grip, he sandwiched my hand affectionately with his left.

I smiled. He said, "Gracias."

It's not the money. It's what you do to get it.

# 3

**Puzzling Gratifications**

If the satisfaction of having money comes from the work you do to earn it, what happens when you work for nothing? Most of the things you do are probably undertaken without regard to compensation, more or less for the pleasure of the experience. Hobbies fall into this category, and there is no more popular one than the crossword puzzle, which many consider to be the world's most popular game. I like a good puzzle, and can usually solve the *New York Times* crossword every week until Wednesday[1]—which ranks my skills far below those normally necessary to compete in the American Crossword Puzzle Tournament. Nevertheless, the tournament offers an ideal testing ground to figure out the source of satisfaction in intellectual challenges. Although anyone can enter the tournament, some of the participants were pros. Really. Some even made a living from crossword puzzles, and with a $4,000 first place prize up for grabs, I had serious competition.

Watching five hundred people cram into the ballroom of a hotel in Stamford, Connecticut, brought flashbacks to taking the SAT.

Foot-high cardboard partitions separated the contestants, who were seated at rows of tables spanning the length of the ballroom. A man sitting across from me had placed a line of mechanical pencils along the rim of his desk. Realizing I had just failed the first rule of test taking—to bring plenty of backup writing instruments— I started to gnaw on my one stubby hotel-issue pencil before remembering that I had found it on the floor of the lobby earlier that day.

The man across from me peered over the partition, eyeing me warily and undoubtedly measuring the competition. He introduced himself as Steve Levy, a bicoastal computer consultant and self-avowed puzzlehead. "First time?" he asked. He shot a quick glance to his left and said sotto voce, "Do you want a tip?"

I nodded expectantly.

"Use lowercase *e*'s."

I think he was testing me, to see if I was a ringer coming in as a rookie. I flashed him a puzzled look, which was enough to put him at ease. He explained, "You can write a lowercase *e* much faster than uppercase." To emphasize his point, he drew an *e* in the air. "See, one fluid motion can save a second. And since *e* is the most commonly used letter, you can save several seconds on a puzzle."

The tournament, then in its twenty-seventh year, was organized by Will Shortz, the *New York Times* crossword puzzle editor. Rules specified that each contestant must attempt seven puzzles over two days. Each puzzle has a time limit, ranging from fifteen minutes for the easiest to forty-five minutes for the most difficult. Ten points are awarded for every correct answer, and a 150-point bonus is granted for each completely correct puzzle. Bonuses of 25 points for each minute are awarded to contestants who finish before the time limit.

"Is accuracy or speed more important?" I asked.

Bruce Morton, a musician and law professor from Stowe, Vermont, who was sitting next to me, chimed in: "Accuracy."

"I disagree," Steve objected. "You have to assume you won't make any mistakes. Go for the time bonuses."

Bruce shrugged and said, "If you make one mistake, you lose two answers and the 150-point bonus, which is equivalent to seven minutes of time bonuses."

As the first puzzle was distributed, Shortz explained the rules. A large digital timer read 15:00, the limit for the first, easiest puzzle. A cloud, rank with Marlboros and Shalimar, floated above the ballroom as contestants began fingering the corners of the puzzles lying facedown in front of them, jockeying to get the best grip on the paper. When everyone had a puzzle, Shortz said, "Go!" and a rustling filled the ballroom as five hundred people simultaneously flipped over their papers.

No less daunted by my prospects, the excitement in the air got my competitive juices flowing. No sooner did I encounter 1-across, a five-letter word for "Penny pincher," than my heart fell. Frozen, I looked at 1-down. Still nothing. I was getting nervous, and the puzzle grid started to blur.

*Focus.*

I took a deep breath and scanned for a clue that spoke to me. In the upper right quadrant, 16-across read "____ Alto, Calif." Yes, Palo Alto. I worked down from there, and the grid started filling in. *Keep moving.* As I began to make progress, people started raising their hands to indicate they were done. I glanced at the clock. Three minutes had passed. *Damn.* Steve raised his hand. I bore down deeper into my puzzle, trying to block out the sound of the growing wave of people filing out to the lobby. When time was called, I had finished about two-thirds.

## Puzzles: A Brief History

I chose to examine crosswords because they are the most popular form of puzzle today, but puzzles, in general, have been around since at least the earliest human writings. The reason is simple: puzzles fill a uniquely human need for intellectual challenge. Puzzles should be clever, neither too easy nor too hard. Regardless of their type, a great puzzle is a work of art—one that seizes the mind, diverts attention from other activities, and presses into consciousness during idle moments, refusing to let go until its solution has appeared, seemingly by the sheer power of thought. And because puzzles more often than not bear the name of their constructor, solving them allows you to prove to yourself and others that you are the puzzle maker's equal, thereby satisfying your competitive appetite.

While we may surmise that puzzles have been around for millennia, their history is itself a kind of puzzle. Riddles were probably the earliest form. The oldest documented riddles could be found in Babylonian texts—for example, "Who becomes pregnant without conceiving and becomes fat without eating?"[2]

The ancient Greeks loved puzzles, the most famous of which was, of course, the riddle of the Sphinx. The riddle, as we know it today, was recorded by Sophocles and appeared around 425 B.C. in his play *Oedipus the King.* As the story went, the city of Thebes was terrorized by the Sphinx, a monster with the body of a lion, the head of a woman, and wings. Sophocles never said what the riddle was, but it was probably well known to the Greeks of that era, since fragments of it had been recorded on texts dating from the sixth century B.C. A later recording rendered the riddle as "What creature moves on four feet in the morning, on two feet at noon, and on three in the evening?"[3] The apparent simplicity of the riddle suggests that it was added to the story for dramatic effect, probably after Sophocles's original version.[4] Were it not for the perfect irony of Oedipus's killing his father and marrying his mother, all of which could be traced back to his solving the riddle, we probably would not know it so well.

The Sphinx was also the pseudonym of England's greatest puzzle maker—Henry Ernest Dudeney (1857–1930), who created puzzles during a renaissance of English puzzle making that began with the word games of Lewis Carroll and continues to the present-day popularity of crossword puzzles.

Dudeney created puzzles that could be stated simply yet got under the skin in an irritating way (even when he gave the answers), like the age of Mrs. Timpkins: *When the Timpkinses married, eighteen years ago, Timpkins was three times as old as his wife, and today he is just twice as old as she; how old was Mrs. Timpkins on her wedding day?*[5] Dudeney's teasers required the solver to look at his puzzles in an unconventional manner. The effect of first solving a Dudeney puzzle is unmistakable—an "Aha!" experience, when everything just clicks into place, and the solution becomes all too apparent. How could anyone not get addicted to puzzles? Maybe the *Aha* feeling is the sensation of dopamine flooding the brain.

Will Shortz has bemoaned the fact that puzzles have lost the aura of dignity they once enjoyed. He's probably thinking of Dudeney's time. Puzzles, Shortz has written, might be an amusement, but they are an intellectual amusement and should be considered alongside other intellectual pursuits.[6] Part of the problem is that most puzzles, especially the elementary ones recognizable to most people, are poorly written. The widespread impression that puzzles are amusements primarily for children comes, I think, from the paucity of artful teasers.

The first modern crossword puzzle appeared in the *New York World*, on Sunday, December 21, 1913. Invented by the journalist Arthur Wynne, it was dubbed a "word-cross" and was constructed in a diamond shape with a hole in the middle. The crossword's popularity continued to grow until it exploded in 1921, when Margaret

Petherbridge assumed the *World*'s editorship of the puzzle. When asked about the reason for the popularity of crossword puzzles, Margaret Petherbridge gave three: "The fascination of words common to an articulate race; self-education; and time-killing."[7] More than anyone else, Petherbridge (later Margaret Farrar) laid down the rules of crossword puzzles and demanded a certain aesthetic quality from the people who constructed them. Aesthetics contributed significantly to the increase in the crossword's popularity. Among other innovations, she required puzzles to be rotationally symmetric and have full interlock—no islands of disconnected words.

## Curiosity Killed the Cat — and Satisfaction Brought Him Back

The brain's need for intellectual novelty manifests as curiosity. Through most of history, curiosity has not necessarily been considered a virtue, as it is more often viewed today.[8] Here is how Saint Augustine, in A.D. 397, described curiosity as "the lust of the eyes":

> For besides that concupiscence of the flesh which consisteth in the delight of all senses and pleasure . . . a certain vain and curious desire, veiled under the title of knowledge and learning, not of delighting in the flesh, but of making experiments with the flesh. The seat whereof being in the appetite of knowledge, and sight being the sense chiefly used for attaining knowledge, it is in Divine language called the lust of the eyes.[9]

It seems that curiosity has always been closely associated with pleasure, and in Saint Augustine's eyes, this was a telltale sign of its power. Even the eighteenth-century utilitarian Jeremy Bentham considered the "pleasures of novelty and the pleasure derived from gratification of curiosity" as one of the prime motivating factors of behavior.[10] Because of its association with pleasure, particularly sexual pleasure, it was another century before curiosity became an acceptable, if still not laudable, trait, and one worthy of scientific study.

Both Saint Augustine and Bentham suggested that curiosity was related to physical arousal, but it wasn't until the nineteenth century that Wilhelm Wundt—the father of psychology in Germany— found that while mild levels of arousal were perceived as pleasurable, too much arousal was unpleasant. This finding led him to theorize that the relationship of arousal to pleasure was an inverted U-shaped curve—where an intermediate level of arousal is the most pleasurable. Although Wundt didn't talk about curiosity, his findings implied that modest levels of it, such as the kind that encourages puzzle solving, would lead to modest levels of arousal and therefore pleasure, or at least satisfaction of some kind.

In the 1950s, the Canadian psychologist Daniel Berlyne rediscovered the Wundt curve, and linked curiosity to arousal, in the process making curiosity a legitimate area of psychological inquiry. Berlyne came on the scene in the midst of the telecommunications revolution and so applied Shannon's information theory to the study of aesthetics. Berlyne believed that the more complicated something is, the more a person will be aroused by it. This idea, cast against Wundt's curve, would suggest that intermediate levels of complexity should be the most pleasurable.[11]

Berlyne was on the right track. Nobody likes to stare at walls, nor is the random complexity in, say, the static of a disconnected television set diverting. Though people do enjoy some intermediate level of intellectual complexity—like a novel whose plot is intricate, but not too intricate—complexity adheres in more than just objects. How you bring order (or disorder) to the complexity of the world defines the rhythm of your life. Work, for example, tends to be most enjoyable when it has an element of novelty but not so much that it is stressful.[12] This desire for order is another way of characterizing the need to predict how the world works. We want to understand, and puzzles tap into this need in more than one way. They foist something unpredictable (will I be able to solve it?) and novel on your brain, reflecting a miniature version of real-world challenges without real-world stress. Beyond challenge, puzzles let you see that the world is not simply random—so complex that you fall off the other side of the Wundt curve—and that you have the capacity to assimilate surprises.

Saint Augustine realized that curiosity has the power to motivate actions that run counter to your best intentions, as if curiosity is itself a demon that takes over your body and commands you to experience a wealth of sensations—both physical and mental. Augustine was no stranger to bodily pleasure, and the encapsulation of curiosity into an internalized force allowed for a convenient explanation of his physical transgressions. Granted, curiosity can leave you with few responses but to obey it: you curse the traffic congestion after an accident while simultaneously slowing down to view the carnage.

As car wrecks illustrate, curiosity does not appear magically in your mind. Rather, it must be triggered by something, and this critical observation suggests a link between curiosity, or novelty-seeking, and the motivational circuits in the brain. It can be argued that people are curious about things they cannot explain, which is the incongruity theory of curiosity. When you are confronted with something incongruous, curiosity presents itself as the means of figuring it out. The incongruity theory bears a similarity to Berlyne's ideas about complexity but considers curiosity an internally motivated drive, so that curiosity derives not from the complexity of the stimulus but from one's expectations about it. Naturally, more complex stimuli lead to more violations of expectation and more curiosity.

George Loewenstein has suggested an insightful modification to the incongruity theory, based on the observation that curiosity often increases with one's expertise in a particular domain.[13] People who are fanatical about trains, for example, might have intense curiosity about a certain steam engine, whereas someone else wouldn't even notice it. Loewenstein suggests that curiosity derives not just from incongruity but from the perception of an "information gap," defined as the difference between what you know and what you want to know. From this definition emerges the addictive quality of curiosity. The more you know about a particular subject, the more you become aware of your ignorance, and this awareness triggers more curiosity.

In Chapter 1, I suggested that novel information has the potential to trigger one of two responses—retreat or exploration. Curiosity is the feeling of novel information taking you down the second, exploratory path, which is the first step toward a satisfying intellectual experience. To get the *Aha!* kick, something in your brain has to change.

## Aha!

A few minutes after the first round of the tournament, Steve Levy returned to his seat, anxious to get to the next puzzle, and said, "That was a great warmup puzzle. How'd you do?"

"I almost finished."

"That's great. Now, it's going to get interesting."

"How so?"

"The even-numbered puzzles are always a little harder."

Indeed. The title of Puzzle #2, "A Comedy of Errors," constructed by Fred Piscop, suggested something impish behind the grid. An extra five minutes was allotted for completing it.

I started, naturally, with 1-across, a three-letter word for "Eur. carrier." The abbreviation in the clue was a standard crossword tip-off that the answer was also an abbreviation. *SAS.* Next, I moved to

1-down, a five-letter word for "Show disdain." *SMIRK?* Seemed right, except the next horizontal answer below *SAS* was *CNN* (clue: "Lou Dobbs Tonight" carrier). I abandoned the first quadrant and skipped over to the next block of answers, which contained the puzzle's first theme clue, a thirteen-letter answer for "The dieter _____."

Crossword puzzles with themes have recently become popular. The usual way in which a theme appears is in three to five long, multiword answers, running horizontally across the grid. These long answers are a bit like a joke, which, if you complete the puzzle from the upper left to the lower right, will lead you from setup to punch line. In actuality, this type of puzzle is difficult for the constructor to pull off, for it requires leading the solver through the grid in the intended order, all the while holding off the best answer for the end.

None of this knowledge, of course, was helping me solve the puzzle at hand. Steve raised his hand after about five minutes, while I was left scratching my head in an effort to discern the theme of this puzzle. I looked at the last theme clue, hoping the punch line would help me in some way—a fourteen-letter answer for "The overhead lighting technician _____ ." Still stumped, I realized that the puzzle contained a lot of three-letter answers, like the first one, and if I started working those, I might be able to fill in enough to arrive at the interlocking theme answers. Steadily, I began to fill in the grid, avoiding the long answers, until I had completed enough of the upper quadrants to seize on the dieter clue: *DROPPED-WEIGHT.* Still unable to recognize how this related to the puzzle title, I pressed on with my strategy in the bottom quadrants.

Time was running out. With less than five minutes left on the clock, and solvers clogging the lobby with boasts of their exploits, I redoubled my efforts to concentrate, and somehow got the answer: *SCREWEDUPABULB. Aha!* I saw it: *dropped* and *screwed up.* The theme answers were colloquialisms of errors, just as the title of the puzzle promised! In the waning moments available to me, the answers snapped into place, and even though time ran out before I could finish the puzzle, I was left with the most satisfying feeling of having figured it out.

.  .  .

It wasn't until I stopped seeing the clues as completions of clichés and instead saw them as variations on the theme of errors that my perception changed, and mystery was met with insight. I think the puzzle actually looked different. How did this happen? Nothing that my eyes registered had changed, so whatever happened had to have occurred in my brain.

Here is another example, drawn from a psychological study, of how insight can change perception: *Describe how you can put 27 sheep into 4 pens so that there is an odd number of sheep in each pen.*[14]

Like themed crossword puzzles, this riddle requires the solver to eschew conventional approaches in order to see information in a different light. Early in the history of experimental psychology, around 1920, scholars in the field engaged in a debate of incredible rancor regarding the nature of perception. Classical psychologists viewed perception, for the most part, as a series of one-way streets that converged in the mind as a percept. For example, the percept of a rose occurs from the convergence of visual information taken in with the eye, smell from the nose, and touch from the fingers. I will go into the nature of perception in more detail in the next chapter, but even in the 1920s this simple idea was being questioned by a trio of Austrian and German psychologists: Max Wertheimer, Kurt Koffka, and Wolfgang Köhler, who called themselves Gestalt psychologists and viewed perception as something altogether different from the mere sum of individual elements that together made up the percept.[15]

Fascinated by the behavior of chimpanzees, Köhler designed the classic experiment of hanging a banana just out of reach and placing a box nearby. Although they'd never seen a box used as a stepping stool, the most clever chimps had the insight to use it as such, moving it under the banana in order to reach the fruit. Interestingly, some of the dimmer-witted chimps, despite having the benefit of watching the smart ones over and over, never figured out that the box had to be set *under* the banana.[16] Merely seeing, Köhler argued, is insufficient to gain insight into a problem. Insight—the *Aha!* moment, which sprang from something besides rational thought—could then be put to work to change the environment.

The solution to the sheep problem, to return to our example, first requires an uncommon insight that, once achieved, alters the way you look at the problem. Most people approach the problem by partitioning the sheep, through trial and error, into four pens—until they realize it can't be done. An odd number can be broken down into an arbitrary number of smaller integers, but there will always be an odd number of odd numbers. The number 5, for instance, can be broken down into 2+3, 1+4, 1+1+3, 2+2+1, and so on. So dividing 27 sheep into 4 pens, each with an odd number, is impossible. The solution is to put all the sheep in one pen and nest this pen within the other pens. Once you arrive at this answer, it is hard to avoid visualizing a bull's-eye of sheep.

## The Psychology of Insight

The Gestalt psychologists laid the foundations for the scientific study of insight, which they thought of as a phenomenological effect necessarily opaque to anyone but the person experiencing it. This belief didn't discourage Köhler from searching in the brain for what he called isomorphisms of insight. He used a 1960s technology, electroencephalography (EEG), which yielded equivocal results. Although today's psychologists are perhaps less caustic in their professional debates than were the Gestaltists, the dividing lines between differing theories of insight remain just as stark.

Some believe that insight is not a distinct psychological process. Advocates of the business-as-usual theory point out that many so-called insights are not insights at all. To classify as an insight, information must be restructured, but some "insights" do not require restructuring, just careful attention to the information at hand.[17] Consider this old puzzle, which appears in one of Dudeney's collections:

> An English officer, after a gruesome experience during the Boxer rebellion in China, fell asleep in church during the sermon. He was dreaming that the executioner was approaching him to cut off his head, and just as the sword was descending on the officer's unhappy neck his wife lightly touched her husband on the back of his neck with her fan to awaken him. The shock was too great, and the officer fell forward dead. Now, there is something wrong with this. What is it?[18]

If, as the puzzle explains, the man really died, nobody could have known what he was dreaming. Understanding this riddle requires careful attention to the facts presented, which leads to the discovery of the inconsistency. No restructuring is necessary. But even if you grant that many problems that initially appear to require insight do not, you must still acknowledge that some do.

A reasonable working theory of insight does, however, exist. In 1926, Graham Wallas proposed the prepared-mind perspective.[19] Wallas outlined four phases of information processing that contributed to insight: mental preparation; incubation—a period of time when the problem is not actively thought about; illumination—which we know as the *Aha!* feeling; and verification—when the solver checks the insight. Insight actually occurs in the third phase. This model pleases both camps on insight: while acknowledging that a particular cognitive/emotional process occurs during insight, it recognizes that the illumination wouldn't be possible without mental preparation and an adequate knowledge base.

What exactly happens during incubation? Colleen Seifert, a psychologist at the University of Michigan, has proposed that, during the working through of a difficult problem, it is at this step that mental bookmarks are generated. These bookmarks can then be reactivated when the person encounters a random piece of information that bears on the problem. Seifert calls this process opportunistic assimilation, a variation of chance favoring the prepared mind. Without the knowledge base, the average person would be unable to come up with insights on, say, quantum mechanics.

But a theory is nothing unless it can be tested, and Seifert has offered several experiments that lend objective support to the idea of opportunistic assimilation, or chance favoring the prepared mind. In one experiment, she gave undergraduates a series of moderately difficult questions, like *What is a nautical instrument used in measuring angular distances, especially the altitude of the sun, moon, and stars at sea?*[20] Most of the questions could be answered, but students found about one-third to be too difficult; for these queries, Seifert generated a list of words, some of which contained hints to the answer. In a second phase of the experiment, the students were shown words and nonwords like *spending, dascribe, sextant, trinsfer, asteroid* and were asked to decide whether each item was a word or not. The students were not told that this task had anything to do with the first series of questions. Then they came back the next day for a repeat session of general questions; some were new and others were ones they previously couldn't answer. Seifert's results demonstrated that exposing people to relevant information almost doubled their ability to respond to questions that had earlier stumped them.[21]

The phenomenon that Seifert studied is known as *priming*. In the extreme, priming can occur with the mere exposure to words, even outside an individual's awareness, and is often sufficient to increase one's performance on a variety of recall tasks. Seifert's questions, fundamentally of the recall type, did not require any particular insight, but subsequent experiments with questions requiring problem solving suggested that the priming effect extends to abstract reasoning. Exposure to new information may facilitate insights.

You can begin to see how the brain's need for novelty may be linked to the satisfying feeling of insight. Everyone has had an *Aha!* experience, and it feels good. Without two elements, however, such an experience would be impossible: first, *Aha!*s do not come passively; they sometimes require substantial mental effort; second, they do not come out of the blue—they are triggered by something, but only after a period of incubation. While new and varied experiences seem to be a prerequisite for insights, mere exposure to them does not guarantee that insight will occur. Moreover, the harder you work at a problem, the more elusive it can often become. Sometimes problems have to be set aside, forgotten about for a while, and allowed to resurface in unexpected moments— when you are in bed, in the shower, or exercising. No aspect of insight is as mysterious as the incubation process, perhaps because the essence of incubation is unconscious.

## Sleep and Insight

Sleep plays a key role in insight. The notion that sleep, especially dreaming, can alter mental associations in awake individuals is over two hundred years old. Freud, of course, thought that the interpretation of dreams led to the royal road of the unconscious, since it is in dreams that true desires are revealed. A modern, neurobiological view of sleep emerged in the 1990s when several lines of converging evidence suggested that sleep, particularly REM sleep, enhances certain types of learning.

Since the development of EEG, which provides precise measurements of physiological changes in brain state, the basic sleep cycle has been well described. In general, sleep can be divided into REM and non-REM periods, with non-REM further subdivided into Stage 2 and slow-wave sleep (SWS). Each phase has a characteristic appearance on EEG tracings. Although REM sleep looks very much like the awake brain, with waves of brain activity in the 4–6 Hz frequency range, it is notable for the almost complete absence of muscle movement (except for the eyes). Brain imaging, which has taken what was visible on EEGs to new depths, has also revealed that the dorsolateral prefrontal cortex, the part of the brain most closely associated with logical, abstract thought, is quiescent during REM sleep.[22]

As you fall asleep, you descend rapidly into slow-wave sleep (what neurologists used to call Stages 3 and 4), and after about ninety minutes, ascend to a brief period of REM sleep, perhaps awakening for a minute or two. The cycle then repeats itself roughly every ninety minutes throughout the night, but with an increasing percentage of time spent in REM sleep toward the morning.

The idea that dreaming occurs only in REM sleep is now known to be a myth. To varying degrees, dreaming occurs in all phases of sleep, although dreams are most prevalent during REM. Freud did not know about the sleep cycle; even so, another of his enduring ideas is that dream content is determined by the previous day's experience, what he called the daily residue. When researchers put this theory to the test by asking volunteers to assess the content of their dreams, with particular attention to the relationship between the dream and their actual experience, most individuals found little resemblance. Instead, dreams appear to be constructed out of discrete fragments of waking experience and assembled into fresh narratives.[23]

In 1994, two papers tipped the field of sleep research by blowing open the idea that sleep and REM somehow facilitated learning, if not insight. In one paper, a team of Israeli researchers, led by the neurologist Avi Karni, reported that REM sleep improved performance on a perceptual learning task. Karni presented volunteers with a computer screen displaying a grid of similar shapes in the form of small dashes, except for three oddball shapes placed randomly. The subjects had to identify the shapes of the oddballs. To make the task difficult, Karni showed participants the screen for only a fraction of a second before replacing it with a grid of jumbled shapes. When the interval between the screen and the grid of jumbled shapes was greater than 100 milliseconds, the volunteers could perform the task accurately, but as the interval between target and mask grid decreased, performance degraded, and at intervals of less than 50 milliseconds, the target grid was essentially imperceptible. With practice over several days, the volunteers could improve their detection thresholds, typically by about 20 milliseconds.

Karni went on to interfere with the volunteers' sleep over seven nights. Some subjects were deprived of REM sleep (by awakening them each time the EEG showed REM patterns) and others were deprived of slow-wave sleep. The REM-deprived people showed no performance improvements over the week of practice, while the others did, suggesting that whatever consolidation of learning occurred happened during REM sleep.[24] Subsequent replications of this experiment have suggested that slow-wave sleep may, in fact, also play a role in consolidation.[25]

In the companion paper, Bruce McNaughton and his postdoctoral student Matthew Wilson, then at the University of Arizona, measured firing patterns in the hippocampus of sleeping rats. The hippocampus, about the size of a pea and lying about a centimeter away from the striatum, is the brain structure most closely linked with memory. Wilson and McNaughton had previously identified the existence of "place cells" in the hippocampus. These cells fire in a particular pattern whenever a rat arrives at certain locations while learning to navigate a maze. Finding that these patterns were replayed during the rats' slow-wave sleep, the two researchers hypothesized that the hippocampus replays activity patterns as part of the consolidation process that eventually transfers memory to the brain's cortex.[26] Were the rats dreaming of mazes? Since rats can't speak to us, Wilson and McNaughton's observations are about as close to an affirmative as we can get.

Not everyone agrees that sleep, and REM in particular, is necessary for memory consolidation and, by extension, insight.[27] The argument against the special role of REM sleep centers on the diverse proportion of sleep spent in REM among different species. Some of the REM-heaviest animals—the platypus, opossum, ferret, and armadillo—are not known for their intelligence. Dolphins and whales, which have shown signs of intelligence seen elsewhere in the animal world only among great apes, may not have any REM at all. Humans are actually in the middle of the spectrum.

The evidence is spotty, at best, for the role of REM sleep in the generation of insight, but sleep, in general, appears to facilitate certain types of learning, especially tasks that do not rely on a memory for facts. Another approach to the sleep-insight problem involves an effect known as sleep inertia. When someone is awakened, by an alarm clock or a persistent researcher, it takes a few minutes for the brain to shift to the awake state. During this transition period, which is presumed to resemble the prior sleep state more than the awake state, cognitive processes can be probed. In one study, investigators had volunteers solve anagrams immediately after being awakened from either REM or non-REM sleep. Solving anagrams requires the type of facility that psychologists call fluid intelligence: the ability to form novel relationships in the mind. In the fully awake state, the volunteers solved about 55 percent of the anagrams, a percentage that was unchanged after they were awakened from REM sleep, but that dropped to 42 percent after non-REM sleep. Investigators have concluded that when the brain is in REM sleep, it is more amenable to cognitive flexibility, but in a way that utilizes circuits differently from its functioning in the awake state.[28]

## The Biology of Insight

Sleep is necessary but perhaps not sufficient for the generation of insight. Until brain imaging came along, the biological source of the *Aha!* moment remained shrouded. In theory, you could design an experiment in which the exact moment in which the solution to a puzzle appeared in someone's mind was found, and the brain activity would be recorded using fMRI. The findings would represent a brain map of insight. If only it was that simple. The biggest confounding factor in such a setup is the protean role of attention. Presumably, flashes of insight are accompanied by dramatic shifts in attention, but in an fMRI scan, there is no way to differentiate between fluctuations in attention and the appearance of a solution. Despite this limitation, some investigators have plowed ahead on the imaging front, searching for the neural basis of insight.

In a relatively early study using positron emission tomography, a group at the University of Pennsylvania measured changes in cerebral blood flow while volunteers solved anagrams. In actuality, the study was designed to examine the opposite of insight—frustration—as an experimental model of learned helplessness in humans. Half the anagrams were unsolvable. Of all the brain regions examined, only the hippocampus had substantially greater blood flow during solvable than unsolvable anagrams.[29] Hippocampus activation was significant, especially since the hippocampus is not generally considered to play a big role in attention, although it is known to play such a role in memory consolidation, a function closely wrapped up with the generation of insight.

A team from China and Japan, this time using fMRI, has taken a similar approach to the imaging of insight and, surprisingly, has come up with a similar result.[30] The experimenters gave volunteers a series of Japanese riddles that required a restructuring of information to solve (rather than just carefully processing the information). For example, what can move heavy logs but cannot move a small nail? *(A river)*. Instead of forcing individuals to exert considerable mental effort in search of the solution, the experimenters simply gave the answer to each riddle, as I just did, after a prescribed delay, forcing insight on the person. When answers were given, the hippocampus was activated, as was a network of cortical regions, including large swaths of the parietal cortex, which is in the back of the head and orients attention. Given the limitations of this study (only seven subjects, for example, and a lack of a control condition), it is hard to know where in this soup insight might lie, but considering that hippocampus activation in fMRI investigations is not very common, its appearance in this experiment is intriguing.[31]

Although I have placed a great deal of importance on the striatum and on dopamine, they are not the only brain structures involved in the generation of the warm feeling of a satisfying experience. The striatum is a major structure when action is involved, but for purely internal thought, the hippocampus plays a key role. Based on a limited amount of brain imaging data, I think that the hippocampus is critical for the generation of insight. The hippocampus is not, however, responsible for the emotional impact of insight—the *Aha!* we've been chasing. That, I believe, does come from the striatum, but the road to insight's emotional impact is a little funny.

I heard this joke a while ago, but I still get a giggle out of it:

> Two cows were standing in a field, and one said to the other, "Those humans are sure getting worked up about mad cow disease. What do you think of it?"
>
> To which the other replied, "Don't ask me. I'm a chicken."

If you got this joke, then you had a type of insight. Although psychologists who study insight have never used humor as a paradigm, jokes meet many of the definitions of insight, not least because they cause a restructuring of what you observe. Ever since I heard the mad cow joke, I can't look at cows the same way.

Historically, jokes served many functions. The eighteenth-century political philosopher Thomas Hobbes thought that humor allows you to express superiority over others; Freud believed that jokes, like dreams, relieve internal conflict; and others have said that humor acts as a safety valve to release pent-up frustration over the effects of social injustice.[32] Whatever the ultimate function of humor, jokes and comedy allow you to see the world differently.

In the first fMRI study of humor, a group at University College in London presented puns and one-line jokes to subjects in a scanner. The funniest of the bunch activated the medial prefrontal cortex—a region often associated with reward—and the cerebellum—a region associated with coordination.[33] But it was hard to know whether these regions were activated because the jokes were funny or because parts of the reward system were responding to the novelty of being told a joke. Presumably, a joke is funny only because it imparts novel information.

In a different study, Allan Reiss, a psychiatrist at Stanford University, presented cartoons to people in an MRI scanner. The cartoons were culled from a variety of sources but were typified by ones from the series *Bizarro*, by Dan Piraro, who is known for his irreverent, twisted outlook on contemporary life. As a control condition, Reiss altered the captions of some of Piraro's cartoons, replacing them with descriptive, nonfunny ones. This manipulation allowed Reiss to control for the visual and language elements of the cartoons, while removing the element of humor.[34] The cartoons with original captions activated a widespread cortical network and also parts of the reward system, including the striatum and nucleus accumbens. It is tempting to conclude that this activity pattern, because it occurred in the reward system, reflects the pleasurable component of humor, but a more parsimonious explanation would be that each of these elements was responding to the novel information in the cartoons and not to the pleasure of the humor. Funny cartoons push more information into the brain because they restructure your worldview.

This same sort of restructuring occurs when a crossword puzzle is completed or a puzzle is solved. The last bit of information that suddenly triggers the restructuring of what you heretofore understood drives your reward system off the scale. It is, after all, the need for novelty that makes puzzles so satisfying to solve.

## Completing the Grid

As the morning wore on at the crossword tournament, the puzzles were getting more difficult, and my mental logjams were no easier to navigate. Steve Levy had been doing quite well. Because he quickly finished his puzzles, he had time to recharge between rounds. A small crowd of boisterous top solvers gathered in the lobby, prompting a reminder from Shortz to be quiet.

As I waited for the third puzzle, I wondered what made for a good puzzle.

"Humor and innovation are the most important," Levy said.

There is an art to constructing crossword puzzles. Good puzzles link answers and clues in unexpected ways. In the hands of the true masters, a crossword puzzle can even make you laugh. Humor, insight, and puzzle solving really do seem to draw on similar cognitive processes and, as I suspected, tap into the basic need for novelty. The people who make crossword puzzles—constructors—are not necessarily the best solvers. Even so, they come to the tournament to mingle with one another and their fans.

Between puzzles, a man came up to Frank Longo, a constructor popular with those who prefer their crosswords on the difficult side, and asked him to sign a copy of Longo's book, *Cranium Crushing Crosswords*. The autograph seeker turned to me and bubbled, "These are the best! I spent hours working these puzzles. His grids are just beautiful."

But when I asked my fellow contestants who their favorite constructor was, the answer was, invariably, "Reagle." Merl Reagle, perhaps the king of crossword constructors, lives in Florida, and his puzzles are syndicated around the country. When Shortz announced Puzzle #3 as Reagle's, the crowd erupted in cheers. Because, at the time, I couldn't recognize his style, I was at yet another disadvantage while solving his puzzle. I didn't know, for instance, that 1-across, a five-letter word for "Holey order?" was *SWISS*; or 17-across, a classic Reagle pun for a ten-letter word, "Bona ____" (answer: *CONTENTION*). During the thirty minutes allowed for the puzzle, the crowd's chuckles maintained a steady rhythm, and Reagle himself stood at the podium wearing a Cheshire cat grin.

When the dust finally settled and the tournament was over, I found myself in a respectable 474th place. Respectable only because I wasn't last out of the 479 entrants. On the trip home, I sat next to a flight attendant dead-heading back to Atlanta, and she pulled out a stack of crossword puzzles. I couldn't help watching her solve them. When she got stuck on a clue, I offered a suggestion, and we started talking about the pleasures of puzzles. Most of the time, puzzles are solved alone, but who said they can't also be sources of social interaction? An entirely different dynamic emerges when you work on a puzzle as a team. In addition to the camaraderie of competing together against the puzzle maker, there is the pleasure of shared insights and—even more rare—the knowledge that another human being sees what you see.

But whether alone or with someone else, the satisfaction of the *Aha!* moment still requires novelty to trigger the mental restructuring that leads to true insight. If you are one that craves *Aha!* moments, then the only logical course of action is to seek out situations in which you encounter something new. Although puzzles provide a limited framework for achieving this, there are other, physical ways as well.

# 4

## The Sushi Problem

If dreams are the road to the unconscious, or, at least the gateway to an *Aha!* experience, then what does it mean to dream about fish?

I dream about slabs of fatty tuna. In this dream, salty air, redolent of fresh fish, circulates from somewhere distant, and the sushi chef parcels this love of mine into thumb-size morsels, presenting a pair of tuna to me with a dab of wasabi and a slice of pickled ginger. The vermillion meat teases, daring me not to chew it, insisting I savor its cool fleshiness before swallowing.

Prepared by a master chef, sushi approaches culinary perfection. Even if its cost were not prohibitive, I would resist regular consumption for fear of growing accustomed to the taste. I could, on the other hand, deprive myself altogether and have sushi only on the most special occasions. Alas, that would be a high price to pay, giving up my favorite dish for the promise of a heightened experience some years from now. I could take the path of the glutton and eat sushi every day. It would be grand at first, sampling

California rolls, hand rolls, inside-out rolls, upside-down rolls, and sashimi, too. But boredom would eventually set in, and the sushi would become as commonplace as, say, a piece of buttered toast.

Somewhere between these two extremes, eating sushi every day and eating it once a decade, must lie the sweet spot. Finding that spot is what I have come to know as the sushi problem, which is not just about sushi. If you really like to do something, how often should you do it? Some of the most satisfying experiences are one-shot affairs; attempts to reproduce them almost always end in failure. The need to predict how things are leads you to novel experiences, but first experiences are always the best, because they provide the freshest information. Repetition lets you refine your predictions, but it is never as satisfying as the first time. With food, though, you have no choice; you must eat several times a day, and so a certain amount of habituation to its pleasure seems inevitable. The only choice lies in what you eat and when you eat it. For this reason, eating is paradigmatic of any activity that must be undertaken on a regular basis. If the secret of a great dining experience could be unraveled, perhaps it could be applied to other realms. And if it couldn't, then perhaps knowing what makes for a satisfying meal is valuable in its own right.

· · ·

You begin life as a pancake of cells, no bigger than a pencil point. Magically, the first step toward becoming human occurs three weeks after conception, when this disk of protoplasm curls upon itself and forms a tube. Everything after that is just an extension of the hollow cylinder: an outpouching for the head and brain, amoeba-like protrusions that become arms and legs, and subsidiary tubes that get pinched off to become the circulatory system.

But we all are still basically tubes, which is to say two-dimensional sheets of tissue making our way in a three-dimensional world. But the truth is even more vulgar, for what glorification can be made of the adult version of a tube that begins at your lips, courses some forty feet through bacteria-laden sludge, and ends ignominiously at your ass?

Your gastrointestinal system is perhaps the most intimate connection you have with the external world. While your skin protects you from the outside world and provides an interface with it through tactile sensors, and your muscles move you about, allowing you to interact with it, your GI tract stands above all other bodily systems in being closely interposed with the outside world. It *is* the outside world, a microcosm alive with foreign substances, many of which flow back and forth freely in your body. To my mind, putting something in your mouth, and swallowing it, is the most intimate of acts, one that brings the world literally inside you. It is a remarkable system that can take such a wide variety of substances and break them down into usable components without destroying itself in the process.

And the GI tract is responsible for some of the most sublimely satisfying experiences that you encounter. Some gourmands would say that nothing—not sex and not drugs—tops a good meal. The secret, as in all things that satisfy, is novelty—novel ingredients and novel sensations.

## Fishing for Taste

In spite of my great love of sushi, I don't fish.

My first memory of fishing is of being dragged down to the fishing hole behind my house by my twelve-year-old neighbor, sweating in the dirt for hours, only to come up with a weedy-looking catfish. I voted to throw it back. Instead, he carried the stinky creature to his house, where he proudly presented it to his father, who, suddenly roused from the television, set aside his beer to demonstrate exactly how to clean it. The procedure lasted into the evening and culminated in the ritual grilling and sharing of the catch.

Nevertheless, I know that some people enjoy fishing, just for the sport of it, and that some are positively obsessed with the pastime. It was by happenstance that I met one of these people, one of today's great outdoor writers, who is particularly keen on fishing.

Peter Kaminsky is a writer and a true outdoorsman, and it was his ideas about food and fishing that helped shaped my thoughts on what makes for a satisfying meal. He has an impressive résumé, with numerous articles in the *New York Times*, *Food & Wine*, and *Field & Stream*, but it was his treatise, *The Elements of Taste*,[1] that really caught my interest.

The work, coauthored with Gray Kunz, the former chef of Lespinasse in Manhattan, lays out a new way of thinking about food. Kunz was the artist using food as his palette, and Kaminsky was the critic deconstructing the artistry; together they discuss the fourteen elements of taste and the ways in which they can be mixed to create inventive dishes. Fourteen? I had been taught that there are four basic tastes: sweet, salty, sour, and bitter. In the West, wider recognition of Asian foods like sushi has led to the acceptance of a fifth taste, umami (Japanese for "savoriness"), which has been portrayed as a pungent taste common to asparagus, cheese, and meat. Kunz and Kaminsky describe the basic five, and nine others too: salty, sweet, picante (spicy hot), tangy (aka sour), vinted, bulby (garlic and onion), floral herbal (rosemary and thyme), spiced aromatic (cinnamon and cloves), funky (cabbage, truffles, and stinky cheese), bitter, garden (aka vegetables), meaty, oceanic (fishy), and starchy.

People tend to think of taste as synonymous with flavor, but it is actually much more. Taste is a multisensory experience that depends on flavor, smell, and tactile sensation. Kunz and Kaminsky nail the multiple sensations contributing to taste, recognizing that picante tastes, for instance, result from the stimulation of pain receptors on the tongue, and that oceanic tastes result as much from salty flavors as they do from the smell of the ocean itself. But even if they were right about the multiplicity of flavors, science was just beginning to catch up with these artists.

Taste is an obvious place to begin the dissection of a satisfying meal, even though the physiological mechanisms of taste have been the least understood of all the senses. It wasn't until 1999 that the genes that code for specific taste receptors were identified; by 2004, forty mammalian taste receptors had been discovered.[2] As every child knows, the human tongue is dotted with taste buds. The smallish ones toward the tip of the tongue that look like sandpaper are called fungiform papillae, and the larger, pimply ones on the back of the tongue are called circumvallate papillae. You can still probably find textbooks that diagram a taste map of the tongue—sweet toward the tip, salty and sour on the sides, and bitter on the back—a map for which there is no evidence. In fact, the various types of taste receptors are distributed fairly evenly across the tongue.

Under the microscope, a taste bud looks like a clove of garlic, but these cloves are actually specialized cells for taste reception. A taste bud has a hundred or so receptor cells, which don't last long under the harsh conditions of the mouth, about ten days. One end of the receptor cell pokes out of the taste bud and makes contact with whatever substance washes over it; the other end synapses with a nerve fiber.

One of the remaining research questions is whether each receptor cell expresses the gene for one type of taste receptor, or whether each cell expresses the genes for different receptors. The answer would determine how many classes of taste you can distinguish. The first taste receptors to be genetically sequenced responded to bitter substances, and they were dubbed $T_1R$ and $T_2R$, for the first and second family of taste receptors. $T_2Rs$ represented a large family of receptors, with at least twenty-five genes coding for variants. The picture that emerged was just as complicated for sweet and umami tastes but involved a different family of genes. One combination of genes resulted in a receptor sensitive to sweet tastes, but another combination produced a receptor sensitive to umami.[3] The detection of salty and sour tastes relied on yet another family of receptors.

Although physiologists were categorizing taste receptors into the five basic categories, the sheer complexity of receptor gene combination suggested that Kunz and Kaminsky were closer to the truth. The number of ways in which the genes for taste combine with one another means that well over a thousand receptors exist on every human tongue, blowing away the idea of four or five basic tastes. Kunz and Kaminsky's fourteen elements begin to appear as a modest expansion of the basic four or five. Presciently, the two writers included odor and tactile contributions to the taste experience. Little did I know how important these sensations are to the dining experience, but I was about to find out in a most uncommon way.

## Food Time

I met Kaminsky at Next Door Nobu, the more casual but no less trendy sister to Nobu—one of Manhattan's hippest and most expensive sushi joints. It wasn't even seven o'clock on a weeknight, but the inauspicious entrance to the restaurant was easily recognized by the dozen people crowding the sidewalk, waiting for tables. I pressed past a man who was yelling into a sliver of a phone, which he held a few inches from his mouth. A quick scan of the restaurant revealed only one empty chair, at a tiny table in the middle of the room where Peter sat, reading a newspaper.

The menu was slightly intimidating, since Nobu alters many of the usual dishes with touches of herbs and sauces. I was leaning toward *omakase*—the tasting menu—when Peter put an end to that idea. "I never get the tasting menu," he said, "because I find the dining experience more enjoyable when I order myself."

But in all things related to sushi, surely the chef knows best, right?

Perhaps, but Peter explained, "Time is very important in the dining experience. You spend time looking over the menu, deciding what you want, and imagining what it will be like. Then, after you place your order, anticipation builds, until it is delivered and you experience it. And then you remember." On cue, the waiter appeared, and Peter ordered for both of us: rock shrimp, spicy tuna roll, salmon sashimi, and Nobu's signature blackened cod.

In *The Elements of Taste*, Kunz and Kaminsky underscore their belief that time is just as important an element in the dining experience as the ingredients themselves. A meal is like a story, they say, with a beginning, middle, and end. Timing, as in all things, is everything.

"Time flies when you're having fun," I said.

"Not really." He picked up a wedge of salmon and carefully laid a piece of ginger across it, eyeing its perfection before swallowing it whole. "When I am really enjoying myself, I call it 'special time.'" Peter has written at some length about this phenomenon, portraying it as "a different reality, one in which I am fully alive, fully focused, where each second is a ripe fruit bursting with juice."[4] He thinks that under the right circumstances you experience "special time" as periods of hyperreality, transcendent moments that burn in your memory. Of course a fisherman should be so aware of time. Cast your fly a split second too late, and the fish will be gone.

Nobu's blackened cod, delivered promptly to the table, yielded easily to our chopsticks. The fish was oily, not in an unpleasant way, and after marinating for three days in a yellow miso paste, it had acquired a sweetness that lingered on the back of the tongue. It had taken three days to prepare this morsel of food, and, in a second, it was gone. The moment you take a bite of something delicious, the combination of flavors, which by themselves might be mundane, is compressed in both time and space. A cosmic convergence at the tip of your tongue.

Maybe Peter was right. There *are* different temporal experiences, and food is just one of the ways to slip into a different current of time. Until that moment, I hadn't thought, at least not consciously, of the alternate realities of a dining experience. But, of course, food has the power to transport us. For some it might be chocolate, for others a twenty-year-old Scotch, and for still others, the perfect simplicity of a freshly picked strawberry. Whatever it is, the right food, at the right moment, has the power to stop time.

The sun had just set as we left Nobu, and a pleasant summer breeze was blowing off the ocean from the south. The salty air whistled through the cables of the Brooklyn Bridge as we walked back toward Peter's home. On the promenade, we passed several young couples in amorous embraces, oblivious to our ramblings about the pleasures of food. Food and love—two of the great pleasures in life whose links are often taken for granted. Much has been written about the aphrodisiac quality of certain foods, like chocolate or oysters, but I was not yet aware of the scientific basis of any such notion. I asked Peter if he knew anything about it.

He shrugged, but it was too dark to make out his expression.

I persisted. "Who might know about the link between food and love?"

Finally, he said, "Francis Mallmann."

The name was unfamiliar.

"Great Argentine chef," Peter explained. "A sensualist, and a true poet."

What came immediately to mind were the possibilities in Argentina, which were tantalizing. I imagined trekking to Patagonia, in search of the reclusive yet brilliant food artiste flanked by legions of women seduced by his meals.

Peter snapped me from my reverie. "He has a place in the Hamptons."

## The Matching Law

Two elements contribute to the difficulty in solving the sushi problem, which is the question of how often you should do something you really enjoy. First, choices are distributed in time. The question is not whether to eat sushi but how often to eat it. Most people have trouble gauging the relative effect of different rates of consumption. I could not, for example, say whether weekly or biweekly sushi was more enjoyable. Moreover, the sheer number of other foods to eat makes choices difficult. On any given day, I could eat a sandwich, pizza, chicken, a salad, or countless other dishes. But more often than not, I restrict my options to make decisions easier.

Second, repeat experiences lead to habituation. Some sensations habituate quickly, like the rapid adjustment to wealth that Phil Brickman documented (see Chapter 2). Other activities, perhaps sex, habituate more slowly, but that, too, remains to be determined. Unless you keep a diary detailing how much you enjoy every event that fills your days, you might never figure out the best way in which to parcel out your pleasures.

It may come as a surprise that a problem of such complexity might actually have a solution. Well, there are many solutions, but both animals and people overwhelmingly adopt one particular approach, which the late Harvard psychologist Richard Herrnstein devoted his career to studying. Instead of sushi, Herrnstein examined pigeons. By measuring the rate at which they would peck for their food, he and his colleagues developed a theory of how animals allocate their decisions when their choices are distributed over time.

Herrnstein kept his pigeons in special cages outfitted with two bars. When pecked on, the bars delivered food, but at different rates. The pigeons easily learned how to distribute their pecks in such an arrangement. If bar A delivered food at twice the rate of bar B, then the pigeons pecked twice as often on A. On the surface, this behavior may seem illogical. If bar A delivered twice as much food per peck as bar B, then why peck at bar B at all? Not only do pigeons respond this way, but so do rats, monkeys, and people. The universality of such behavior led Herrnstein to dub his observation the matching law, which states that animals allocate their rates of response to different choices in a ratio that *matches* the rates at which they get goodies.[5] It is one thing for a rat or a pigeon to behave this way, but when humans allocate their choices in the same manner, a deeper process, one not totally dependent on intelligence, must be at work.

Making the matching problem more complicated, though, is the process of habituation. The enjoyment of sushi habituates to some degree, as does everything. The trick is to keep habituation in check so that you can continue to savor the pleasures of the activities you really enjoy. After a week, perhaps a month, of daily sushi, I might not like it as much. When, say, a sandwich becomes more appealing than sushi, I would switch to eating sandwiches as often as I had eaten sushi. When I got tired of sandwiches, I would switch back to sushi until I found a stable alternation of the two. Then I would be in equilibrium between my choices, matching the frequency of my selections to the intensity of the enjoyment they brought me. Herrnstein labeled this process melioration, an apt term, given the fact that this biological process reduces great experiences to the level of mediocrity and elevates the mundane.

While melioration leads to a stable mixture of choices, it is also a trap. As soon as you start overconsuming one item and thus move away from an equilibrium point, tension builds, like an unseen hand on the tiller, steering you back to the comfortable mix defined by the matching law. The need for novelty, though, directly opposes this process, periodically kicking you out of matching behavior. You feel this as boredom and the itch of curiosity.

. . .

About halfway through our Kool-Aid experiment, Read and I got the idea that maybe the striatum played a role in matching behavior. As I have described, the striatum is linked to both action and reward, so it was not far-fetched to think that the striatum might have something to do with the way you allocate your choices. We took as our inspiration the behavior of bumblebees. Bees may not be very intelligent, but they still have to make decisions about which flowers to visit. In an elegant series of experiments, the ecologist Leslie Real constructed enclosed bee colonies and filled artificial flowers with various amounts of nectar. In one experiment, blue flowers contained two microliters of nectar, and yellow flowers contained six microliters. But there was a catch: only one-third of the yellow flowers had nectar and two-thirds had nothing. Blue and yellow flowers would, on average, have the same amount of nectar—the same expected value—so the bees should not exhibit color preference.[6] But they did, visiting blue flowers 84 percent of the time.[7] Bees, like humans, prefer a sure thing.

Read had been programming computer models of simple choice behavior, specifically how bumblebees decide to allocate the time they spend at one flower or another. His computer simulations suggested that the way in which dopamine is released in the brain might explain why bees are risk averse and why humans are prone to getting stuck in matching behavior. One day he showed me a simple computer game he had developed. The screen contained two large rectangles signifying buttons to push; the one on the left was labeled A and the one on the right B. A vertical reward bar was positioned between the two buttons.

"Use the mouse buttons to select either A or B," Read

instructed. "You can go as fast or as slow as you want, but the object is to get the reward bar to move as high as possible."

Sounded simple enough, so I clicked A, and the bar nudged up a little. I clicked A a few more times, and each time the bar moved up a little more. It seemed too easy; so, out of curiosity, I clicked B. The bar zoomed up by almost double. Naturally I stayed with B for a while, but after half a dozen clicks there, the reward bar started going down. Frustrated, I went back to A. And so it went, until I had settled into a stable ratio of two B's for every A. Without me knowing it, Read had sucked me into pure matching behavior.

He had set up the game to give rewards based on the percentage of A's and B's in the last forty clicks. With about 30 percent A's, the reward yield was the same for A and B, so there was no clear incentive to pick one rather than the other. Increasing the allocation of A's, from 30 to 50 percent, caused a decrease in the rewards. If only I had stayed with A longer, I would have discovered that picking A more than 50 percent of the time would have led to higher rewards, and picking A 100 percent of the time would have been the best response of all. Instead, the rubber band that represents matching behavior kept pulling me back toward a stable 1:2 mix.

After some of our volunteers had completed the MRI scan, we asked them to play Read's computer game. If they got stuck at the matching point, as I did, we categorized them as Conservative. If they escaped the matching point and picked A more than 50 percent of the time, we categorized them as Risky. With their fMRI data in hand, we compared the striatal responses of the Conservatives and the Riskies. Not everyone behaved as conservatively as I did. About half of the participants escaped the matching point and discovered the secret to the game. Read thought that the Riskies and the Conservatives might have different set points in their dopamine systems. I wasn't so sure, but since our Kool-Aid experiment was already under way, it seemed a simple thing to look into.

I should emphasize that we combined two different experiments: the fMRI measurement of how predictability modulates striatal activity (the Kool-Aid test) and a behavioral test of decision making. When we plotted each person's propensity to risk on the computer game against the strength of response in his striatum to unpredictable squirts of Kool-Aid and water, the points fell on a straight line.[8]

Lest you think that your striatal response somehow hardwires you into a risk-taking profile, a follow-up experiment showed that risk-taking or novelty-seeking can be influenced by other factors in the environment. In another group of subjects, a computer algorithm determined who was Risky or Conservative and, midway through the game, started giving the person juice squirts in an attempt to change his behavior. Risk-takers were given juice squirts when they picked B, which pushed them back toward the matching point, and Conservatives were given juice squirts when they picked A, pushing them away from the matching point.[9] Far from being hardwired, the propensity to risk—novelty-seeking—turned out to be malleable.

This was good news, for I was about to get a whopping taste of novelty in my pursuit of the perfect dining experience.

## Cooking Lessons

I finally met the Argentine chef at his home in the Hamptons, on eastern Long Island, on a dreary winter morning. The drizzle of sleet outside made Mallmann's home an inviting refuge after the long drive from Manhattan. A fire crackled in the den, and the unmistakable voice of Maria Callas, singing a duet from the *Marriage of Figaro*, filtered into every room.

The son of an Argentine physicist, Francis Mallmann acquired an early appreciation for the chemistry of food and became well acquainted with the physics of cookery. In the academic household in which he grew up, his parents entertained frequently. But more than the intellectual jousting common to such gatherings, Francis was fascinated with the culinary preparations that went into hosting parties. He left home at age seventeen to cultivate his calling as a chef and spent several years bumming around the Haight-Ashbury district in San Francisco before returning to Argentina to help run a restaurant. He broadened his skills by getting classical training in France, resulting in a brand of cooking that has been hailed as a unique blend of French and Argentine influences.

Busy in the kitchen, a practical room, with well-worn pots stacked on open shelves and an eating area in the center, Francis filled the room. His longish, thinning hair and intensely blue eyes reminded me of Marlon Brando in *Last Tango in Paris*. He had the aura of someone who had experienced life's deepest emotions. His academic roots hadn't been completely abandoned, though, as he announced, "Every day begins with a cooking lesson."

He was placing pieces of Valrhona chocolate in a double boiler, handling the chunks as if they were gold. "Chocolate is the most sensuous of foods," he said as he added the last of what looked to be about a pound. "It melts at precisely the temperature of the human body."

It was indeed a happy coincidence that one of the most beloved of foods is matched so closely to the human body. A piece of high-quality chocolate placed on the tongue will actually feel cool because the process of melting it absorbs energy from the mouth without raising the temperature of the chocolate.[10]

"You don't want to overheat it," he said as he creamed together butter and sugar in an electric mixer. His gaze never left the boiler, waiting for the magical moment when solid transformed to liquid, an almost instantaneous process because of chocolate's abrupt melting point. "That would ruin the texture."

When the chocolate had cooled, he carefully added it to the butter and sifted in flour. He did this a few tablespoons at a time, until the batter dripped slowly off a spoon in a continuous stream. After folding in beaten eggs, he placed the batter in a round baking pan and popped it into the oven. "Don't let me forget about that," he said.

While the torte baked, we sat at the kitchen table and sipped hot tea from glasses. The glass was shaped like a tumbler but with a much thinner wall. Each glass was filled about halfway with an herbal tea, rich with the scent of jasmine.

"I love these glasses," he said, holding them up for me to see.

"Do you always drink tea out of a glass?" I asked. It seemed a little odd; I thought that tea was always drunk from a teacup.

"The shape of the glass affects the taste in many ways," he explained. "With wine, it is even more important. The weight of the glass, its curvature, how it presents the liquid to your eye, and how the glass delivers it into your mouth, all contribute to the enjoyment of even a glass of tea."

I looked at the tea with a new appreciation. Tea looked different when you could see it through and through. The glass's heat contributed to a multisensory experience that relied on my mouth and tongue to savor the infused herbs while my mind's eye took in the colors, and the heat filled my hands. Something in my brain stem began to tingle.

## Feeling with the Mind's Eye

We all know there are five senses—sight, hearing, touch, taste, and smell—but as Francis made clear with his glasses, all of them—not just taste—play a role in the dining experience. Although Francis was approaching the construction of a multisensory experience from the vantage point of a chef, a great deal of neurobiology uncovered in recent years, in fact, conforms to his techniques.

The multitude of sensations in your body results from the conversion of various forms of energy into electricity, which gets transmitted to your brain. Your eyes are connected to your brain through the optic nerve, and your ears through the auditory nerve; smells reach the brain through the olfactory bulbs above the nose; and tastes through several nerves that go to the tongue and throat. Unlike the other sensations, touch is spread throughout the body; no single nerve transmits touch sensations to the brain. Neuroscientists have thought that each sensation goes to a particular part of the brain, where the raw signals are decoded and then passed on to higher cognitive centers where they are integrated. In fact, scientists still speak of the visual cortex and the auditory cortex as distinct anatomical locations in the brain. Nevertheless, multisensory regions exist between the primary stations in several parts of the parietal cortex, a sort of no-man's-land between the back of the brain and its sides, where raw sensations are brought together and merged into a unifying concept.

A rose, for example, has color, smell, and texture. Somehow all the sensations are integrated in your brain to produce the singular notion of roseness. The parietal cortex performs part of this function. Damage to this region results in a veritable sideshow of bizarre neurological syndromes, ranging from the inability to identify one's fingers to the alien hand syndrome, in which one hand seemingly has a will of its own (think *Dr. Strangelove*).

At first glance, pathways of sensation seem to be one-way streets, with information flowing from the sense organs to the brain and not in the other direction. Neuroscientists have broadly categorized nerves as either afferent (going into the central nervous system) or efferent (going out of the central nervous system). Nerves of sensation are all afferent. But once sensory information reaches the brain, the direction of information flow can actually become confusing.

Vision is the easiest system to study. Visual stimuli can be precisely controlled by the experimenter and presented to people in an MRI scanner. The visual cortex is in the back of the brain, and each location in the retina maps to a specific location in the visual cortex. The first part of the cortex that receives vision inputs is dubbed, appropriately, $V_1$. Neurons in $V_1$ tend to respond to rudimentary aspects of vision, like edges and differences between light and dark. $V_1$ then projects to higher-level visual processing regions—called $V_2$, $V_3$, and $V_4$—that extract progressively more complex representations of what the eyes see, like motion and color.

It is tempting to think of the way you see as resembling the way a video camera operates, but the analogy is poor. Whereas a camera faithfully renders whatever is placed in front of it, human vision is full of holes; what you "see" is as much the product of your imagination as it is the result of what your eyes physically take in. For example, the moon appears larger when it is near the horizon than when it is overhead because objects on the horizon make you think the moon is closer than it actually is. The big question for scientists is the degree to which the act of seeing can be altered by nonvisual processes. Can your mind affect what happens in $V_1$ itself, changing what you see before you are even aware of the image? The answer has startling implications for the perceptions during a great dining experience. As Peter Kaminsky said, anticipation— the way you conjure up the food before it arrives—may actually affect how you taste a meal.

Imagination really can have an impact on what you see. Using fMRI, a group of cognitive scientists in London showed that low-level vision can be affected by other parts of the brain. When participants were asked to detect shapes in different parts of their visual fields, their performance on the task could be improved if they were first touched briefly on the hand, indicating on which side the target would appear. It is a long way from the hand to the eye, about six inches in the brain, and yet the London group found that activity in the visual cortex could indeed be influenced by touching the subject on the appropriate hand.[11] The parietal cortex plays a key role in this process, receiving both tactile and visual signals and sending the appropriate parts of the mixed information back to their respective brain regions, with touch changing visual processing in real time.

Does this process work in the other direction? Can what you see change the way you feel? Using a different technology, a colleague of mine in Atlanta, Krish Sathian, showed that both touch and sight are two-way streets. Krish has used transcranial magnetic stimulation, TMS, to disrupt the visual cortex while subjects determined, by touch, in which direction a series of metallic ridges was placed on their fingers. TMS works by passing electrical current through a doughnut-shaped device. When electricity flows in such a circle, it creates a magnetic field through the hole of the doughnut. The more loops of wire and the stronger the electrical current, the stronger the magnetic field. When the doughnut is placed over the scalp and the electrical current turned on, the resulting magnetic field disrupts the neurons just beneath it. The disruption is only temporary, and the neurons return to normal when the current is turned off. TMS has become popular in research circles because the temporary brain lesions it induces allow scientists essentially to take a part of the brain off-line and see what effect this has on normal function. When Krish disrupted the visual cortex, his subjects' ability to distinguish touch dropped almost to the level of chance.[12]

The senses are clearly not as distinct as was once thought. If what you understand as touch can mutate under your eyes, and vice versa, the boundaries of sensation, like watercolors on a canvas, can bleed into each other, creating a multisensory experience different from the sum of its parts. But Francis, of course, already knew this.

## A Merging of Senses

The perception of each sense is clearly malleable, and most neuroscientists and psychologists now accept the evidence for the ability of one sense to affect another. Normally, the interaction of sensation occurs seamlessly and without any conscious effort, but in a small percentage of people, senses can become so scrambled that tastes have shape or sounds have color. *Synesthesia* is the union of sensation and refers to a condition that is reported to affect about one in two thousand people.[13]

Although synesthesia had been documented for centuries, scientific dissection of the condition began in the 1980s when the American neurologist Richard Cytowic published two books in which he described several patients and their forms of synesthesia.[14] Every patient had a distinct form, although associations with color were the most frequent. Lexical synesthesia, in which letters or words are perceived as colored, was particularly common. The classical explanation of synesthesia implied either that the patients were faking their experience (after all, nobody but the patients themselves could know what they perceived) or, more generously, that these folks were speaking in metaphors, like *blue Mondays*. A number of studies, however, have confirmed that synesthetes indeed perceive what they say they do.[15] How does the phenomenon occur? To some researchers, the answer lies in cross-wiring, in which the parts of the brain that normally represent letters, for example, get crossed with the parts of the brain that represent a sensation like color.[16] Brain imaging studies support this idea, because, in synesthetes, color regions, which are outside $V1$, are activated by spoken words.[17]

The cross-wiring is presumed to have occurred sometime early in development. Most synesthetes report experiencing the phenomenon since childhood, but if synesthesia could emerge in adulthood, then there might be a latent synesthete in all of us, and, I thought, it might be unmasked during a great dining experience.[18] Drugs like LSD often cause synesthetic-like experiences, and there is some evidence that infants are synesthetic; thus the mixing of senses might occur, under the right conditions, in anyone.

· · ·

While the torte baked, Francis prepared a demonstration, or perhaps performance is a better word, of the power of a multisensory experience to unmask the inner synesthete.

In his den, he had placed a galvanized steel vat at the foot of a plushy sofa. Were it not for the lemons he was slicing into it, the ten-gallon vessel would have been more at home next to a garden shed. Francis beckoned for me to sit down and place my feet in it. The vat was filled with very warm water, which in the middle of winter felt intensely hot on my naked, bluish feet. The infusion of lemon contrasted with the sharp aroma of onions and fennel.

"Are you comfortable there?" asked Francis.

"Very," I replied.

He then placed a blindfold around my eyes and handed me a set of earphones that were plugged into a CD player. A composition in a minor key faded in, a single synthesizer plucking plaintive tones. With a slight reverb, I heard Francis's voice in Spanish, *"Que tus ejércitos militen el oro y la tempestad, Magnus Barfod."* Later he told me that this was the first line of the poem, "El enemigo generoso" ("The Generous Enemy") by Jorge Luis Borges.[19] Of course it is only fitting that Francis should begin with a poem by the greatest Argentine poet, but the significance of the poem's homage to a short-lived Norwegian king, Magnus Barefoot, would become

discernible to me only later, halfway across the Atlantic. Regardless, I sat there letting myself get into the experience, a unique
blend of poetry, music, aromas, and tactile sensations.

The voice began speaking in French, shifting from a calm bari-
tone to an urgent tenor. *"J'ai tant rêvé de toi que tu perds ta réalité,"*
which translates beautifully as: "I've dreamed of you so much that
you're losing your reality."[20] Just as I caught a snatch of something
to do with a sundial, Francis switched to English, reciting a poem
by Robert Graves which begins: "He is quick, thinking in clear
images; I am slow, thinking in broken images."[21]

After an indeterminate amount of time, Francis refreshed the
bath around my feet with an infusion of lemon and fennel. I was in
a different time—maybe even Kaminsky time—an internal hyperreality as sharp as an arrow. Francis continued, alternating between
Spanish, French, and English at a quickening pace, before finally
transitioning into a duet of "Cucurrucucú Paloma," a song by Cae-
tano Veloso made famous in the Pedro Almodóvar film *Talk to Her.*
Francis carried a surprisingly good tune.

Each of the poems Francis had chosen spoke of its own realities,
some sharper, some more real, but each a world constructed within
the mind. The juxtaposition of these worlds, whether conscious or
not, against the sensory inputs to which he subjected me created an
experience so different from the sum of its parts that it is not clear
how to characterize it. Was it dining, or poetry, or music, or aro-
matherapy?

Francis had performed this ritual for the first time in his restaurant in São Paulo, Brazil. "São Paulo," Francis said. "It's quite hor-
rible, but I really like it. It's very industrial, very powerful. But they
are a very happy and patient people." In the full experience,
patrons were not only blindfolded, as I was, but fed small portions
of food that Francis had created.

"Some people couldn't cope with it," Francis explained. Those who were able to tolerate the intense novelty received something special indeed. "When you show something different, people are very eager to take it."

## Champagne Dreams

It was time for lunch. As our chocolate torte cooled, Francis unwrapped some duck breasts. While they lay naked on the butcher paper, he scattered them with sea salt and herbs.

I uncorked a bottle of champagne as he seared the duck on a griddle. Together, we made a salad of romaine lettuce dressed with balsamic vinegar, extra-virgin olive oil, truffle oil, and a grating of parmesano reggiano. In the time it took to make the salad, the duck was done. Francis roasted sliced almonds in the pan and scattered them across the breasts, which he had placed on simple white dishes.

We toasted our collaboration and pledged to bring our fields closer together. The duck tasted of autumn, fragrant with smoke, and the almonds crunched like fallen leaves. The champagne made me light-headed, as it always does, and maybe I was too much into the multisensory experience, but a lunch of duck and salad, prepared without pretension, transcended mere sustenance.

Perhaps it was the champagne. The effects of alcohol need no elaboration, for as Brillat-Savarin, the first physiologist of taste, said, "Alcohol is the prince of liquids, and transports the palate to the highest pitch of exaltation."[22] Royal or not, alcohol has an undeniable effect on the palatability of food. But almost two hundred years after Brillat-Savarin's observation, the marriage of the two is still not fully understood.

Alcohol can be considered a component of the human diet because of its high energy content: a gram of alcohol provides seven calories of energy, second only to fat. Beyond its raw energy value, alcohol has the curious property of stimulating appetite. Whereas a glass of wine might contain about an ounce of alcohol, or two hundred calories, compare its effect on appetite with eating the caloric equivalent, a pat of butter. While fat sates, alcohol stimulates.

Whatever alcohol does has little to do with its energy content. Alcohol's effect on the brain occurs mainly through its interaction with the gamma-aminobutyric acid, or GABA, system. GABA is an inhibitory neurotransmitter: it makes other neurons less likely to fire. GABA neurons are found all over the brain; they keep, for instance, the cortex from firing out of control in epileptic fits. Alcohol, however, exerts its effect mainly through GABA receptors in the striatum and brain stem. Over 90 percent of the striatum is composed of GABA neurons, a proportion several times greater than in any other part of the brain. When drugs that block the GABA receptor are infused directly into the brain stems of rats bred to like alcohol, their alcohol consumption, but not their overall food intake, decreases, demonstrating that the addictive properties of alcohol occur in the striatum.[23]

Although the bulk of the striatum is composed of neurons that release GABA, those same neurons have the highest concentration of dopamine receptors in the brain, and, as I described in the first chapter, they receive most of their input from the cortex. Alcohol enhances the effect of GABA—essentially turning up the volume in the striatum—and through mechanisms that are not completely clear, stimulates appetite. This effect on appetite, however, is not uniform; alcohol tends to stimulate the intake of salty and fatty foods. In one study, subjects consumed 9–17 percent more calories after a single drink; a disproportionate number of them came from potato chips.[24]

Francis's duck was no potato chip. The fatty skin had turned a deep brown, and its crispness surpassed anything eaten out of a bag. The champagne was surely working its magic on my striatum, but there was something else, something lingering from the multisensory experience I had just indulged in.

As Francis's multisensory experience demonstrated, removing vision emphasizes the other senses. Alcohol reduces the prominence of the vision system, too, by making you less attentive to objects you see, while amping up the striatum. Under such circumstances, the other sensory systems become free to associate with one another in novel ways. Humans are, after all, visual animals. Take away sight, or at least diminish its preeminence, and the tastes, smells, and sounds of a meal become that much more powerful. Perhaps alcohol's palate-enhancing effects are, in part, a result of the unleashing of the synesthete within each of us. Add novelty to this mix—say, in the form of a new recipe, restaurant, or dining companion—and you have a formula for really turning up the striatum. But to top off the experience, you need one other element. Chocolate.

## Chocolate Love

The duck satisfied our midday hunger, leaving us with little desire for anything else. Except for the chocolate torte. As every child insists, and to which every parent is resigned, there is always room for dessert.

What makes chocolate so good? Fat, for one. More than half the weight of the dried bean comes from fat. When separated from the cocoa bean, the fat is called cocoa butter, whose chemical properties are responsible for its abrupt melting point, just about the temperature of the human body. These same chemical properties also make cocoa butter desirable for nonfood purposes, such as in cosmetics and pharmaceuticals. Because of these more lucrative uses, most cocoa butter does not end up in the chocolate you eat. Manufacturers of low-quality chocolate substitute cheaper vegetable solids for cocoa butter, so that only 15 percent of this inferior product contains actual cocoa solids. In contrast, high-quality chocolate contains up to 70 percent cocoa solids.

There has been one imaging study of the effects of chocolate on the brain. Dana Small, a neuropsychologist specializing in taste, investigated what happens to the brain when substantial quantities of chocolate are eaten. Because you must swallow it, having chocolate placed on your tongue would be expected to result in dopamine release and striatal activation. The question that Small addressed, however, was more subtle: does the amount of enjoyment you get—the pleasure component—change the way chocolate tastes? By having participants eat squares of bittersweet or milk chocolate between scans, Small pushed its consumption beyond the pleasure point. As the participants got sick of eating it, as anticipated, there was less activity in the striatum. More interesting even than this, the brain regions corresponding to taste, the insula and the somatosensory cortex, showed decreasing activity as more chocolate was consumed, suggesting that the pleasure of chocolate isn't confined to reward centers but that pleasure affects taste itself.[25]

. . .

Francis opened a bottle of Pinot Noir and proceeded to slice modest wedges of cake. He served them with a dollop of plain yogurt and *dulce con leche*, a spread of caramelized milk. The cake burst with chocolate, sweetened just enough to cause ocular gyrations but not so much to make your teeth hurt. The yogurt provided a cool, tangy balance, and its color offered a stark contrast to the cake itself. The *dulce con leche* completed the trio, a holy trinity of tastes. I only wished that my wife, Kathleen, had been there, too—to enjoy a dish that was clearly meant for lovers.

"I believe everything has to do with romance," Francis told me. "From the moment you wake up. Everything."

The association between food and love is an ancient one, but we must thank Comte Donatien-Alphonse-François, aka the Marquis de Sade, for elevating chocolate to its status as supreme aphrodisiac. Sade was a great fan of chocolate, probably the first chocoholic. At one of his more infamous parties, it was reported, he fed his guests chocolate candies laced with Spanish fly. The guests became so inflamed with passion that they couldn't contain themselves. As one contemporary described, "[The party] degenerated into one of those licentious orgies for which the Romans were renowned. Even the most respectable of women were unable to resist the uterine rage that stirred within them."[26] Several guests were reported to have died from sexual excess.

The truth was probably a bit tamer, as Sade, in addition to his love of chocolate and sex, had an even greater fondness for storytelling. The tale circulated widely enough, and chocolate's link to passion became permanent. I think, however, that there may be something more to this business of chocolate and love. Fat does play a privileged role in activating the dopamine system. Combine chocolate with a little alcohol, and you've got rocket fuel for the striatum—a conflagration waiting to be ignited by novelty. Beyond novelty, chocolate may, in fact, have aphrodisiac effects on the brain.

Until 1994, nobody knew exactly how the body communicated its nutritional status to the brain. It was known that the sensation of satiety did not arise solely from the mechanical stretching of the stomach but rather from several signals released by the gut after a meal. Insulin was an obvious candidate, because the pancreas secretes insulin after any meal that contains carbohydrates. Once released into the bloodstream, insulin helps cells soak up the energy just consumed, but insulin's effects on satiety depend on other hormones.[27]

The first strong candidate for an endogenous satiety hormone was leptin, a protein secreted by fat cells. Leptin's role in appetite became clear after the gene for it was inactivated in mice. The mice, known as ob/ob mice, overate and became obese. Leptin's effects, unlike insulin, are not temporally linked to a meal. Instead, leptin is secreted in a circadian rhythm, with more of it occurring at night, suggesting that leptin signals the body's overall energy needs on a daily basis. Once released into the bloodstream, leptin circulates to the brain and acts on the hypothalamus, a small region known to regulate feeding and reproduction. Since leptin is made in fat cells, the more fat stores a person has, the more leptin is released, although women, even after controlling for differences in body fat, secrete twice as much leptin as men.[28]

The fat cells that release leptin do so in spurts lasting about thirty minutes. The only other major hormone that behaves in this way is luteinizing hormone, LH, the substance secreted by the female hypothalamus that triggers ovulation. Right before the time of ovulation, the leptin and LH pulses synchronize with each other.[29] Leptin serves as a direct link between the nutritional status of a woman's body, her ability to support a growing fetus, and her brain's "decision" to reproduce. While you may not be a slave to your hormones, it may be that the biochemical basis to chocolate's aphrodisiac quality flows through leptin.

. . .

Although I had set out to find a solution to the sushi problem, instead I found something deeper. Kaminksy was right about Francis. He is a sensualist. And even more than being a poet, he is a romantic.

A satisfying dining experience, in particular Francis's vision of it, goes beyond mere sustenance. It transcends taste, too, for even with the best ingredients, you need something else—something novel. Francis creates special meals through careful attention to all the senses, in the process delivering a multisensory experience to the diner. At the same time, he enhances the novelty effect by supercharging the meal with alcohol and chocolate. In the best of circumstances, such an experience is meant to be shared with a lover, for if there is such a thing as an aphrodisiac, this is it.

As for the sushi problem, the key ingredient of novelty precluded repeating, at least exactly, the meal I had just enjoyed so much. And so I am left with only this conclusion: peak dining experiences are exceedingly rare, and they require just the right mix of elements. If you are lucky enough to have one, savor it for what it is, but do not attempt to repeat it. The next time, try something different.

# 5

———•———

# The Electric Pleasuredome

Neuroimaging, especially fMRI, is a great tool for peering into the functioning of the brain, but because so many parts of the brain are interconnected, investigators often have difficulty isolating the function of one part from another. In the last chapter, I mentioned transcranial magnetic stimulation, or TMS, which allows researchers to take individual parts of the brain temporarily off-line. By disrupting a part of the brain, TMS does what even fMRI cannot. It reveals the direct contribution, to human behavior, of a particular brain region. I can think of nowhere more tantalizing to use TMS than in the striatum; the technique enables us to observe the motivation system at work. Unfortunately, the striatum is buried deep in the brain, almost in the geometric center, and it is impossible for the magnetic pulses of TMS to reach that far. To see what happens when we start mucking around with striatal function, experimenters have to implant an electrode there. While this is done all the time in rats, there is no reason for doing so in humans.

But that doesn't mean it hasn't been done. In the 1950s, at Tulane University in New Orleans, one renegade psychiatrist dropped electrodes into all parts of the human reward system, turned on the juice, and, while a camera was rolling, watched what happened.

The records of these experiments have all but turned to dust, relics of an era in psychiatry that many would like to forget, even though most of the key physicians and patients are dead. I traveled to New Orleans in the hopes of learning something about the human reward system, something forbidden, by watching the only remaining films that document direct human striatal stimulation.

Coming into the Big Easy, I saw tombs and mausoleums rising on all sides. When the road dips below sea level, as it often does, the gauntlet through the cemeteries folds oppressively upon itself, distracting me from the purpose of my visit. The tombs range from mundane boxes to magnificently ornate monuments. Since much of New Orleans lies below sea level, corpses have been known to float to the surface, requiring the creation of cities of tombs aboveground. Nowhere else do the living walk among the dead as they do here.

Tulane Medical Center thrusts upward from the swampy plain into a vulgar amalgamation of crusty granite buildings, one of which, Charity Hospital, has served the indigent population of the city since 1726. Leaching out from the core of the sprawling medical complex, the onetime world's largest hospital still stands proudly, even as it, too, sinks slowly into the muck of the Mississippi delta. The upper floors of Charity seem to be stained with a sooty material, as if a fire had recently gutted part of the building. I soon realized that I had observed an optical illusion: the granite fascia becomes progressively darker toward the upper floors.

As I walked across Bourbon Street to the medical center, a hooker beckoned me from a doorway. She was a curvy black woman, wearing a skintight white dress that stopped an inch or two below her crotch. From the shadows I heard, "Hey honey, what's your pleasure?"

She had no idea.

## Lobotomies for All

More than a decade after his death, the persona of Robert Heath permeates Tulane. Here Heath founded, in the early 1950s, the first combined psychiatry and neurology department in the country. Decades ahead of his time, he envisioned this form of medicine as one that combined the biology of the brain with the process of psychoanalysis. Controversy still swirls around Heath's work, in part for the audacity of what he did, but in larger part for the misunderstanding among the public and his colleagues of what he found.

From the outset, Heath was criticized for attempting mind control. Many scientists were repulsed by what they deemed to be his inhumane experiments on psychiatric patients and prisoners. Heath's critics publicly vilified him not just for his experiments on the effects of deep-brain stimulation but also for his work on hypnosis and mind-altering drugs, including marijuana and LSD. In later years, his detractors alleged that Heath worked for both the army and the CIA to develop brainwashing techniques.[1] For those fond of conspiracy theories, Heath's work provided endless fodder. Regardless of his reputation, Heath remains one of the few scientists to have investigated the effects of direct stimulation of reward centers in the human brain.

After being discharged from the army in 1946, but before he arrived in New Orleans, Heath completed his medical training at Columbia University, which he chose because it was, at that time, the only place where he could receive simultaneous training in psychiatry and psychoanalysis. To the present day, the psychoanalytic profession maintains a discreet distance from medical schools—a tradition descended from Freud's banishment from Viennese universities—except at Columbia University. Heath learned neurophysiological techniques from some of the pioneers of the field; at the same time, he opened a psychoanalytic practice on Park Avenue under the supervision of an avant-garde analyst, Sandor Rado.

Rado, an iconoclastic Hungarian, was recruited from Berlin in 1931 to establish the New York Psychoanalytic Institute. The hallmark of his analysis was the introduction of biological elements as an alternative notion of the forces that Freud had described, like the eternal conflict between the unconscious id and the semiconscious ego. When Rado's ideas became too radical for the Freudians, he split with the New York Psychoanalytic Institute to create a model for psychoanalysis based on the merging of biology and traditional analytic techniques. To do so, he went across town, from the Upper East Side to Harlem, and set up the Columbia Center for Psychoanalytic Training. Rado, and later his protégé Heath, believed that they could locate the id deep in the brain. Heath would conduct this search by adapting his newly acquired neurophysiological skills to humans.

Around the same time, one of the darker chapters in psychiatry was winding down. Walter Freeman, an American neurologist and psychiatrist based at Saint Elizabeth's Hospital in Bethesda, Maryland, had become a sort of traveling salesman for prefrontal lobotomy, selling the procedure to hospital administrators with growing populations of mentally ill patients. As the coinventor of the so-called ice-pick lobotomy, Freeman was proud of the fact that the procedure could be taught to anyone, with or without medical training, in an afternoon. He and his collaborator James Watts, a neurosurgeon at George Washington University, developed the simple technique for treating mental illness. It required no anesthesia and no messy operating rooms, with their expensive staffs of assistants and nurses. The Freeman-Watts lobotomy could be performed in about five minutes, with nothing more than a flat table and, yes, a common ice pick. A well-honed ice pick, inserted between the upper eyelid and the eyeball, created a slightly upward trajectory until the pick encountered the thin layer of bone above the eyeball. A sharp tap from a hammer pierced the pick through the skull and into the brain. With a quick sweep left and right, the procedure was done, and the frontal lobe was disconnected from the rest of the brain.

Because the brain has no sensation, and few nerves exist above the eyeball, Freeman billed his procedure as painless, but the ice pick lobotomy's effects were as immediate and dramatic as the way it was performed. Previously agitated, delusional, and psychotic patients became docile. Use of the prefrontal lobotomy soon expanded from the most seriously ill schizophrenics to patients with only mild disorders, including anxiety, obsessive-compulsive disorder, depression, and mental retardation, especially in children.

From the mid-1930s to the early 1950s, about 100,000 lobotomies had been performed,[2] but not all physicians were convinced that the procedure improved the lives of their patients. The lobotomy eliminated disruptive behaviors, but it also removed much of the internal dialogue that we associate with being human. Many lobotomized patients passed their days in a perpetual present, with no sense of the past or of the future. Although the administrators of psychiatric hospitals benefited from a docile patient population, the growing chorus of complaints from the patients' families led the Columbia psychiatrists to initiate a study. The researchers at Columbia teamed up with their colleagues at Greystone State Hospital in Morristown, New Jersey, to determine, once and for all, whether lobotomy worked.[3] As a consultant for the Columbia-Greystone Project, Heath learned firsthand the damage that lobotomy wrought.

Heath's problem with lobotomy went deeper than the damage inflicted upon the patient. As a treatment for schizophrenia, lobotomizing a patient presupposed that the illness lay in the brain's cortex. Proponents of the procedure argued backward: because disconnecting the frontal lobes eliminated many of the symptoms of schizophrenia, the disorder must therefore reside there. Heath saw it differently.

Under Rado's influence, Heath proposed a theory for schizophrenia based on the idea that higher thought was located in the cortex, while emotion emanated from the brain stem. Cortical activity, Heath believed, was dominant when a person's sense of self was in tune with the real world—not psychotic or delusional, as in schizophrenia. Subcortical, or emotional thinking, became dominant during periods of fantasy, pleasure, and rage. When the cortical (thinking) and the subcortical (emotional) systems became unbalanced, severe disturbances in arousal occurred. Heath was convinced that schizophrenia originated not in the cortex, as the lobotomizers thought, but in the more primitive brain stem systems. Rather than cut off the cortex through lobotomy, physicians could provide a more efficient and humane treatment to restore balance by using electricity to turn up activity in the brain stem.[4]

When the chairmanship of the psychiatry department at Tulane University opened up, Heath almost passed it by. Deep in the South, not to mention in one of the poorest states in the country, Tulane and the city of New Orleans held for Heath a certain European appeal, but with few other resources to offer someone of his stature. New York had never suffered from a lack of psychiatrists, and the density of colleagues in the city made it impossible for Heath to do innovative work without tripping over a dozen other shrinks. More than anything else, Heath moved to Tulane to work unimpeded and to refine, in relative isolation, his ideas about schizophrenia.[5]

## Deep-Brain Stimulation

The striatum, a structure vital to motivation, sits in close proximity to the brain stem, which is where the history of deep-brain stimulation begins. The brain stem is a four-inch segment of tissue that serves as a transition zone between the cerebral cortex and the spinal cord. Its small size belies its importance; not only does the brain stem funnel almost all the information between the cortex and the body, but it contains several dozen clusters of neurons that together have unique functions. Breathing, for example, is controlled by a small collection of neurons in the brain stem. Heath had a particular interest in an area adjacent to the brain stem called the septal region. The septal region is trapezoidal, extending forward from just above the brain stem to the base of the cortex and sideways for about five millimeters, and includes parts of the striatum.[6] Animals that experience damage to this part of the brain are hyperexcitable and prone to intense anger, a phenomenon known as septal rage. Conversely, when the septal region is electrically stimulated, the animal becomes docile, retreating into an internal world of pleasure. Heath hypothesized that electrically stimulating the septal region of schizophrenics would have a similarly soothing effect.

To understand why electrically stimulating the septal region should have this effect, you need to understand how you can infer that something is pleasurable to an animal. Observing an animal (or another human, for that matter) and trying to figure out what motivates this living thing can be a frustrating exercise. Why, for example, do most people eat when they are hungry and not whenever food is available? A simple, although incomplete, explanation suggests that humans have innate drives—hunger being one of them—that periodically must be acted on. From watching an animal's behavior, we can infer its drives; we cannot measure them directly. If a rat is offered food pellets but doesn't eat, then the rodent must be in a low motivational state for food. Withhold food for twelve hours, and the rat will ravenously consume whatever is put in front of it. For animals, we can conclude, food itself is not the source of pleasure; rather, the sating of a particular drive—in this case, hunger—is. Drive-reduction theories, which were popular in the nineteenth century, influenced Freud's development of the id as an innate, primitive drive with particular needs that must be satisfied. Now that we know that there are drives other than physical ones—for novelty, for example—the source of the other drives reveals something important about human behavior.

By the 1950s, experimental psychologists, following the behaviorist tradition of the Russian physiologist Ivan Pavlov, had discovered that both animals and humans can also be motivated by what they learn. Infants, for example, are not born craving money; as they grow up, children absorb the idea of money as valuable. This fact seemed to contradict drive theory because, in the strictest sense, drives were considered innate rather than learned. In their place, B. F. Skinner espoused operant learning theory, which posited that animals can learn from the consequences of their actions.[7] As interest in drives waned, scientists focused on behavior in order to understand what reinforces it. While the feeling of reward is an internal state, the related concept of reinforcement can be defined by observation. If a rat learns to press a bar for the receipt of a food pellet, then the food can be said to reinforce bar-pressing behavior. Even so, observing the reinforcement offers no entrée into the animal's state of mind—that is, why the rat should continue to press the bar. If, as I believe, an innate drive for novelty exists, then drive theories and learning theory aren't far apart. But this was not the predominant view in the 1950s.

In 1952, a bright young psychology student named Jim Olds received his Ph.D. from Harvard and moved to Montreal to work on the neurobehavioral substrates of motivation at McGill University. At the time, the reticular activating system (RAS) was the hot area of the brain to be studying, because it seemed to be critically involved in the regulation of consciousness. The RAS is a diffuse collection of neurons scattered throughout the brain stem, and Olds was particularly interested in RAS's role in motivation. Perhaps, he thought, he could modulate an animal's motivational state by stimulating the RAS. With the help of an undergraduate, he rigged up a simple stimulation device and implanted an electrode into the RAS of a rat. After the rat recovered from the surgery, he placed it in a large box, with corners labeled A, B, C, and D. Whenever the animal ventured near corner A, Olds gave a brief electrical shock to its RAS. Remarkably, even when the current was turned off, the rat kept returning to that corner. At first Olds thought that he might have stimulated some type of curiosity center, so he started giving the rat shocks when it took a step toward corner B. Sure enough, the rat lost interest in corner A and started spending time in corner B. Within a few minutes, Olds was able to steer the rat around the box; he could arbitrarily reinforce behavior by electrical stimulation of the brain stem.[8] This feat was remarkable because it seemed to identify a pathway into the brain through which natural reinforcers, like food and sex, might also act.

Still not sure as to why the shocks should be reinforcing, Olds placed the rat in a Skinner box. The box, developed by the psychologist, is a cage fitted with a variety of lights and levers as well as several means of delivering rewards and punishments. The box is designed to let an animal naturally discover what the experimenter reinforces. In Olds's experiment, when the rat accidentally touched a lever in the Skinner box, it got a brief jolt to its RAS. Within two minutes, the animal was purposely hitting the same lever to receive more jolts in an effort to self-stimulate. Over the next several years, Olds and his colleagues systematically mapped out the brain regions that governed self-stimulation. It was a surprisingly restricted brain circuit, with less than a dozen discrete elements, and has come to be known generically as the reward circuit. Some parts of it, notably regions of the hypothalamus and septum, were associated with extraordinarily high rates of stimulation, up to two thousand times an hour.[9]

It certainly appeared that the rats found the stimulation pleasurable, but a rat's subjective experience of the world may have only the slightest relationship to the human experience.

## A Shock from the Past

Heath's laboratory, even ten years after his death, still bears his name. An observation window looks forlornly into another empty office, and the surrounding corridors are eerily quiet, unusual for midday at a busy academic medical center. In a small room connected to his lab, I thread a series of sixteen-millimeter films through an old-style movie projector.

The first film opens with Heath standing in front of a curtained window. He appears to be in a laboratory. A shabby, low-slung vinyl couch has been pushed into a corner to the right of the curtains, and the rest of the decor is sparse and institutional. The curtains, which appear as if they frame the observation window in the office I just left, are parted slightly, though no light seeps through.

Heath turns to the camera to explain what is about to transpire. Notably handsome, his charisma penetrates even the fifty-year-old film. Looking about forty years old, Heath has a full head of distinguished gray hair that sports an attractive fringe of black above the ears—a stylish haircut, distinctly unlike the flattops and crew cuts of the other young doctors and assistants.

The curtains part, and a young woman is revealed, lying on a hospital gurney. Her head is swathed in bandages, making it difficult to tell her age, but I'd guess she is in her mid-twenties. She has a roundish face, large eyes, and the corners of her mouth are turned downward attractively. Though her face is devoid of emotion, she does not appear apprehensive. A bank of electronic equipment fills the wall behind her.

A small indicator light on the electric panel is situated above the patient's head. Heath's assistant explains that the light will glow each time an electrical pulse is delivered to the patient's septal region. At this point, the image filling the screen is split in two: the patient is on the left, and the dozen electrical tracings from her brain that begin spewing out on paper are on the right.

The light above the young woman's head begins to flash about once a second. With each flash, an electrical spike occurs on the tracing labeled "RP Sep" (right posterior septal region).

The patient smiles.

Heath asks, "Why are you smiling?"

"I don't know," she responds. Her voice is high-pitched and childlike. "I guess I've cracked up all the way." She begins to giggle.

"What are you laughing about?"

The woman banters back, "I don't know. Are you doing something to me?"

"Why do you think we're doing something to you?"

She laughs again. "I don't know, but I usually don't laugh."

Heath begins chuckling, too. "I don't understand this," he says. "What do you mean?"

The woman pulls herself together and says with a smile, "You must be hitting a good spot."

The technician voices over, "One-twenty," indicating that 120 pulses have been delivered. Two minutes have passed. Heath and the woman continue chatting, and despite the difference in their ages, the erotic undercurrent continues unmistakably.

"One hundred eighty pulses," says the technician.

No sooner has the woman said that her hands and feet are feeling cold than she smiles and says, "But in my head I feel like something."

Intrigued, Heath presses on, repeating what the woman has just said, and then suavely changing the subject. "Do you feel like talking to me about that Italian you liked so well?"

The woman laughs again, for she clearly likes this attention, but weakly she protests, "Why are you doing this to me?"

Again, Heath becomes coy. "Huh? What do you mean, what are we doing?"

"Well, you're up to something," she replies. "You must be pulling some type of sneaky. Are you pulling a sneaky?"

"What kind of a sneaky? Hmm?" Heath is toying with her. "Tell me what you think."

"I don't know. Maybe you're stimulating something. Maybe you're stimulating some type of goody place."

"What kind of goody place? What makes you think we're stimulating a goody place?"

The woman laughs again, and she glows with the attention lavished upon her. "Well, why would I be laughing?"

"Two hundred and forty pulses," the technician drones. The exercise lasted four minutes before concluding with a sputtering thwack as the last piece of film flips around and around.

· · ·

Viewed in the context of Heath's other patients, many of whom I also saw on film, this young woman's response to septal stimulation, which I would describe as sexual, appeared idiosyncratic. Years later, Heath wrote in a self-published monograph that even though most of his patients regarded septal stimulation as pleasurable, not all felt it as sexual.[10] In fact, response to deep-brain stimulation was highly variable and seemed to Heath to be as much a product of the person's state of mind as of the stimulation itself. Rather than creating emotions where none existed, stimulation acted more like an amplifier of emotion. For instance, if the patient was hungry, Heath observed, septal stimulation increased the pleasure associated with food.

Only a few of Heath's subjects experienced obviously sexual effects, as determined by direct report, erections, or orgasms, and when they did occur, Heath documented them extensively. There was comparatively less documentation of more mundane responses. As Heath himself wrote, most subjects just "felt good" with septal stimulation and were unable to describe the feeling further.[11] It is not clear if Heath could, in fact, have enhanced these nondescript responses. When pleasurable responses did occur, they provided Heath with evidence that the power of the id could be used to shape behavior. He had, after all, been trained in the Freudian psychoanalytic tradition, which, in the late 1940s, when he received his training, considered the id the repository of suppressed sexual drives. Heath simply carried this line of thinking forward by looking for their biological source.

Brought to their extremes, Heath's experiments suggest that deep-brain stimulation could alter human traits previously thought to be psychological rather than biologically based—sexual orientation, for example. Patient B-19, whom Heath wrote about extensively and who appears in many of the films, was described as a twenty-four-year-old male who suffered from temporal lobe epilepsy. The son of a retired U.S. Army officer, patient B-19 was discharged after one month of military service because of "homosexual tendencies." He landed in Heath's care after several years of drug abuse, chronic depression, and multiple suicide attempts. Patient B-19 began his drug experimentation with the ingestion of vanilla extract and from there worked his way through amphetamines, marijuana, nutmeg, inhalants, and occasionally LSD. He was admitted to the Tulane hospital under Heath's direction, ostensibly for treatment of a severe personality disorder and, secondarily, for treatment of homosexuality. Patient B-19 reportedly had never engaged in heterosexual intercourse. As part of his treatment, he was implanted with multiple deep-brain electrodes. Only the septal electrodes evoked the feelings of pleasure, alertness, and sexual arousal that he reported during stimulation sessions.

Taking a cue from Olds's experiments in which rats, when given control of the electricity, avidly stimulated their septal regions, Heath rigged a self-stimulation device for patient B-19. One film demonstrates how the device worked. The intracranial self-stimulation mechanism, or ICSS, is a metal box, about four inches square, and small enough to be attached to a belt around the waist. Three push buttons are located on the face of the box, each controlling electric current into one of three brain regions. When patient B-19 was permitted to wear the device, he stimulated his septum up to 1,500 times in a three-hour period. The sessions were necessarily limited to three hours, at the conclusion of which the patient protested, pleading to be allowed to self-stimulate just a few more times.

During the second phase of the experiment, for which I could not locate the films but about which Heath wrote, he introduced behavior modification. While undergoing septal stimulation, the patient was shown pornographic films of heterosexual intercourse. During the first week, the patient was repulsed by the films, but after ten days of watching them, he became increasingly aroused, and the patient became interested in the female staff members of the hospital. His treatment then culminated in Heath's procurement of a prostitute for the patient. On the appointed afternoon, the patient was allowed to self-stimulate his septum for three hours. He was then introduced to the prostitute and guided to a specially prepared lab, where they could have privacy. His electrodes, however, were connected to recording devices, so that the natural electrical activity in several areas of his brain, including the septal region, could be measured. As Heath described:

> In the immediate preorgastic stage . . . striking changes occurred
> in the left and right septal leads resembling an epileptiform dis-
> charge. . . . With onset of orgasm, the septal and thalamic
> recordings evolved into spike and slow-wave activity [a seizure].[12]

Throughout Patient B-19's appearances in Heath's films, he never appeared mentally ill.[13] To the contrary, B-19 struck me as rational, able to make good eye contact, to express a full range of emotions, to carry on a cogent conversation, and to display no evidence of delusions or hallucinations. More than anything, Patient B-19 appeared manipulative. He spent most of the time strikingly unconcerned with the procedures being done to him—evidence of which I found in his oddly distant, almost mocking tone of voice and constant smirks. He relished what appeared to be his addictive tendencies, so that the septal stimulation treatment appeared to be merely a substitute for what he might otherwise seek from other sources.

While the young woman in the earlier film experienced what appeared to be an amplification of her attraction to Heath when he tickled her septum, B-19 was able to control the septal stimulation and use it as a way of fulfilling his hedonic needs. The fact that he normally preferred homosexual intercourse appeared, at least from the film, immaterial. If the experience was accompanied by septal stimulation, he could probably have sex with anything placed in front of him.

The pattern I saw emerging from both patients was that direct brain stimulation of the septal region amplified, rather than changed, underlying characteristics of personality and mood. It was as if Heath supplied the brain's need for novelty in the form of electrical stimulation and so, by short-circuiting the natural pathway for such things, provided more than the brain needed. Whereas a little stimulation might have been beneficial to these patients, too much stimulation turned out to be very, very bad.

## Bad Trips

The majority of Heath's patients reported positive feelings with septal stimulation, but a few had the opposite effect. In patients with a personality that tended toward anger, deep-brain stimulation unmasked responses not unlike those of septal rage in animals. In 1952, Heath showed a film of one such patient to his colleagues at Tulane. The audience's reaction, in keeping with the film's content, was extreme, and Heath was accused of treating his patients inhumanely and attempting mind control over them.[14]

Patient A-10 landed in Heath's care in 1952, after several behavioral problems in the army. Repeatedly disciplined for disobedience, fighting, and erratic behavior, he was diagnosed as a paranoid schizophrenic. The film opens with him lying on a hospital gurney. He is a small, wiry fellow, weighing perhaps 140 pounds, but clearly not someone to get into a scrape with. He is wearing a stocking cap from which a few thin wires snake out.

Heath turns to the camera to explain that he has implanted a deep electrode into A-10's tegmentum, an even deeper part of the brain stem than the septal region, an area that Heath had not yet plumbed. Heath reached for the tegmentum because he believed it could provide a more direct pathway into the septal region. As the stimulation begins, the patient's eyes flutter up and down, back and forth. Shaking his head a few times, like a dog stung by a bee, he appears to go into an epileptic seizure, except for the fact that he is fully conscious.

Heath's assistant asks him, "What's the matter?"

The patient doesn't answer, and instead contorts his face into a series of grimaces.

"What's the matter?" the assistant repeats. "Do you see things double?"

The patient starts to wave one of his arms around, clenching and unclenching his fist. He repeatedly rubs his face. "I'm seeing double," he finally answers. He is breathing heavily now.

A technician calls out his blood pressure: "One-forty over one-ten."

The patient starts to groan, "I feel so uncomfortable." His eyelids flutter again.

"What is so uncomfortable?"

Silence.

Finally, the patient gasps, "The back of my head."

Just to make sure he is still oriented to space and time, the assistant asks, "Do you know what day it is? Can you tell me what day of the week it is?"

The patient writhes on the gurney as the interviewer repeats the question. Finally, the patient spits out the correct date, "November twenty-fourth."

"November twenty-fourth? What day of the week?" the interviewer demands.

The patient sighs heavily and moans, raking his face with his hand.

"What's wrong now?" Concerned that the patient will pull out the electrodes, he commands, "Don't put your hand up there."

"I feel so uncomfortable. It's in my head, in my feet, in my eyes."

The interviewer presses him more, asking him to describe how he feels. The patient just continues to breathe heavily and squirm on the gurney for about ten seconds.

Finally, he rasps, "I can't see straight. I'm seeing double or something." He groans and says, "I'm going black in the head."

"Tell me more about that."

Instead of uttering a word, the patient makes a claw with his right hand and begins to curl up into a fetal position. The stimulation has now been going on for about three minutes.

Increasingly frantic, he exclaims, "I can't think of nothing when my brain is turning up like that. Oh, no . . . before I pass out! I don't want to pass out . . . Oh, my brain!"

Suddenly the patient's voice changes. He screams in a pitch so high it is uninterpretable. Then he starts tearing at his clothes, trying to rip off his shirt, and gets up from the gurney.

The interviewer says, "You're tearing at your clothes. Do you know you're tearing at your clothes?"

On the verge of incoherence, in a falsetto voice, the patient screams, "I don't care! I gotta do something! I don't care. I don't care!" Pausing for a moment, he starts to get off the gurney again before yelling, "I'm gonna rip you up!"

Several hands come into view and hold the patient down, tying his hands. "Stop!" the interviewer commands. "Stop!"

The patient stares into the camera and hisses, "I don't give a goddamn. I'm gonna kill you. Let me up. I'm gonna kill you and rip you to goddamn shreds!"

## The Price of Discovery

The films of these three patients illustrate the awful power that Heath wielded. In some cases, electrical stimulation made his patients feel better, while in others it had the opposite effect. According to the films, no single part of the septal region (or brain stem) is responsible for whether stimulation feels good or bad. Instead, we see how the subjective experience was highly malleable, but in an unpredictable way. The malleability and the arbitrariness of the experimentation, I think, got Heath into trouble. Allegations that his patients were, in fact, prisoners seeking a reduction in their terms didn't help,[15] but mostly the controversy arose because Heath's investigations occurred at a time when there was public fear of brainwashing and Manchurian candidates.

When Heath began his research, the outlook for patients with chronic mental illness was grim. Many, as we've seen, were incorrectly diagnosed with schizophrenia, the mainstay of treatment for which, in 1950, was lobotomy, insulin shock therapy, or unmodified electroshock treatment.[16] From 1950 to the early 1970s, Heath implanted deep-brain electrodes in 110 patients. Sixty-six of the devices were implanted deep in the septal region. Several patients simultaneously received small tubes for the direct infusion of chemicals into the area. The other 44 patients were implanted with another version of the deep-brain stimulator seen in the films. Called the cerebellar pacemaker, it was introduced by Heath in later years, because he hypothesized that parts of the cerebellum could serve as a gateway to the septal region. Some of the patients with cerebellar pacemakers are still alive and show up at Tulane from time to time when their pacemakers malfunction.

The discovery of drugs with powerful effects on mood have rendered deep-brain stimulation obsolete for decades. Just as Heath unveiled the benefits of electrical stimulation, his technique was pushed aside by pharmacology. Antipsychotic medications like Thorazine and Haldol paved the way for more humane treatment of schizophrenia, and the discovery of antidepressants and lithium radically changed the way mood disorders are understood and treated. Although chemistry seemed, for some time, to have overtaken Heath's techniques, his observations about the functioning of the area around the striatum nevertheless endure.

But even drugs have limitations. They are not suitable for everyone; they have side effects; and sometimes they simply stop working. It shouldn't be surprising that after half a century of psychopharmacological discovery, deep-brain stimulation is making a comeback. It is now employed as a common treatment for Parkinson's disease, a condition that Heath also investigated, and approximately ten thousand vagal nerve stimulators have been implanted for the treatment of epilepsy and, more recently, depression. But even if Heath's theories could ultimately be proven, the allegation of mind control still hangs over his work.

. . .

As I walked out of the Tulane Medical Center and a hazy twilight settled over the French Quarter, Bourbon Street came to life. Miniature herds of tourists and conventioneers, gulping watered-down hurricanes in disposable cups, bounded from one bar to another, while, at a safe distance from the drunken mobs, horse-drawn carriages pulled families with young kids. Bourbon Street wasn't seedy anymore. Even the strip clubs, advertising all-nude bottomless dancers, were a parody of themselves. This downgrading of decadence into excess offers as good a paradigm of the hedonic treadmill as I can think of.

Heath's work and the films documenting it provide insights into that treadmill. As individuals, we may have difficulty understanding why we do certain things and end up concocting explanations after the fact. We grapple with the source of our motivations and drives; we arbitrate between conflicting desires; and sometimes we choose the easiest course of action, while at other times we opt for the arduous one, if only because we expect rewards in the future. Heath did an end run around this morality play and, in a Faustian bargain (which, it could be argued, he lost, even while some of his patients ultimately gained), attempted to control drives directly. Perhaps on a whim, he chose what his patients would experience. By short-circuiting what the striatum normally does, Heath disconnected subjective experience from action.

Heath's taking the reins of nature is what makes his films so creepy. After viewing them, I am not surprised by the reactions of several generations of his colleagues. I think the outrage against him springs more from the simultaneous fascination and revulsion of watching Heath evoke his patients' pleasure and pain and less from a queasiness at the ethics of his research program. Perhaps as a backlash response to their own voyeurism, scientists have, sadly, buried Heath's findings. In addition to whatever prurient fascination can be attributed to him, Heath stumbled onto a deep truth about the way the brain works.

Electrical stimulation of parts of the septal region, as I saw in Heath's films, induces pleasurable sensations, but move the electrode a millimeter or two in one direction, or turn the current up a little, and what was pleasurable suddenly becomes painful. The fickle nature of deep-brain stimulation, especially in humans, means that pain and pleasure do not reside in distinct parts of the brain but, rather, share elements of the same circuit. If Heath is to be remembered for nothing else, he should be remembered for this observation. Without knowing it, Heath tapped into the brain's need for novelty, and in the case of his explorations in the septal region, he stumbled onto the one area that links action to outcome, that cements motivation, and keeps human beings hungry for more information—the striatum. While I had come to these conclusions separately, based on brain imaging, Heath's films drive home the point: deep in the brain, pleasure and pain are not so different from each other. All that matters is novelty.

# 6

## It Hurts So Good

Pain comes in so many forms that it almost defies classification other than by its universal unpleasantness. Sometimes it is sharp, like the thwacking of a thumb by a hammer, or the pricking of a finger with a needle. Sometimes it is like being stung by a bee—a combination of pricking and chemical burn. And sometimes pain wells up slowly, like the visceral ache of a bruised testicle or a uterine cramp. Pain stalks you, ready to bite should you misstep. And pain, even that which is alleviated, begets more of the same: anxiety, the distress it heaps upon loved ones, visits to doctors, insurance bills, lawyers.

In the 1970s, Ronald Melzack, a psychology professor at McGill University, and Patrick Wall, a biologist at MIT, proclaimed in a landmark paper that there was no pain center in the brain.[1] While Heath was searching for the pleasure centers, Melzack and Wall were seeking the equivalent for pain—even if it didn't reside in a single location. With the advent of deep-brain stimulation and the host of research studies using it, no evidence could be found of a specific structure that functions as a pain center. Melzack and Wall's concept, which relied on the observation that the brain can exert control over noxious impulses at multiple levels in the nervous system, has come to be known as the gate-control theory. The two investigators concluded that pain arose from the interactions of three systems: the peripheral sensors at the ends of nerves, a gate-control system in the spinal cord, and an action system that engaged the muscles to move away from pain. The gate-control idea has held up, more or less intact, for four decades—an impressive feat for any psychobiological theory.

Everything I had been taught in medical school suggested that pain is a bad thing. Pain indicates inflammation, a sign of tissue damage, the source of which must be discovered. If we fail to identify its cause, then we can only alleviate the symptom with painkillers. No other animal seems as preoccupied with pain and its avoidance as humans; certainly other animals hurt, but they muddle through their discomforts, or they die.

Sometimes people purposely inflict pain on themselves. Remember Jane Fonda thrusting her pelvis into the air, admonishing women to "feel the burn"? Anyone who has tried that exercise knows that it hurts; and yet a satisfying sensation coexists with the pain. There is a simple solution to the pain-pleasure conundrum, although it is semantic. We could all agree that pain and pleasure are mutually exclusive, as does the International Association for the Study of Pain (IASP), which defines it as "an unpleasant sensory or emotional experience associated with actual or potential tissue damage."[2]

But under certain circumstances, a noxious stimulus, like a burn, may not be perceived as painful, while an innocuous stimulus, like a cool breeze, might, under other circumstances, be painful. The IASP definitions leave us with the unsatisfactory conclusion that pain is a state of mind. But as I dug deeper into the morass of pain, some interesting findings emerged—that pain, under the right circumstances, could both be satisfying and sate the need for novelty.

## A Satisfying Pain

Weeks after returning from New Orleans, I stood before a nondescript industrial park in Atlanta. The squat building stretched out in a straight line, windows and steel doors alternating on the facade. I had driven by the area at least a thousand times and had never given it a thought. During the daytime these anonymous structures blend into the suburban cityscape, but at night this building acquired a personality. Call it industrial Goth.

For many years its tenant, a well-known S and M club, flourished. As I quickly learned, nobody called it "S and M" anymore, except plain vanilla folk not involved in The Scene. To the connoisseur, it is just SM. Saturday night is the big one for both the fetish and the SM crowds, and judging by the overflow of parking onto the street, I had picked a good night to check it out.

Kathleen accompanied me on this particular venture, and she was prepossessingly clad in a low-cut V-neck sweater and leather pants that came to a pleasing taper over some pointy-toed boots. I went native, too, donning a pair of black chinos and a black Lycra shirt topped off by a leather jacket. For the ten-dollar cover charge, we wanted to see some pain and pleasure.

Stainless steel platforms, about four feet high, were positioned throughout the interior, and flat black curtains cloaked several passages that led to rooms unseen. A large iron cage in the shape of a spaceship appeared to have landed in the center of the dance floor, a pair of manacles dangling from its fins. Except for the blood-red lipstick worn by the women, the patrons' appearance was drawn from a monochromatic palette—primarily black leather, latex, and vinyl covering pale white skin. Techno music reverberated through-out the chamber, while people of indeterminate gender gyrated absentmindedly, oblivious to one another.

A couple pushed by us. He was thin and neatly shaven, looking a bit like Anthony Perkins. From the waist up, he wore a latex tunic, bedazzled in D-rings, and culminating in a four-inch-high Eliza-bethan collar. Below, he had on what appeared to be a latex kilt. The pencil-thin woman, with a waist perhaps twenty inches around, had a mousy face and a blond ponytail pulled as tight as a sausage. She was squeezed into a black latex catsuit that clung so firmly that bending at the waist surely must have cut off all sensation to her legs. The couple regularly spritzed each other with a small water bottle they shared, highlighting their latex sheen.

These two burrowed their way into one of the passages, disap-pearing behind a curtain. Intrigued, Kathleen and I followed. The corridor led to a room with several reproductions of torture devices. In one glance, I took in a man being tied to a wooden rack in one corner. A group of four men were binding a woman to an X-shaped crucifix in another, while, aways off, a man was bent prone over a crossbeam in the center of the room, his baboon-red ass attracting a sizable crowd.

A busty woman in a French maid uniform screamed at him, "You piece of shit!" She then took out a riding crop from behind her back and swatted his butt cheeks. The guy cried out in pain, which only provoked more wrath from the maid.

"I said shut up!" She pulled out a vinyl strip with a rubber ball in the center and said, "I think you need to be gagged." She stuffed the ball into his mouth and resumed her whipping.

I lost sight of the latex couple, but a crowd of thirty-something males had gathered around the maid and her subject. Most leaned catatonically against the wall, showing little interest in the tableau, preferring instead to sip their beers with indifference.

Kathleen whispered to me, "Is this for real?"

I pointed to the quarter-size bumps that had risen up on the guy's thighs. The welts looked genuine. There is an old adage in medicine, *rubor, calor, tumor, dolor,* which is Latin for the four cardinal signs of inflammation: redness, heat, swelling, and pain. Without laying hands on the man's ass, I ventured to say we were looking at all four.

When tissue is damaged, the cells leak out chemicals, including histamine, bradykinin, and a class of compounds called chemokines, which attract other cells to gobble up the debris. The same chemicals cause blood vessels to dilate, hence the redness and heat, and to pass fluid into the affected area, hence the swelling. The cells that repair the damage—macrophages, mast cells, and neutrophils—release chemicals that coordinate the immune response. These chemicals, large proteins called cytokines, are extremely potent. Tumor necrosis factor, or TNF, is released first, and it causes mast cells to make interleukin-1 (IL-1).[3] Both TNF and IL-1 elicit demonstrable effects in the brain, promoting what has been termed sickness behavior, a constellation of flu-like symptoms we all know: fatigue, aches, and depression.

Too large to diffuse across the blood-brain barrier, cytokines can seep into the brain through a few sites in the ventricles. If you are injected with a dose of cytokines, as some cancer patients are, you will be in for an unpleasant experience. Because of the untoward effects of cytokines, the satisfaction derived from physical pain must come from something else. Besides coordinating the immune response, cytokines also interact with the stress system.

Stress, I think, unfairly gets a bad rap. Although some investigators have suggested that stress damages the brain,[4] without it, animals would lack the ability and motivation to escape from predators. Humans tend to think of stress as something to be avoided, because it feels bad, although such trepidation overlooks a rather obvious point. Conquering small amounts of stress actually feels good, and conquering physical stress feels the best of all.

Our man on the crossbeam was telling us something. His welts provided incontrovertible evidence that tissue damage was occurring. And his screams supported the observation that his ass-whooping hurt. Exhibiting all the classic signs of inflammation, from redness to pain, he still could have stood up and walked out anytime. Why didn't he? The obvious conclusion is that he derived some satisfaction from this transaction with the buxom maid. A brief side trip into the history of SM places the neurobiology of pain and pleasure into a psychological context.

## Sadomasochism

After spending thirty-seven years in prisons, the Marquis de Sade (1740–1814) died as a "patient of the police" at Charenton, the French asylum for the insane.[5] We are left with only fragments of his considerable literary output, almost all of which were penned during his incarcerations, and much of it destroyed in the years surrounding the French Revolution. Yet this remarkable figure remains as controversial and enigmatic two hundred years after he unleashed his authorial prowess as when he was alive. The colloquial meaning of *sadism*, deriving pleasure from inflicting pain, has become culturally entrenched, but Sade's writings were either banned or assumed lost until Guillaume Apollinaire rediscovered them in 1909—although it wasn't until the last few decades that most of Sade's work was translated into English. Several recent academic and popular investigations into Sade's life have elevated the Marquis above the prurient background noise of common pornography, with which his work is often mistakenly linked.

In contrast to the Marquis de Sade, whom most people have

heard of, the namesake of *masochism*, Leopold von Sacher-Masoch (1836–95), is virtually unknown. This Ukrainian novelist, with a taste for being tied up and whipped by fur-clad women, wrote more eloquently about the pleasures of pain than even Sade did. How these two figures became conflated to form the one-dimensional framework of sadomasochism is a curious tale of twentieth-century psychiatry.

The singular construct sadomasochism (SM) is interesting because neither Sade nor Sacher-Masoch saw the two behaviors as complementary. Certainly Sade, writing one hundred years before Sacher-Masoch, knew well of masochistic pleasure. According to police records, Sade's first arrest occurred after hiring a prostitute and demanding that she whip him with an iron cat-o'-nine-tails that had been heated in a fire.[6]

In 1785, while imprisoned in the Bastille, Sade finished assembling the first of his books, *The 120 Days of Sodom*. More encyclopedia than story, the work uses a fictional premise to catalog a variety of sexual acts for future reference. Most of *120 Days* was probably more a product of Sade's imagination than of actual events, although personal experience undoubtedly contributed. Cribbed onto sheets of paper five inches wide and glued together into a roll forty-nine feet long, *120 Days* is shocking even by today's standards. The book chronicles the escalating antics of four libertines: a duke, his brother, a judge, and a financier. Sade tells us that in their pursuit of pleasure, the libertines had already been habituated to the usual manner of sexual acts. So they hire four prostitutes to instruct them in extreme forms of behavior. Sade cataloged 150 simple passions, 150 unusual passions, 150 criminal passions that "most outrage the laws of both nature and religion," and, finally, 150 murderous passions. Moreover, the prostitutes were instructed to find other men and women for the libertines' pleasure of acting out their self-styled menu of debauchery.

While Sade evoked sympathy for, and could even identify with, the victims, Sacher-Masoch reversed the roles of victim and torturer. For Sacher-Masoch, the victim was in control. In *Venus in Furs*, he writes about his obsession with an icy Russian beauty named Wanda. A red-haired goddess with eyes that pierced like green lightning, Wanda is likened to the Venus de Milo. Her skin is described as marble, and she is as cold as marble, too: introduced to the reader, she is draped in furs and sneezing. Wanda could never reciprocate Sacher-Masoch's feelings, for she could not love someone who loved her, which of course made her all the more alluring. The imagery used in describing Wanda emphasizes her inaccessibility and indifference for the author. Wanda warns Sacher-Masoch, "An Olympian divinity, such as I am, requires a whole army of slaves. Beware of me!"[7] Sensing his curiosity, she asks huskily, "Do you want to be my slave?"

Remarkably little of the contemporary imagery of SM has changed since Sacher-Masoch: the icy distance between "subs" and "doms" persists as the accepted form of relationship in the SM scene today.[8] Only the fur has been replaced by latex and leather. Sacher-Masoch was clear about the nature of his relationship with Wanda. She was not a sadist, and she gave no hint of enjoyment in the pain she inflicted upon him; she simply served his purposes by standing in as a neutral instrument of his desire. He, the victim, was in control, a fact expressed by his submisson to her.

The contract is central to the nature of SM, because it explains the degree to which the sub is actually in control. The contract is so important that Sacher-Masoch reproduced it in the novel. It begins:

AGREEMENT BETWEEN MME. VON DUNAJEW
[Wanda]
AND SEVERIN VON KUSIEMSKI
[Sacher-Masoch]

Severin von Kusiemski ceases with the present day being the affianced of Mme. Wanda von Dunajew, and renounces all the rights appertaining thereunto; he on the contrary binds himself on his word of honor as a man and nobleman, that hereafter he will be her slave until such time that she herself sets him at liberty again. . . .

Mme. von Dunajew is entitled not only to punish her slave as she deems best, even for the slightest inadvertence or fault, but also is herewith given the right to torture him as the mood may seize her or merely for the sake of whiling away the time. Should she so desire, she may kill him whenever she wishes; in short, he is her unrestricted property. . . .

Mme. von Dunajew on her behalf agrees as his mistress to appear as often as possible in her furs, especially when she purposes some cruelty toward her slave.[9]

Although the contract appears in the context of his novel, Sacher-Masoch had similar contracts in real life, both with his wife, Wanda, and his mistress, Franny Pistor Baddanow.[10] If Sacher-Masoch truly, without hesitation, enjoyed pain and humiliation, he would simply have turned himself over to her whims rather than draft a contract that stipulates what the two of them must, and must not, do. The French philosopher Gilles Deleuze presciently identified the source of the masochist's pleasure as not just pain or humiliation but also suspense and fantasy. The delay of pleasure through the endurance of pain heightens the result. No matter how uncomfortable, the sub is assured through the contract that the dom will not push the scene beyond the agreed-upon limits. This safety net is what allows the sub to "let go," and the SM literature is replete with out-of-body experiences.[11]

In the SM experience, anticipation, rather than consumption, is everything. For example, think of a pleasurable event. It doesn't have to be sexual. Now, try to remember the moments leading up to the experience. If you had to choose between the feeling of anticipation or the actual event, which would you pick? If you chose the anticipation, then perhaps you have more SM in you than you realize. The need for novelty asserts itself in sometimes unexpected ways. Delicious anticipation can stem from bits of antecedent information, which, in the case of SM, might be the smell of leather or the sight of a riding crop. By themselves, these elements may be of no importance, but, to varying degrees, they can evoke the anticipation of forbidden acts, setting the brain's reward system into overdrive contemplating what will happen next.

•   •   •

The merging of sadism and masochism into sadomasochism can be traced not to Freud but to a lesser-known nineteenth-century Viennese psychiatrist, Baron Richard von Krafft-Ebing, who coined the terms *sadism* and *masochism*. In a monumental compendium of sexual pathology that would make Sade proud, Krafft-Ebing described over two hundred cases of perversion.[12] A substantial number relate to sadism and masochism, including a description of Jack the Ripper (Case 17). The definition of *sadism* that the Viennese physician favored was "the experience of sexually pleasurable sensations produced by acts of cruelty, bodily punishment inflicted on one's own person or when witnessed in others." He defined masochism as the opposite of sadism.[13] Krafft-Ebing went to some length to defend his coinage of the term *masochism*, citing evidence that Sacher-Masoch was not merely a novelist but was "afflicted with this anomaly." A decade later, Freud muddied the picture by concluding that masochism could not be reconciled with the pleasure principle and that it was actually sadism turned inward, toward one's ego. In Freud's view, masochism was like a snake consuming its tail, the fullest expression of what he proposed as the death drive, Thanatos.[14]

While the Freud/Krafft-Ebing conceptualization of SM has remained entrenched in popular culture, there are signs that it is giving way to a more balanced view of masochism. The SM club I visited is hardly an anomaly, and with racier depictions of masochism on broadcast television, it was a rather tame version at that. What seems to have been lost in SM's popularization is the element of anticipation. As Sacher-Masoch portrayed it, and Deleuze later recognized, the pleasure of pain derives from suspense, which, I believe, has its origin in the brain's craving for novelty. Postponing an outcome, which creates suspense, is just another way of injecting uncertainty into an experience, making the ending that much more satisfying. Any good movie uses the same technique.

## The Pain Machine

After my time at the SM club, I wondered whether pain itself could be the source of satisfaction, or whether it felt satisfying just to cease what had caused the pain. It was a confusing problem, for the relief of pain *is* satisfying. Was the man on the crossbeam rapturous from his anticipation of relief, or was he really getting satisfaction out of being whipped?

To answer this question, I sought out Dan Ariely, a professor of behavioral economics at MIT. Tucked into a corner of MIT's Media Lab, behind an inauspicious blue door, his lab offers another entry into a world of pain and pleasure.

In a seemingly incongruous marriage between economics and the study of pain, Ariely investigates how physical sensations affect the decisions humans make. Until recently, the science of decision making has focused on cold cognitive processes, like rationality and risk aversion. Some have argued that emotion is as much a part of decision making as rationality,[15] but Ariely has taken this question to its logical extreme by determining how physical pain and pleasure affect judgment. In the wrong hands, this investigation might be dismissed as a perversity on the order of a modern-day Sade or Heath, but Ariely is different. His firsthand knowledge of pain occurred when, at age eighteen, he sustained an excruciating burn injury while serving in the Israeli army. When I met him, a warm handshake and a piercing gaze put me at ease, in spite of what I knew would come next.

The lab is a small room, perhaps ten feet square, chock full of computer equipment and high-tech thermal pumps. A large steel vat—a pasteurization tank, I was told—occupied almost half the space. A maze of tubes and pumps connected the tank to the thermal devices, which I recognized as standard operating room equipment for circulating water in cooling blankets, a procedure to lower body temperature during some types of surgery. Dan noticed me eyeing them.

"I hold the water in the tank at a comfortable temperature," Dan said as he patted each of the thermal devices. "Then these two pumps raise and lower the temperature." A reclining chair was positioned between the thermal pumps and the pasteurization tank. Opalescent hoses connected the tank to the pumps, and from the pumps, two more tubes were coiled up, waiting to be connected to something else.

Dan handed me a pile of black neoprene material. "Put this on."

"What is it?" I asked.

"It's a flight suit used by helicopter pilots to keep their body temperature comfortable." I nodded appreciatively, and Dan added, "But I've made a few modifications."

I stripped down to my underwear and wriggled into the suit. "What sort of modifications?"

Busy adjusting the temperature controllers, Dan obviously did not hear my question. The reason I was here was that I had traced, to Dan's lab, rumors about experiments into the pain that results from raising and lowering core body temperature. When I asked him about the motivation behind such experiments, he explained his interest in measuring pleasure objectively. But pleasure is difficult to induce in an experimental setting; cynical humans are not prone to fits of pleasure, especially not in a laboratory. Dan reasoned, therefore, that the most reliable way to induce pleasure was by first imposing, then removing, pain.

I wasn't so sure. Pleasure is not the same as relief at the removal of pain. But who really knows? Maybe pain and pleasure are relative.

The suit was a good fit, snug but not too tight. The left sleeve had been cut away, leaving me standing there like a twenty-first-century gladiator, without a shield for my left arm. I was well insulated and started to warm up right away, a temporary respite from the cold air. Small tubes were woven into the fabric of the suit, all designed to circulate water around the body. Dan hooked the ends of the tubes to the thermal pumps. He opened a valve, and cold water started flowing through the suit. A mild chill enveloped my legs and expanded to the rest of my body—like the sensation of being dipped into ice water. When the water hit my torso, I felt as though someone had punched me in the stomach.

"What temperature did you set?" I asked.

Dan was busy at the computer and pointed to the digital readout on the pump. Four degrees Celsius.

"Sit in the chair," Dan said, "and make yourself comfortable."

"Are you serious?"

"Not really."

A piece of PVC pipe, about four inches in diameter and two feet long, stood on end in a drainage pan. Dan ducked behind the pumps and opened up several valves. The noise of *whooshing* water filled the room, and a high-pitched dripping sound came from inside the PVC pipe as it began to fill up with water. Dan asked me to put my unsleeved arm into it. At first the water flowing through it would be as cold as that circulating through the body suit. To limit any convective effect from the surrounding air, which now felt quite warm, Dan wrapped me in a Mylar blanket, a sort of reverse insulation.

After ten minutes of the cold treatment, I started to shiver. "I thought you told me that you were going to make me hot."

"Change of plans," Dan said. "Personally, I find hot to be more unpleasant than cold, but you seem more affected by the cold, so it's a better test."

Dan tapped a few keys on the computer, and the water around my arm warmed up by a few degrees. I could feel capillaries flashing open, and a tingling sensation crept up to my armpit.

"How does that feel?" he asked.

It was pain and pleasure wrapped in a single embrace. My arm felt good. Really good. But the contrast with the rest of my body was almost unbearable. I found myself directing all my attention to my arm, as if I were pouring my very existence into the one part of my body that didn't feel pain. Psychiatrists call such behavior dissociation.

•　•　•

Acute pain—pain caused by a momentary noxious event—is detected by specialized sensors in the skin. These sensors, called nociceptors, are actually specialized nerve fibers, not unlike the nerve fibers that conduct other tactile sensations from the skin to the spinal cord. But nociceptors are not the same as the nerve endings that pick up other touch sensations: they do not respond to innocuous sensations, like the brush of a feather; they respond only to noxious stimuli. In fact, nociceptors are now regarded as the sixth sense—the sense of pain.[16] A nociceptor can be activated by a mechanical force, like a spanking, but it can also be activated by thermal injury, such as temperatures above 45 degrees Celsius, or chemical injury, like bee stings and exposure to acids. Employing a mechanism still not completely understood, the nociceptor converts a noxious stimulus into an electrical signal that is transmitted to the spinal cord, and then to the brain. The best guess for the identity of nociceptors is a family of proteins known, curiously, as the vanilloid receptor, or VR1. VR1 is a protein that winds itself into the membranes of cells, and when deformed, allows charged atoms to flow into the nerve fiber, conducting electricity in the process.

Before reaching the brain, all sensory signals, including nociception, pass through a structure of the brain, about the size of a key lime, called the thalamus. Since the 1920s, most neuroscientists have believed that the perception of pain originates in the thalamus, because damage to specific parts of it blocks the sensation of pain.[17] But functional brain imaging has revealed that a wide network of brain regions is involved in the subjective perception of pain. There is an ongoing debate about whether the primary sensory region of the brain, called S1, is activated by painful stimuli. Most brain imaging studies suggest that it is, but, in fact, the level of activation can be increased by directing attention to the injured part of the body and decreased by directing attention elsewhere.[18] Pouring consciousness into my arm while in Ariely's pain suit offers an example—at the time, the S1 region of my brain was probably firing on all cylinders. While S1 appears to be involved in the processing of sensory attributes of painful stimuli, other brain regions integrate pain's emotional and visceral components. The innermost folds of the brain, along the midline, notably the anterior cingulate and the medial prefrontal cortex, appear to anticipate pain as well as to process it emotionally.[19]

· · ·

Again Dan asked how I was doing. Truthfully, I didn't like having one part of my body feeling good and the rest feeling awful. I looked down at my toes, which had turned dusky blue. "I'm ready to get out now."

As I stripped out of the pain suit, the previously cold air felt like a blast of warmth. *That* was pleasure. As I pulled on my clothes, I noticed Dan smiling.

"See," he said. "The removal of discomfort is quite nice. No?"

Sacher-Masoch would have agreed, right down to the coldness and the way pain was used to delay the gratification of—in my case—being pain-free. Removing the suit felt great, but only because I always had the option to do so. Although Dan was in control of the temperature, I was, in fact—by virtue of my agreement to wear it in the first place—the one in control of my bodily sensations. I could determine when the experiment was over. Just like SM. But what if I didn't have control of the pain?

## Pain Control

Before you can comprehend how pain can be turned into satisfaction, you must examine the conditions under which pain is lessened rather than removed altogether. The understanding of both the biology of pain and its psychological dimensions has shifted away from the idea that pain and pleasure lie at opposite ends of a spectrum. The biological pathways through which pain and pleasure reach the brain are similar, reaffirming what the SM crowd knows: that pain itself can, under the right circumstances, be satisfying.

Instead of thinking about pain and pleasure on a single continuum, I find it useful to picture them as two independent dimensions of one subjective experience. Imagine a graph with two lines at right angles to each other. The horizontal line represents pleasure; the vertical line, pain. Most of the time, you sit around the intersection of the two lines, feeling little pain or pleasure. Burn a finger on the stove, and you shoot up the vertical pain axis; eat chocolate mousse and swing out the horizontal pleasure axis. Now consider a deep tissue massage. It hurts. But it also feels good. So the massage would be high on both the pain and pleasure dimensions, at a point lying in the upper right of your imaginary graph.

Mental states like hypnosis can decrease the perception of pain, but can thought alone change one dimension into another?

After Melzack and Wall formulated their theory of the nervous system's multiple levels of pain control, Melzack developed techniques of measuring pain objectively. He constructed a series of questions based on three hypothesized dimensions (sensory, emotional, and cognitive)—now known as the McGill Pain Questionnaire, or MPQ.[20] Melzack asked people to rate specific qualities of their pain, using terms like "throbbing," "lancinating," and "gnawing" to describe pain's sensory components. The emotional component was assessed with terms like "suffocating," "punishing," and "vicious." The cognitive component was assessed with "discomforting," "troublesome," and "unbearable." MPQ patients circled appropriate descriptors and assigned an intensity value from 1 to 5. By adding up the intensities along the three dimensions, Melzack categorized types of pain according to characteristic pain profiles. With the MPQ, for example, menstrual pain could be distinguished objectively from a toothache. It seems obvious that there are different types of pain, but even today most physicians simply ask patients to rate the severity of their pain. Reducing a multifaceted experience to a single physiological parameter misses other components related to the way a patient feels when experiencing pain. Anxiety, for instance, heightens attention and makes pain seem worse.

As one might expect, the three dimensions of the MPQ are not completely independent of one another, a point that has been the major criticism of the theory. Some scientists have argued that two dimensions are sufficient to capture the pain experience: stimulus intensity and unpleasantness.[21] Stimulus intensity is perhaps the most important, because sensations that are pleasant at a mild intensity, like a light scratching of the skin, become painful at high intensity.

When you are in pain, your first instinct is to remove its source, reducing its intensity. If the source of the pain is external, like a splinter, this is easy to do. But at other times, the source of the pain cannot be removed. A burn, for example, causes lasting tissue damage that is a continual source of pain. Applying ice, while helpful, doesn't reverse the damage; it just reduces the inflammatory response. Tissue damage can take anywhere from days to weeks to repair itself; any possibility of pain control must then be directed farther up the nervous system, either at the level of the spinal cord or in the brain itself.

It turns out that the nociceptors in the spinal cord can be inhibited by signals originating in the brain. Two brain stem systems, the periaqueductal gray (PAG) and the rostroventromedial medulla (RVM), contain high concentrations of morphine-like substances, and the neurons in these regions project down the length of the spinal cord to release small amounts of these opioids right at the locations where the noxious signals enter. The PAG and RVM act as a descending pain control system, reducing stimulus intensity almost at its source. So even after tissue damage has occurred, pain can be controlled from within the nervous system. PAG and RVM's critical roles in blocking pain occur in the spinal cord, but the cell clusters themselves are located high in the brain stem—between the brain and the spinal cord; for this reason, they interact closely with cortical systems. The cortex's modulation of the PAG and RVM allows pain to be controlled through thought itself. If your mind can control pain, why not transmute pain into something pleasurable?

• • •

Physicians sometimes refer to pain control as "pain management," a modest admission that pain cannot actually be controlled. But anyone who has had major surgery in the last decade or so will be familiar with patient-controlled analgesia, or PCA. In the late 1970s, anesthesiologists got the idea that letting postoperative patients mete out the dose of their narcotic might give them more effective pain relief. Before the development of PCA, patients would wait a certain amount of time since their last dose, usually of morphine, until they could ask the nurse for another. Calling the nurse—who would then have to go to the pharmacy—introduced delays, during which the patient's pain would often grow more and more intense. PCA eliminated the delays and let patients control their pain. Feeling better, patients would then ease off the dosing if side effects like sedation and nausea became too severe.

To nurses and physicians, the efficacy of PCA goes beyond simply giving patients the amount of narcotic they need. Many believe that the benefits of PCA stem from the transfer of control from doctor to patient. When people are given control over their pain, they often experience it as less intense. Under the right circumstances, the mere perception of control may be enough, especially for patients who are confident of their ability to reduce their pain.[22]

More generally, the ability to regulate a stressor of any type makes all the difference in the world. Uncontrollable stress can be external, like the boss yelling at you, or being in a traffic jam when you're on the way to an important event. Or it can be internal, like headaches and stomachaches—which, although they originate in your body, feel as if they are outside your control. Yet other stressors, like a hard workout, are controllable by virtue of your willingness to endure them in the first place.

Uncontrollable stress is almost always perceived as unpleasant, but controllable stress may be endurable, even enjoyable. A classic series of investigations on rats proved that the ability to control stress has a major impact on physical well-being. A rat given random shocks from an electrified cage will experience stress. When the rat is trained to hit a lever that turns off the electricity, many of the adverse effects can be eliminated. In some elegant experiments, pairs of rats were housed together in cages with dividers down the middle. One of the rats in each pair had access to an OFF lever, but the other did not. Each time the cage was electrified, the rat in control turned off the shock for both. Though the two rodents received identical shocks, only the yoked rat showed signs of chronic stress: weight loss, ulcers, and increased susceptibility to cancer.[23] Control protected against debilitation. The beneficial physiological and mental effects of controlling a stressor, at least in rats, appears to depend on a small part of the striatum (the nucleus accumbens) and to come from dopamine.[24]

Independent of its role in controlling stress, dopamine has pain-alleviating qualities of its own. In fact, the analgesic effects of drugs that release dopamine, like cocaine and amphetamine, have been known for decades. One of the oldest treatments for intractable pain was called the Brompton cocktail, an elixir of morphine and cocaine, very popular in the nineteenth century but no longer in use. When drugs are injected that block dopamine receptors in the accumbens, the analgesic effects of dopamine disappear, indicating that the pain-relieving effects of dopamine most probably are exerted in the accumbens.[25] The analgesic effects of dopamine can be seen in other parts of the human brain, but individuals with high pain thresholds have more dopamine in their accumbens.[26]

Once again, the story of how pain and pleasure combine comes back to the striatum, of which the nucleus accumbens is a small but important part. The striatum may not be the site where pain or pleasure is determined, but it appears to be the key element of a brain network that gauges the importance of all information you encounter, which includes pain and pleasure.

## Is It Pain or Is It Pleasure?

So far, nothing that I've said about pain would suggest pleasure. But two brain imaging studies have shown that, under the right circumstance, noxious stimuli can directly activate the striatum.

Hans Breiter, a Harvard psychiatrist, was the first to demonstrate the effect of pain on the striatum. I saw Hans for the first time in a bar in Acapulco, long after the day's meeting of psychiatrists had concluded. Knowing him only through publications, I was surprised to find Hans an imposing figure, balding with an odd reddish beard, and gripping a ten-inch Cuban cigar.

Immediately plunged into his world, he held nothing back. I wanted to talk about his recent study on the effects of cocaine in the human brain, but instead I found myself caught up in a story about pain. Hans described an fMRI investigation that he had just completed with his Harvard colleague David Borsook, a neurologist specializing in pain treatment. In their experiment, Borsook and Breiter had used a thermal probe to rapidly heat the back of their subjects' hands. They then switched back and forth between the application of a warm stimulus and a hot one. When Borsook and Breiter compared the brain responses to hot stimuli and to warm ones, they saw activation in not only the brain's classic pain network, including $S_1$, thalamus, insula, and anterior cingulate but also the activation of a reward circuit, which included parts of the striatum, amygdala, and brain stem. Their observations led them to conclude that the reward system, which was activated by noxious stimuli, is not limited to processing pleasant things.[27]

A few years later, another fMRI study isolated, even more precisely, the role of the striatum in signaling impending pain. A group in Toronto, led by Shitij Kapur, used brief electrical shocks to the finger to find that the striatum was activated not by pain per se but by the appearance of a light on a computer screen that signaled when a shock that would cause pain was coming.[28] Since striatal activation preceded the pain itself, Kapur's findings suggested that the striatum acts as an early warning system to the brain that something significant is about to happen and that action must be taken.

Some researchers still might argue that the striatum is purely a pleasure center. For instance, in Kapur's experiment, the striatum merely indicated the anticipation of relief from the impending shock. But Kapur did a follow-up experiment in which he focused on what happened in the striatum when the light was turned off—the signal that the trial was over and that the person was safe. Because it was not the disappearance of the light that drove the striatum but rather its appearance, Kapur concluded that the striatal activation could not, as previously thought, have stemmed from the anticipation of relief. Rather, the striatum was signaling the imminent occurrence of something important.

Until this point, the idea that the brain cares primarily about information, and not so much whether it is good or bad, had been based on experiments using positive reinforcers—things that feel good. The studies by Borsook and Breiter, and by Kapur, show us that the need for information, especially novel information, cuts across the arbitrary dichotomy of good and bad. This doesn't mean that, for your brain, distinguishing between pleasure and pain is insignificant. It does mean that the key structure in your brain that motivates behavior—the striatum—cares less about bodily pleasures than about how it can use each bit of information it encounters to predict the future.

## Flying with Cortisol

The striatum is a crossroads for various types of information, but it still plays a role in the way pain is either eliminated or turned into pleasure. How this happens is not completely understood, but the inflammatory response has an important role.

As I saw at the SM club, three of the cardinal signs of inflammation—redness, swelling, and heat—indicate that cytokines have been released in the vicinity of the tissue damage. But cytokines don't stay sequestered in peripheral tissue. They wend their way to the brain, where the hypothalamus senses their presence and sends corticotropin releasing factor (CRF) into the pituitary gland.[29] The pituitary, which dangles from the underside of the brain, secretes adrenocorticotropic hormone (ACTH) into the bloodstream, which then flows to the adrenal glands, located in a glob of fat atop each kidney. In addition to releasing adrenaline, the glands secrete cortisol, the prototypical stress hormone and the body's frontline steroid.

Doctors have long known about the psychotropic effects of steroids. Synthetic steroids like prednisone are ten times more potent than the natural steroids, like cortisol, and sometimes result in bizarre changes in mood and thought. For many years, both synthetic and natural steroids were thought to alter moods in a negative way. In the 1990s, however, two classes of steroid receptor were discovered in the brain, each with a particular effect on mood. The mineralocorticoid receptor (MR) is a steroid receptor concentrated in the hippocampus, while the glucocorticoid receptor (GR) is found throughout the brain but especially in the limbic system and the striatum. The overall effect of steroids on mood appears linked to the ratio of activated MRs and GRs.[30]

The mood-altering effects of steroids, particularly cortisol, result from their interaction with the dopamine system in the striatum. For example, when animals in a laboratory are stressed, they release cortisol, but if given the means, they will readily self-administer dopamine-releasing drugs like cocaine. Much of this drug-seeking behavior can be stopped by giving chemicals that block not dopamine but cortisol, which can be inhibited with several well-known medications. The antifungal drug ketoconazole blocks the synthesis of cortisol, and the abortifacient RU-486 binds to the glucocorticoid receptor and prevents cortisol from affecting neurons. These medications, when given to rats that have been made dependent on cocaine or amphetamine, decrease their drug-seeking behaviors.[31]

The interaction of cortisol and dopamine may well hold the key to the satisfaction of pain. And, I suspect, cortisol has something to do with the pleasure of SM. For decades, psychiatrists have used hormonal stress tests to diagnose depression. In the classic test, dexamethasone, a synthetic glucocorticoid, is injected into the bloodstream. In a healthy individual, dexamethasone acts like cortisol on both the hypothalamus and the pituitary and suppresses the release of ACTH. Without ACTH, the adrenal glands do not make cortisol. Hence the procedure is called the dexamethasone suppression test, or DST. Endocrinologists use the DST to diagnose problems with both the adrenal and the pituitary glands, but severe forms of depression are also associated with an abnormal DST. The test is used extensively in psychiatric research to elucidate the links between stress and mood.[32]

Cortisol moves freely into the brain, including directly into dopamine neurons. When compared to a placebo, cortisol significantly elevates mood, increases concentration, and even improves memory under the right circumstances.[33] The dose of cortisol that produces these beneficial effects appears to be between twenty and forty milligrams, or about the daily amount secreted by the adrenal glands under normal conditions.[34] Injecting more than forty milligrams at one time impairs concentration and often leads to overstimulation and anxiety. If I'm right about the dopamine-cortisol connection, then the appropriate dose of cortisol should make pleasurable things, well, more pleasurable.

You can buy cortisol in any supermarket. Hydrocortisone, the primary ingredient in many brands of anti-itch creams, is chemically the same as cortisol. Before you slather up, I should point out that the amount of cortisol that finds its way into the bloodstream through the skin is minimal. To get a good-size dose of cortisol, you either have to inject it or take it orally—neither of which is possible with over-the-counter creams. In prescription strength, cortisol comes in tablets. At doses of twenty to two hundred milligrams a day, it is prescribed for the treatment of adrenal insufficiency. Similar doses of cortisol are sometimes used in treating a variety of inflammatory conditions like dermatitis and asthma.

For advice on cortisol, I needed to approach Mike Owens, a pharmacologist at Emory University and an expert in neurophysiology, who uses stress hormones in his research. I walked into Mike's office and found him reclining in his chair, steel-pipe cycling legs propped on a desk surrounded by pictures of professional cyclists.

"I want to do a DST," I announced.

He nodded nonchalantly and said, "That's easy enough."

"But I want to do it with cort instead of dex."

Mike pondered this for a moment and said, "Won't work. You can't measure the endogenous cortisol suppression with cort on board."

"That's okay," I replied. "I just want to raise my cortisol to a stress level and see what it feels like."

"If you want to raise your cortisol level, why don't you just go exercise?"

"Because that would hurt." I wasn't afraid of pain; I just didn't want to mix up the effects of cortisol with the stressor that released it.

With a sigh, Mike opened a drawer and pulled out a handful of small plastic vials and said, "Use these to put your saliva on ice." Because of the ubiquity of cortisol in the body, it can be measured in pretty much any bodily fluid, including saliva. Mike kept a handful of spit vials for himself and said, "I'm doing a hard cycling workout tonight. Let's see how much I raise my cortisol compared to you."

Cortisol secretion follows a circadian pattern that is highest right before waking but is cut in half by bedtime. At three in the afternoon, I was approaching the nadir of my daily cortisol secretion. I settled on twenty milligrams as a test dose. Twenty milligrams would be equivalent to the amount released during a hard workout, like running a 10K race. Considering that several studies of cortisol used injections of one hundred milligrams without any adverse effects, twenty milligrams was a small dose and would be safe.

To get a baseline cortisol level, I spit into the first vial and then swallowed two ten-milligram tablets before heading home.

The hormone crept up on me. Not euphoria, not a buzz, but clarity. It was like one of those early spring days before summer settles in, a day with cumulus clouds flitting across the sun, each piece of light revealing a landscape in too-sharp focus. The tulips were spilling reds and yellows like acrylic onto a carpet of awakening grass. Maybe I just imagined it.

When I got home, my children bounded up with a little more enthusiasm than normal and gave me an extra-long hug and kiss, and I noticed their smiles lingering a millisecond longer than usual. Kathleen looked beautiful, and our spaghetti dinner tasted a bit more spaghetti-ish.

I thought, *this* must be the secret to unlocking the satisfaction in pain, and I began to understand how the people at the SM club were experiencing pleasure. No doubt about it, cortisol acted synergistically with dopamine—even the dopamine released during an ordinary day—to create something very close to the feeling of a satisfying experience. Cortisol comes from stress, especially physical stress, and dopamine from novelty. Put the two together, and it is easy to see that novel physical challenges might be the best way to get the feeling of satisfaction we all crave.

# 7

•

## Running High

The cortisol high didn't last long. By nine o'clock, I was crashed out in a sweaty, tired heap, not unlike my kids, who, just four hours earlier, had bounded up to meet me. The dinner that seemed so wonderful remained lodged in my stomach. I diagnosed myself as having all the symptoms of a mild case of adrenal insufficiency: nausea, fatigue, and weakness. Not so different from a hangover.

The next day, Mike ran the salivary cortisol assays. For three hours following ingestion, my cortisol levels were raised to ten to twenty times what is normal for that time of day. Mike's workout—without the benefit of artificial elevation—was almost as impressive, resulting in cortisol levels five to ten times higher than normal. Considering that I took the daily amount of secreted cortisol in one dose, and that cortisol has a half-life of a few hours, my values were about as expected.[1]

Enlightening as my experience was, it is not a viable path to activities that would prove satisfying in the long run. A catabolic steroid, cortisol has degenerative effects on several body systems. Patients with conditions that require the long-term use of steroids like hydrocortisone suffer a panoply of side effects, including weight gain, gastrointestinal bleeding, diabetes, hypertension, and bone loss. But as Mike's workout demonstrated, there are other ways to release cortisol besides consuming it orally.

Any stressor, especially a physical one, results in the release of cortisol. The biochemical interaction of cortisol and dopamine in the striatum suggests that these two chemicals are involved in the achievement of satisfaction, perhaps even transcendence. Alone, neither compound can provide a state resembling satisfaction. Dopamine may be associated with transient euphoria, but you need cortisol to get that satisfying feeling. And because cortisol is released most effectively by stressful situations, the road to satisfying experiences must necessarily pass through the terrain of discomfort.

## Flow

Not everyone would agree with the contention that discomfort is a necessary ingredient for a satisfying experience. Perhaps discomfort is too strong a word. In 1990, the University of Chicago psychologist Mihaly Csikszentmihaly (pronounced chick-sent-me-high-ee) published *Flow*. Based on two decades' worth of research, Csikszentmihaly's book argues that happiness, which he linked to the achievement of the state he calls "flow," arises from two elements: skills and challenges.[2] Flow takes place when challenges match one's skills; if one is an accomplished pianist, for example, then flow occurs when playing a challenging piece, whereas a more modest pianist could achieve flow from playing a less complex arrangement. A sense of dynamism is central to the notion of flow: to achieve this state, one has to be challenged, and, through that challenge, change.

Challenges, by their very definition, evoke a certain disquietude, and it is here that discomfort arises. Finding the right level of challenge is a difficult balancing act; if the challenge is too great, not only is it unconquerable but the uneasiness engendered in attempting it can spill over into naked, paralyzing anxiety. Conversely, if a challenge is inadequate, boredom ensues. Between these two extremes, Csikszentmihaly found the flow channel.

There is an underappreciated aspect of this idea. If flow (or, for present purposes, satisfaction) arises from going just beyond one's current level of skills, then personal growth is inevitable. Anyone who has played the piano for some period of time knows that mastering "The Entertainer" ceases to be satisfying after the twentieth recital. In other words, natural evolution dictates that you move on to increasingly difficult pieces to attain the same level of satisfaction. Once you have achieved a state of flow, you experience the desire for more complex challenges. What I am describing is a treadmill of a sort different from the hedonic treadmill. Both, however, are rooted in the brain's need for novelty.

Achieving states of flow through intellectual means is possible, like the mental groove of completing a good crossword puzzle, but I have struggled to find a mental challenge that is ultimately as satisfying as a physical one. In the end, physical activity seems to be the most effective way to attain a flow state that concludes with the fuzzy warmth of satisfaction. Physical activity, especially involving a challenge, is the surest way to release a combination of dopamine and cortisol in the brain.

Running is one such challenge, and the growth in its popularity attests to the satisfaction that people realize from it. There are degrees of running, of course, ranging from jogging a few miles a week, to participating in a marathon. Beyond the marathon, though, a small but increasing number of people are attracted by the challenge of the ultramarathon—running 100 miles. Not only does the race require sustained physical effort for twenty-four hours, but the mental exhaustion at its completion begs the question of why anyone would undertake such an endeavor. Early on, I mentioned that novel information changes the brain at a molecular level. Physical activity does the same, and ultramarathons are just an extreme version. Beyond this, the physical and mental transformation that occurs during such a prolonged period of exertion tells us something important about how our brains work—and what we find satisfying.

## A Long Run to Satisfaction

The Western States 100 Mile Endurance Run is the granddaddy of ultramarathons, not because it is the hardest but because it is the oldest. Since the 1970s, three hundred or so runners have lined up every June at the starting line in Squaw Valley, California, to run 100 miles due west. Those who complete the course in fewer than twenty-four hours receive a coveted silver belt buckle emblazoned with the phrase "100 miles—one day." Those who reach the finish line under the time limit of 30 hours receive a bronze buckle stating "100 miles." There is no prize money, just the personal satisfaction of completing the race and the respect of one's fellow runners.

The run has its origins in the gold rush of 1849. As the story goes, James Marshall was building a sawmill for John Sutter on the American River, about halfway between Sacramento and Lake Tahoe, when Marshall discovered a few nuggets of gold in the riverbed. Eventually half a million people, the forty-niners, descended on those foothills in search of instant wealth. For those coming from the East, their path was an arduous one. Construction on the Transcontinental Railroad did not even begin in Sacramento until 1863, so the only route to gold country was on foot or on horseback through the Sierra Nevada.

The trail blazed by the forty-niners came to be known as the

Western States Trail. It begins in Squaw Valley near Lake Tahoe and ascends steeply to Emigrant's Pass, at 8,774 feet. There is a monolith of volcanic rock at the pass, which the miners, in the early days of the Civil War, named Fort Sumter.[3] From Emigrant's Pass, the trail follows the ridges of the Sierra Nevada as it splays out west. The trail occasionally dips into the steep canyons, but for the most part it parallels the American River, before ending in the town of Auburn. In the winter, because of the high country's deep snow, the trail is all but impassable. For those who doubt the trail's cruelty, the fate of the Donner Party two years before the gold rush, and twenty miles north, serves as a grim reminder of the dangers of this part of the West.

·    ·    ·

To run, hike, or ride the Western States Trail is to step back in time, for large portions of it remain untouched by development. It may, in fact, be the only historical east-west trail that exists in much the same condition as it did a century and a half ago. The Western States Trail Foundation was formed, in part, to preserve this natural resource and to celebrate the spirit of the early pioneers. In addition to its conservation efforts, the foundation sponsors two major events: the Western States 100 Mile One Day Ride, aka the Tevis Cup, and the Western States 100 Mile Endurance Run.

The Tevis Cup began in 1955, when horsemen celebrated the spirit of the Pony Express by challenging one another to cover the trail in one day. Today, it is still the ultimate test of horsemanship, a challenge of strength and stamina, with awards granted to both riders and horses. The Endurance Run began in 1974, when Gordy Ainsleigh, a veteran rider of the Tevis Cup, found himself without a horse. Rather than forgo the ride, Ainsleigh covered the course on foot—in 23 hours, 42 minutes. By 1977, the first official run was in place, with fourteen men lining up to race against the horses. Apart from water, the runners were responsible for their supplies. Only one runner finished under 24 hours, but two others continued unofficially, to finish in 28:36. Based on the determination of these two runners to complete the trail, the absolute cutoff of 30 hours was established. In 1978, the run broke off from the ride, and, ever since, each has been organized independently.

Organizing a 100-mile, point-to-point race through remote mountainous terrain presents logistical challenges. But because of its popularity, the Western States attracts over 1,300 volunteers each year, roughly 4 volunteers for each runner. A network of twenty-five checkpoints and aid stations ensures that runners are well supplied and never far from medical assistance. Even with such carefully calibrated support, things can and do go badly.

In 2003, Floyd Whiting, a 61-year-old longtime ultra runner from Reno, Nevada, dropped out at mile 98 when his kidneys became clogged with myoglobin, a breakdown product of muscle. After 98 miles of pounding, some muscle breakdown is to be expected, but in Whiting's case, his myoglobin rose so high that it blocked the filtration mechanism of his kidneys, resulting in the production of almost no urine, and what was produced was dark brown. Whiting's condition was so severe that he had to undergo dialysis for more than a week until his kidneys recovered.

More common than kidney failure, but no less dangerous, are hyperthermia and heat stroke. Temperatures in the canyons can get up to 100 degrees Fahrenheit; failure to prepare for the heat has caused many runners to drop out. Adequate fluid intake is a necessity; over 24 hours, runners can be expected to consume up to one-third of their body weight in fluid. But drinking only water is a recipe for disaster. Replacing fifty pounds of body fluid with water would dilute the naturally salty plasma, resulting in a potentially fatal condition called hyponatremia. When the concentration of salt in the body falls rapidly, the effect on internal organs is identical to that of soaking in a bathtub. Tissues swell, particularly in the brain, and when the brain swells, the only direction for expansion is down—through the foramen magnum, at the base of the skull. When this happens, the person almost always dies. With mild cases of hyponatremia, one usually escapes with just nausea and some vomiting.[4]

## Ultimate Challenges

Every December, the run organizers hold a lottery for 369 entry spots. Historically, most of the runners live in California. In 2004, five entrants from Georgia won places in the run, and I met with two of them several months before. Janice Anderson, a 38-year-old systems engineer for Home Depot, has been running ultras for over fifteen years. She finished tenth in the 2003 Western States Endurance Run, earning her an invitation for 2004 (the top ten male and female finishers from the previous year are exempted from the lottery). In 2000, Janice posted five of the six fastest times for women running the 100-mile distance, including the world record for a 100-mile trail run, earning her the title of Female Ultrarunner of the Year. Ragan Petrie, also 38 years old, is a professor of economics at Georgia State University, and a friend and training partner of Janice's. Ragan had qualified for the Western States by completing the Vermont 100-mile run, her first, in less than 18 hours. The Western States would be her second.

Having never known anyone who ran distances of this length, I wasn't sure what to expect. Serious long-distance runners tend to be rail thin, and half expecting two skeletors, I was relieved to see that Janice and Ragan were, well, normal-looking. We met at a vegetarian café one evening after they had finished a training run. Janice was a petite woman with shoulder-length brown hair and a quiet intensity. Despite her stature in the realm of ultrarunning, she did not dwell on her accomplishments and, in fact, dismissed my praise—perhaps because I am not an ultramarathonner, or, having run for so many years, the novelty factor wore off long ago. Never for a moment, though, did I take her humility as a sign of noncompetitiveness. Come race time, I suspected, Janice was fierce.

I immediately liked Ragan. She had long dark blond hair and a heart-melting radiance. Although relatively new to the field of ultrarunning, she exuded a determination of a different sort from Janice's. Two months earlier, she had broken her collarbone in a running mishap with her dog, but she had made up her mind to run the Western States—and finish under 24 hours. Ragan started running ultras when she was a graduate student. For her, they provided a defined goal. "An ultra has a start and an end," she said, "in contrast to a dissertation, when there is no end in sight."

When I pointed out that a race of more modest length also has a start and an end, both Janice and Ragan replied that they liked the challenge of an ultra. No matter how much one prepared for an ultra, pain was an integral part of the experience.

"These runs hurt," Janice emphasized.

And although neither of them said so, I imagined that the pain of a 24-hour run was very different from the comparative discomfort of a mere marathon. Short of taking up the sport myself, the next best thing was to see one of these runs up close.

## Squaw Valley

A tense atmosphere settles over Squaw Valley as the Western States runners flock to Race Central. The quaint Olympic Village, the former site of the 1960 Winter Games, is paved with cobblestones and is off-limits to cars so that the racers can amble about with their support crews—mostly friends and family. The runners are easily distinguished from the smattering of hikers and mountain bikers by their sinewy legs, beat-up feet, and the de rigueur T-shirt from another ultrarun, usually faded and stained from endless miles of training. One shirt boasted: Ask me how I lost 14 lbs in one day!

A group of first-timers had congregated on a grassy lawn at the base of the tram to the summit. Mike Sweeney, a 49-year-old veteran of the race and top-ten runner, was leading a prerace briefing.

"This is about you versus the course, and you versus the elements," Sweeney trumpeted. He stared back at the crowd and warned, "And you versus your own personal problems."

Sweeney continued to give advice about specific portions of the course, like Devil's Thumb, a steep, 1,500-foot climb at the halfway point. "There is a creek before Devil's Thumb," he said. "If your water bottle is low, fill it up. You won't have to worry about giardia for another four days."

The crowd laughed uneasily at the prospects of diarrhea, and Sweeney continued, "There is a medical checkpoint at the top of Devil's Thumb. They will ask you some trick questions like, 'What's your name?'"

The crowd laughed again, but their nervous glances said more.

Sensing the concern of this group of virgins, Sweeney explained, "They are looking for confusion, like how long it takes you to answer. Your blood pressure drops as soon as you get on the scale to be weighed, so hold onto someone if you have to.

"Rucky Chucky [the river crossing at mile 78]," Sweeney said. "The water is fifty degrees [Fahrenheit], so you can get hypothermic in the time it takes to cross. Put on a long-sleeve shirt and keep moving as soon as you get through. Your natural body motion will heat you up again."

As he said this, I realized that there was no way these runners were going to remember this.

"From Robie Point [mile 99], you can have as many people as you want run with you. Family. Kids. Whoever." Sweeney paused and in an inspiring tone about the finish said, "Remember this: *There is nothing quite like running into that stadium.*"

## Changing the Brain

Set aside ultrarunning for a moment; even moderate exercise affects the brain, although we are just beginning to discover how this happens. The correlation between mental and physical fitness was recognized almost fifty years ago, when physically fit adults were found to perform better on a variety of paper-and-pencil tests. These findings remained consistent over the decades, but only recently has the issue of causality been addressed. Does exercise improve mental function, or are fit individuals also smarter? Structuring an experiment that might answer the question would be difficult, because first you'd have to find an unfit population in which to introduce exercise; second, you'd have to develop some means of testing whether the individuals became smarter as a result of exercise.

In any event, a wealth of data have been collected from the experimentalist's favorite animal, the rat, clearly pointing to the beneficial effects of exercise on cognitive function. For a rat, the enrichment of its environment by the addition of climbing devices and places to explore results in more synapses, increased capillary development, and neurogenesis—the creation of neurons in the brain.[5] Giving rats an apparatus to climb on, while providing a means of physical activity, also provides novelty, but exercise itself has growth-enhancing effects on the brain that go beyond novelty. In the early 1990s, William Greenough, a neurobiologist at the University of Illinois, Urbana, found that when rats were encouraged to run on an activity wheel, rather than simply to traverse rope bridges and climb over obstacles, the density of capillaries in the cerebellum rose.[6] According to subsequent studies, in rats and in monkeys, aerobic exercise increases vascularization in the cortex. By itself, more blood flow in the brain does not prove that exercise improves cognition. But a few studies in rats have shown that exercise boosts certain types of learning, especially of spatial relationships, like mazes.[7]

Until recently, most neuroscientists accepted as dogma the idea that neurogenesis does not occur in adults. Most of the brain, however, is not made of neurons but rather of cells that surround neurons, called glial cells. Since the 1960s, scientists have known that cells are created in the adult brain, but until the discovery of genetic labeling techniques, nobody knew whether the cells were neurons or glial cells. Injecting an animal with a chemically related analogue of one of the building blocks of DNA would eventually solve the mystery. Bromodeoxyuridine, or BrdU, is one such substance; it is taken up by cells that are actively dividing and can be visualized under a microscope with fluorescent labels.

The BrdU technique confirmed that cells in adult brains do, in fact, divide, making neurons in the process. Among the earliest studies using this approach, an enriched environment was found to enhance neurogenesis in the hippocampus, a structure critical for memory.[8] Several investigations that have replicated the results have furnished evidence for neurogenesis in other parts of the brain, such as the prefrontal cortex. By 2004, enough evidence had accumulated that adult neurogenesis does indeed occur; the new neurons are located in the parts of the brain most important for processing recently learned information and for laying down memories—the hippocampus and the prefrontal cortex.[9] Running, even more than simply providing an interesting environment, is effective in increasing neurogenesis; one study suggests, in fact, that exercise might even double the rate of neurogenesis in the hippocampus.[10]

Prior to these studies, the effects of all types of stress were thought to inhibit neurogenesis. Sufferers of combat stress—or posttraumatic stress disorder, as it is now called—have smaller hippocampi than normal, and the shrinkage increases with the length of combat exposure.[11] According to many researchers, the agent causing the shrinkage was none other than cortisol. Patients with Cushing's syndrome, in which too much cortisol is produced, also have smaller hippocampi; as in soldiers with combat stress, the degree of shrinkage can be correlated with the level of cortisol in the blood. When rats are injected with cortisol, neurogenesis decreases in the hippocampus. All these findings might confirm the notion that stress is bad for the brain[12]—except the particular brand of stress brought on by exercise.

By any definition, exercise is stressful. All the usual stress markers, like cortisol, increase during exercise. Despite the rise in cortisol, exercise does not inhibit neurogenesis but actually enhances it. Either other factors that protect the brain are released during exercise, or the stress-is-bad-for-the-brain hypothesis is wrong.

The best guess as to how exercise leads to neurogenesis is that it does so through the release of growth factors.[13] Physical activity increases brain-derived neurotrophic factor (BDNF), a protein synthesized in neurons that, in addition to creating synapses, promotes neurogenesis and protects against stress-induced cell death in the hippocampus.[14] Exercise also releases erythropoetin, a protein secreted by the kidneys, and vascular endothelial growth factor (VEGF), both of which promote the growth of brain vasculature and are necessary to support the metabolic demands of more neurons and more synapses. In the striatum, exercise protects animals against the degenerative effects of Parkinson's disease—a benefit traced to yet another growth factor (glial cell line-derived growth factor, or GDNF).[15]

Any way you look at it, exercise is good for the brain. Apart from improving overall health, exercise promotes neurogenesis—quite literally remaking the brain. More than even mental gymnastics—for instance, doing crossword puzzles—exercise confers protective effects. And although the exact mechanism of these effects is unknown, the implication is clear: exercise protects the brain from sources of both physical and nonphysical stress—a panacea for all that ails you. Feeling depressed? Exercise. Stressed out? Exercise!

But even these conclusions don't explain the appeal of ultrarunning. None of the neurogenesis studies imply that one has to run a hundred miles to get the benefits of exercise. Fairly modest levels of activity should suffice.

## Brain Food

Bob Lind, the medical director of Western States since its beginning, was the next at bat. Based at Appalachian State University, in North Carolina, Lind and his students are one of the few groups of researchers to study the biochemical changes that happen to the body during an ultraendurance event. Even in 2005, few data on this exist; for example, most of the long-distance studies have not controlled for the significant effects of going without sleep for 24 hours.

The lack of data, I suspect, comes from the limited availability of funding for this area of research. Ultrarunning is not a disease, at least not in the conventional sense. Most of the research done on it is motivated by the passions of its scientists—many of whom are ultrarunners themselves—and is conducted on shoestring budgets cobbled together from a variety of private donors and a portion of the Western States' race fees.

Even a seemingly basic question, like how much food should be eaten during the race, has not been answered. Although the metabolic costs of running have been known for decades, they have been estimated under ideal conditions, like running on a track. Such studies have resulted in the estimate that running one mile burns 100 kcals (a calorie of food is actually 1 kilocalorie of energy—a kcal), but this rough approximation applies to an average, 150-pound male running on a flat track.[16]

During the 2003 Western States, Charles Dumke, a physiologist also at Appalachian State, attempted to measure his metabolism

under realistic trail-running conditions. Energy in the body is produced through either aerobic metabolism (requiring oxygen) or
anaerobic metabolism (not requiring oxygen), but since endurance
running is almost exclusively aerobic, the metabolic rate can be calculated from the measurement of oxygen consumption and carbon
dioxide production. Measuring oxygen and carbon dioxide has,
until recently, required bulky equipment that limits studies to
treadmills in the laboratory; only recently have portable systems
been used. Dumke's experiment—really just a test of feasibility,
since he performed it only on himself, in the Western States Run—
suggested that the metabolic requirement might be as high as 134
kcal/mile, or 34 percent higher than most runners assumed and
probably met.

But whether the runners expended 100 or 130 kcal per mile,
multiplying the appropriate figure by 100 miles indicates that they
were burning anywhere from 10,000 to 13,000 kcals during the
race.[17] The vast majority of energy reserves in the human body are
stored in fat, so that even lean adults like ultrarunners have more
than 80,000 kcals of energy stored in their fat cells.[18] In comparison, only 2,500 kcal of energy is available in the form of glycogen—
a carbohydrate that can be burned aerobically to yield a rapid
source of energy. Glycogen stores are found in muscle and liver,
but after they are used up, the body switches over to burning fat for
energy. The popular Atkins diet, which deprives the body of carbohydrates, forces the metabolic switch to fat.

Both carbohydrates and fats are utilized as energy sources, while
several factors determine the relative contribution of the two.[19]
Only extreme circumstances, like low-carb diets and endurance
sports, deplete the body of carbohydrates, forcing it to increase its
utilization of fat. At moderate intensity, like the pace of fast marathon runners, most energy comes from carbohydrates, specifically
the glycogen stored in the muscles. Once muscle glycogen is de-
pleted, athletes "hit the wall" and experience the sudden onset of

fatigue.[20] Given the energy demands of a 100-mile race, either runners must consume upward of 8,000 kcals of carbohydrates while they run or they have to burn fat.

Fortunately, exercise increases lipolysis, or fat expenditure, up to ten times the rate at rest; as a result, exercise is a more efficient way to lose weight than dieting. Although the exact mechanism has not yet been identified, endurance training itself increases the efficiency of fat utilization during exercise, making the body a better lipolysis machine. These details are important because the source of the fuel used by the body has specific effects on the brain that, in turn, might shed light on why so many people feel a compulsion to run long distances.

Carbohydrates—glucose and glycogen—burn cleanly. The aerobic metabolism of glucose yields energy with only carbon dioxide and water as waste products. Fat is also composed of carbon, hydrogen, and oxygen, and, like glucose, is ultimately burned down to water and carbon dioxide, but fat metabolism is complicated by the way fat is transported to the tissues. The energy in fat is locked up in triglycerides, which are large molecules found in fat cells. Although fat cells contain a high density of energy, its distribution to the vital organs has to overcome a fundamental problem: fat and water do not mix. At any given moment, a human being has about four liters of blood circulating. Red blood cells constitute about one-third of this volume, and the rest is plasma—a solution of water, electrolytes, proteins, and suspended fats. But transporting fat in water is tricky. The body has evolved mechanisms to sequester the fats in droplets so they won't glob together (these are the low-density lipoproteins, or LDLs). Although LDLs transport fats around the body, many organs—notably the brain—can't metabolize fat directly.

A guiding tenet of endocrinology states that the brain is a privileged organ. The body will do whatever it takes to please the brain and to keep it alive. What does the brain like most? Glucose. When glucose starts running low, other organs adjust their metabolism to use less of it, saving what is left for the brain; when glucose stores run really low, the brain shifts, somewhat reluctantly, to an alternative source of energy. Although the brain can't use the energy locked up in fat, parts of the brain can, under certain circumstances, use a by-product of fat metabolism for energy—ketones.

The liver plays the chief role in this process, because it orchestrates the conversion of glucose and fat. The first step in fat metabolism occurs in fat cells themselves, where triglycerides are split into two components: a small glycerol molecule that can be converted into glucose and a large, free fatty acid. Unlike triglycerides, fatty acids are slightly soluble in water and can be transported in the blood. Once in the liver, fatty acids are split and partially metabolized into two smaller molecules called acetoacetate and beta-hydroxybutyrate, both of which belong to the class of chemicals called ketones. Ketones are soluble in water and are small enough to diffuse into any tissue, including the brain.[21]

Ketones were first discovered in the urine of comatose diabetics, and acetoacetate, which spontaneously converts to acetone, is responsible for the fruity breath of someone in diabetic ketoacidosis. Naturally, ketones got a bad rap for being associated with diabetes. But by the 1960s, ketones had overcome their bad reputation as scientists realized that they served critical functions under normal circumstances in the body.[22]

The brain especially likes ketones. When they are injected directly into the body, the brain immediately starts using ketones for energy. And you don't have to be starving, either. After infusing beta-hydroxybutyrate into human volunteers, Danish neurologists found that the brain decreased its use of glucose by 33 percent in favor of ketones.[23] Use of ketones, though, varies from one part of the brain to another. The brain stem, where dopamine neurons are located, does not use ketones as much as the cortex.[24]

For millennia, ketones have been used medically, notably in the treatment of epilepsy. Antiepileptic diets advocated by the Greeks and Romans involved starvation and the consumption of potions designed to induce vomiting, a combination guaranteed to elevate ketones in the body. The modern variant of the ketogenic diet, introduced in the 1920s, required the consumption of roughly four times as many calories from fat as from carbohydrates.[25] Although no controlled trials exist, the ketogenic diet has been reported to reduce seizures in over half of epileptic patients, an efficacy that may be even higher in children.[26] According to one theory, the brain's shift to ketones for fuel results in downstream effects on neurotransmitters. Ketones stimulate the production of GABA—the inhibitory neurotransmitter previously encountered in my food adventures—and the major neurotransmitter in the striatum.[27] And for good measure, ketones have even been shown to protect against neurodegeneration in Alzheimer's and Parkinson's diseases.[28]

The potential benefits of ketones for those suffering from Parkinson's disease are intriguing, especially since the substance holds out hope that the loss of dopamine, as a result either of disease or of normal aging, need not have such dire consequences for the attainment of satisfying experiences. From about age twenty, humans lose dopamine neurons, and so anything that can be done to protect them is a good thing. Above and beyond the general benefits of exercise, perhaps it is the production of ketones during extended bouts of physical activity that gives the extra boost to the dopamine system. Ultrarunners certainly get their share.

## Altered States

The day before the race, I was assigned to an aid station at mile 93. Since my job was to monitor the medical status of runners as they came through, I was curious to see how they looked before the race. At the weigh-in the same day, their starting weight and blood pressure were recorded on bands secured around their wrists. At each medical checkpoint, the runner's weight would be compared with the starting weight. Depending on how hot the day got, runners could be expected to lose anywhere from 3 to 5 percent of their body weight, all in water, by the end of the race. Runners who lost more than 5 percent could be forced to rehydrate at an aid station. Losing 7 percent of the starting weight brought the risk that the runner might be pulled from the race altogether.

As I watched the runners file through the scales, their weights appeared surprisingly uniform. Almost everyone, regardless of sex, weighed between 130 and 160 pounds, confirming my initial impression that these were not the superthin body types of Olympic runners. The body's requirements for running 100 miles differ from those required for running a marathon. Most moderately fit individuals can probably run a marathon if they have the mental fortitude to endure the pain. Even if it takes five hours, with a modest intake of carbohydrates, the body has enough available energy to go 26.2 miles. But 100 miles requires training of an entirely different sort. The slightly heavier weights of the ultrarunners reflected their bodies' need for ongoing, or stored, energy during a 24-hour run.

By about ten in the morning, many of the runners had checked in and headed off to relax, meditate, or otherwise get their heads into race mode for the start the next day. I set off from the starting line to experience the first few miles of the race.

The sun was already high, and without a cloud in sight, it beat down relentlessly on Emigrant's Pass. I hiked the initial part of the trail beneath the idle lifts, following the Sno-Cat roads used to groom the ski trails in winter. Every bit of moisture seemed to have evaporated from the air, and although I was just walking, the liter of water I toted felt barely adequate.

As I huffed my way up through the thinning atmosphere, small groups of runners, unwilling to take even one day of rest, jogged their way past me. After about an hour and a half at a decent clip, I passed the tree line and found myself in a meadow surrounded by snow-lined crags. A piece of yellow tape, signifying a change in the trail direction, had been affixed to the base of a steep granite incline. Chalk arrows pointed up. I had thought that this was supposed to be a run, not a climbing expedition. After 100 meters of climbing the rock face, I found myself on the only snow-covered portion of the course, an icy drift nestled in the shadow of Emigrant's Pass. This was fortunate; in comparison with 1995 and 1998, when the first 24 miles were covered in snow, this year the runners would have to worry only about the heat.

From the top, the trail snaked its way west through canyons that stretched to the horizon. I turned around and saw that a blue mist had settled over Lake Tahoe. Someone was hiking up through the snow.

"How youz doin'?" he said.

He introduced himself as Nick "Where's my soup?" Palazzo, a 57-year-old truck driver from Long Island and irrepressible fan of and participant in ultrarunning. His nickname comes from what he describes as a cranky moment during the 1999 Badwater 135, which was immortalized in Mel Stuart's documentary *Running on the Sun*. Badwater is probably the most difficult of the ultras, run over 135 miles in July from the lowest point in North America—Death Valley—to the highest point in California—Mount Whitney. The moment that coined his name occurred 106 miles into the run. Unable to hold down any solid food, Nick carped at his crew, "This is fucking ridiculous. I'm fucking hungry!" When two of his friends returned from being dispatched 15 miles up the road in search of soup, they were greeted with a testy "I don't wanna ask where youz went. I walked twelve miles since you left." Just before Nick gobbled down a cup of clam chowder, he added wearily, "I'm about to deplete here."

As we walked back down to the valley, Nick boasted of running twenty-six ultras. I asked him why he does it. As we passed through the tree line, he looked up at a strand of California pines and, in answer to my question, asked, "How long do you think these have been here?"

At least two hundred hundred years, I thought.

Without waiting for an answer, he said, "Longer than we will be." Nick continued, "I do it for the challenge. It fills a void."

Although he wasn't running the 2004 Western States, Nick was there to pace a friend for the last 40 miles. He explained that the mental part of the race is the most difficult, which is why runners need someone to join them. "You gotta distract the mind. Just get your runner to the next aid station."

"What happens out there?" I asked.

Nick shook his head and replied, "Out on the trail, people don't talk. They confess."

"Do people hallucinate?"

"Oh, yeah," he said. "Especially at night. Shadows start looking like people. Or animals."

Sleep deprivation will do that. Decades have passed since the last hardcore physical research on sleep deprivation, but its psychological effects have been well documented. At some point, probably after about ten days, total sleep deprivation results in death. As you can imagine, it is hard to determine whether sleep is a purely physiological, or just a psychological, essential; finding out entails some creative approaches.

As an animal (or human) is deprived of sleep, increasingly noxious stimuli are necessary to keep it awake. Until the 1980s, nobody knew whether the deleterious effects of sleep deprivation arose from the loss of sleep itself or from the external proddings necessary to maintain wakefulness. In 1983, researchers at the University of Chicago devised a method of controlling for the effects of keeping animals awake.[29] They housed rats in a Plexiglas cage filled with water. On one side of the cage, half a circular disk protruded, forming a ledge that the animals could use to stay out of the water. The other half of the disk jutted out into a neighboring cage. Whenever the target rat began to fall asleep, the disk rotated, awakening the rat and forcing it to walk in the direction opposite the rotation, to keep from falling into the water. With the rats yoked in pairs, the disk rotation was rigged to keep only one rodent awake. Although the control rat was awakened by the disk rotation, too, it was free to sleep when its partner was awake and the disk was still. All the sleep-deprived rats became debilitated: they stopped grooming, and their fur became yellow; skin lesions appeared; their paws swelled; they had problems with coordination; and, finally, just before they died, their EEGs flatlined. The sleep-deprived rats lived from five to thirty-three days, and when their bodies were examined, the researchers found signs of overwhelming infection: fluid-filled lungs, stomach ulcers, internal bleeding, and, in most, enlarged adrenal glands. Although the control animals had been subjected to the same awakening stimuli, they did not experience any of these symptoms. The results indicate that sleep is, indeed, a physiological necessity.

Short of death, extended sleep deprivation in humans has been hypothesized to produce psychosis.[30] On closer examination, sleep deprivation causes visual misperceptions and hallucinations, although psychotic behavior has never been seen in laboratory settings. In one study, at UCLA in 1967, four volunteers were sleep-deprived for 205 consecutive hours (8.5 days). After the third day, visual misperceptions, like those Nick Palazzo described, became commonplace. In the late 1980s, a study performed at the Walter Reed Army Institute of Research, in Washington, found that visual distortions increased sharply after just 24 hours of sleep deprivation. After 48 hours, 80 percent of people experienced either a visual distortion, like that of a video monitor swimming around, or a hallucination, such as seeing "the decaying corpse of the research assistant."[31]

But there is a bright side to sleep deprivation. Psychiatrists have known since 1971 that sleep deprivation has mood-elevating effects. As little as one night of wakefulness can snap someone out of severe depression, a simple treatment, if there ever was one, with a 60 percent response rate—comparable to most antidepressants.[32] Alas, the effect is generally short-lived; in about half the patients who responded to sleep deprivation, the effect was lost after one night of sleep. The biology of the euphoria has consistently been linked to an increase in dopamine in the striatum following sleep deprivation,[33] which must certainly contribute to the satisfaction of running an ultra.

## Race Day

The runners milled about the starting line with nervous energy. At 4:55 A.M., daylight had not even broken, but the resort had turned on some of the floodlights, normally used for nighttime skiing, and they stretched like Christmas lights four miles up the face of the canyon.

Greg Soderlund, the race director, offered an Olympic blessing to the runners: "Ask not for victory, ask only for courage. For if you endure, you have brought honor to yourself. More importantly, you have brought honor to us all."[34]

Someone flipped a switch, and the sound of Steppenwolf's "Born to Be Wild" blared from the PA system. Bob Lind raised a shotgun in the air and fired the blast that started the race.

The top runners took off in a dash, to the whoops and hollers of their crews, while the rest of the pack ambled along, conserving energy for what was to come. When the last of the runners had gone, I did what any normal human being would do—I went back to sleep.

It wasn't until after eight o'clock that the sun rose above the eastern rim of the valley, and, with it, light came streaming into my hotel room. The runners had already been out on the course for three hours, and the leaders were probably approaching the first major checkpoint, at Robinson Flat, 24.6 miles into the race. I took that estimate as my motivation to get down to Highway 49, my assigned aid station.

Situated at the crossing of the Western States Trail and Highway 49, mine was the last of the medical checkpoints, a mere 6.7 miles from the finish. Although it was mile 93 on the trail, driving from Squaw Valley took a significantly more circuitous route, and it wasn't until two in the afternoon that I pulled into the site of the aid station. The air was still bone-dry, although, by this hour, considerably hotter in the canyon and heavy with dust from a rock quarry across the highway.

Heidi Ryan, the spitfire captain of the aid station, pointed to a stack of tables for me to set up. A large RV formed the core of the station, and as other volunteers trickled in, they spread out a smorgasbord of food, a gustatory gauntlet for the athletes to run through.

By seven o'clock, when we expected the first runners, the aid station was in full operation. As Nick had made clear, many of them wouldn't be able to keep down solid food; at this point, therefore, soup provided the most important sustenance. Heidi unloaded a pallet of gallon-size cans of chicken soup from the RV and poured them into a ten-gallon pot perched on a propane stove. Every aid station had a signature dish, and she began frying hers, a delectation fit for Elvis: peanut-butter and bacon sandwiches. The remainder of the buffet was filled out with more conventional runner's fare: M&Ms, bananas, saltine crackers, and an electrolyte replacement drink called GU2. Gatorade was so '70s.

Scott Jurek, a 30-year-old physical therapist from Seattle and winner of the last five Western States runs, blasted through the aid station at a little after 7:30 P.M. On record pace to win his sixth, he didn't hang around long. After jumping on the scale for his weight check and refilling his water bottles, he was off with his pacer. He went on to win the race, setting a new course record of 15 hours, 36 minutes. The next runner didn't come through for another hour, and as the evening wore on, the participants' sporadic appearances increased to a steady trickle of one about every ten minutes.

As the flow of runners through the station picked up, the encampment of support crews, which easily looked as weary as their runners, grew. The crew members had been awake as long, driving from one aid station to another, offering comfort food, fresh socks, and moral support along the way. By two in the morning, the station was hopping. To make the 24-hour mark and get the coveted silver belt buckle, runners had to come through no later than three. The temperature at this hour had dipped to about 50 degrees Fahrenheit, and many crew members, unprepared for the chill, huddled under blankets and sleeping bags, waiting for their runners.

I kept busy weighing the athletes as they entered the station, asking how they were doing, and looking for signs of mental confusion. At this point in the race, all those on pace to break 24 hours looked strong. Some, sensing the nearness of the finish line, were giddy with euphoria. A short blond woman who nearly toppled off the scale was immediately surrounded by a trio of tow-headed girls, the oldest no more than ten, yelling in unison, "Mommy!" I almost wept as she scooped them up, their presence somehow imbuing her with a new source of energy. She kissed each one and bounded away, saying, "I'll see you at the finish in a couple of hours!"

Ragan came through around two-thirty. She looked strong and alert, although she was clearly in pain as she swallowed a couple of tablets of ibuprofen. By that point, she told me later, she was mentally out of it. With her quadriceps shot, the slightest incline on the trail slowed her to a walk; coupled with overall fatigue and the darkness, her condition was producing weird visual perceptions. She would, however, make her goal, finishing in 23 hours, 20 minutes. Janice was about an hour behind Ragan.

## Transformation

When determining whether to pull a runner from the race, Bob Lind once said, "You look into their eyes and see if their souls are separating from their bodies."

Something does happen to runners out on the trail. Out-of-body experiences, hallucinations, mystical enlightenments—whatever the description, the phenomenon seemed to me, a bystander, like an acid trip. Arnold Mandell, a psychiatrist who trained under Heath in the 1950s and who was in the thick of hallucinogenic research during the heyday of its psychiatric use, in the next two decades, once told me that he likened the runner's high to the expansion of consciousness that occurred with peyote and mescaline.[35]

The term *runner's high* probably originated in the 1970s during the explosion in popularity of running. But even now, deciding whether the high exists, and if it does, what its nature is, has been more of a debate than a scientific study. When I asked Ragan and Janice about the runner's high, they both gave me quizzical looks. Janice dismissed the idea as a notion created by casual runners who confused their exhaustion at the end of a run with some sort of transcendent experience.

Much of the confusion over what the runner's high is, I think, comes from the conflation of endorphins and running. Beginning in 1973, with the discovery of opiate receptors in the brain, and culminating, three years later, in the identification of naturally produced opioid substances, the endorphin link was latched onto by the popular running press when describing the runner's high.[36] The explanation was fueled by the growth in popularity of so-

called organic, or nonhallucinogenic, ways to expand consciousness. The discovery that not only does the brain have receptors for
morphine-like chemicals but that it produces opioids must have
reinforced the myth. Running is obviously painful, so, the logic
went, the brain must release endorphins that allow an athlete to
continue on for marathon distances.

When scientists examined the blood of long-distance runners,
they indeed found elevated levels of endorphins.[37] The term *endorphin*, however, is imprecise; it refers to any opioid-like substance
produced by the body that mimics the effect of morphine. Subsequently, several distinct classes of peptides, including beta-endorphin
proper, enkephalin, and dynorphin, have been found to have this
property.

Each of the three peptides begins as a much longer protein,
from which the active component is cleaved.[38] Beta-endorphin, for
example, starts as a 267-amino acid precursor called proopiome-
lanocortin, or POMC for short. POMC is produced in only a few
locations in the brain, primarily in two tiny brain stem nuclei: the
arcuate nucleus and the nucleus of the solitary tract, the latter
receiving the majority of sensory information from the tongue and
therefore a critical way station for taste. The arcuate nucleus, a
pea-size collection of cells in the hypothalamus, is even more interesting, because in addition to synthesizing POMC, its neurons
have receptors for leptin. Mice whose leptin receptors have been
inactivated in these cells become obese, indicating the critical
interplay between leptin, body energy storage, and POMC.[39] The
arcuate nucleus has widespread connections throughout the limbic
system of the brain, where POMC is released and affects mood,
motivation, and the perception of pain.

From the middle part of POMC comes the 39-amino acid
adrenocorticotropic hormone (ACTH)—which I introduced in
Chapter 6—and from the end of POMC comes beta-endorphin,
itself only 31 amino acids long. As described earlier, ACTH is the

hormone that signals the adrenal glands to release cortisol. It is no coincidence that levels of beta-endorphin rise during stressful exercise. Any condition that releases POMC will increase the production of both ACTH and beta-endorphin. Since activation of the cortisol system is necessary to maintain energy balance during exercise, the extra beta-endorphin may come along as a by-product of ACTH. If this speculation is true, then beta-endorphin might be unrelated to the runner's high.

But the early blood assays did not distinguish between these compounds and the biologically inactive proteins from which they were cleaved. When assays were developed that separated true beta-endorphin from the chaff, increases in true beta-endorphin were found in only 50 percent of subjects undergoing intense exercise.[40] Even if exercise releases true beta-endorphin into the bloodstream, scientists don't know what good it would do there, because the opiate receptors are in the brain and the spinal cord. What matters is whether exercise releases endorphins into the central nervous system.

All of this is not to say that the runner's high doesn't exist. I think that it does, but it doesn't come from endorphins. However one describes the mental state that occurs during running, no component of it resembles the effect of opiates. Opiates like codeine, morphine, and heroin induce a mental fogginess that can bring on a state of detachment from both internal and external sources of unpleasantness. But I never met a runner who described the sport in any way resembling opiate-related euphoria. Mandell thought that the first runner's high came during physical fatigue, invigorating the athlete like a bolt of lightning.[41] As the fatigue falls away from your legs, the air becomes cleaner, trees become sharper, your mind churns out ideas, rough-and-tumble upon each other, and a cacophony of grand schemes suddenly seems possible, only to be washed down the drain as soon as you hit the shower. It sounds like dopamine. And cortisol.

## Final Steps

By sunrise, many of the remaining runners looked to be in bad shape. The trail, which emerged from the trees and snaked downhill about 100 meters to where we were positioned, produced runners who broadcast how they were doing by their gait. Brian, an emergency medical technician and my compatriot at the weigh-in, nudged me from a catnap and pointed to a hunched figure walking toward us. "Look at this guy," he said. "That is what you call a blister walk." With every step, the poor fellow winced in pain. He sat down for a few minutes but refused our offer to treat his blisters. "Just duct-tape them," he said.

As the early morning hours wore on, we approached the 30-hour cutoff. Any runner not making it to our aid station by 9:15 A.M. would be disqualified. Sweepers patrolled the trail on horseback, looking for runners who were not on pace to make the 30-hour mark, pulling them up into the saddle if necessary. While the winner had showered and enjoyed a full night's sleep, the folks coming through in the early morning had been out on the trail for well over 24 hours. Until that point, nobody had lost more than 3 percent of body weight, but shortly after dawn, we started seeing runners down more than 5 percent. One guy, reeking of ketones, indicating that he had not consumed enough food, was down 6 percent of his starting weight. We made him sit down, against his will, and wouldn't let him leave the aid station until he drank a cup of fluid. His pacer shook his head and said, "What's the difference? He's just going to vomit it down the trail. Let him go." We did, and he finished.

The most heartbreaking moment came at 9:15. A man in his early sixties came staggering in just before the race official was to blow the horn. The rules state that runners must leave the aid station before the horn blows, although they can return if they need to and not be disqualified. We all gathered around him, like a pit crew around a NASCAR racer. Heidi told him that if he got out of the aid station in the next minute, he could come back and refuel and continue on. I wanted him to get up, but he shook his head and said, "It's over."

"Are you sure?" I said. "You can still make it."

"No. It's all right. Really."

As aid station captain, Heidi had the responsibility of cutting off his wrist band, officially disqualifying him from the race. As she did so, she hugged him and said something in his ear.

In the end, 278 people finished the race, a remarkable 75 percent completion rate. Ragan did very well, breaking 24 hours and finishing as the thirteenth woman and sixty-fifth overall. Janice didn't do as well as she had hoped but did finish in a little over 25 hours, the nineteenth woman and ninety-sixth overall.

It was a powerful experience—certainly for the runners, but also for the observers. You cannot help but be affected by the sheer force of will that compels these athletes to push their bodies to the limits, nor can you overlook the outward effects of the crucible of physical pain and exhaustion that we know alters the brain. The body heals, but I think the impact on the brain may be more lasting. Though we don't know exactly where the change comes from, we do know that dopamine and cortisol are likely suspects. Anything you can do to promote the release of these two hormones in tandem, even in small amounts, might lead you to transforming experiences. Change, after all, is the goal, and the best way to sate the need for novelty.

# 8

―――・―――

## Iceland: The Experience

As I observed, while watching ultramarathoners complete a race in spite of evident pain, unpleasantness can be obviated, and even transformed into pleasure, through the act of controlling its source. Even if control is only an illusion, maintaining the illusion might be sufficient to trick the brain into producing a flood of dopamine. The variety of ways in which the dopamine system malfunctions, whether through major depression or Parkinson's disease, illuminates the tenuous link between dopamine, mood, and motivation, all of which are necessary for the creation of satisfying experiences. Watching people like Ragan Petrie grind out 100 miles, while staying awake for 24 hours or more, underscored one facet of this equation: the intimate relationship between sleep and mood and its bearing on the ability to find satisfaction. As I explained in Chapter 3, sleep is also necessary for the *Aha!* experience. To help me figure out the source of sleep's pleasures, I turned to Dave Rye, a neurologist friend and colleague at Emory and one of the world's experts on sleep disorders.

I can say with certainty that I have never found sleep particularly satisfying; through most of my life, I probably would have preferred to do something else. Clearly I am in the minority, because when I ask my students to list activities they find rewarding, having sex and eating top the list, followed closely by sleeping, as is typical for people in their early twenties. But at least I wasn't alone in my preferences, because Rye echoed my opinion about sleep, but for a reason different from mine. His was a dopamine problem.

At full attention, Rye stands just over six feet, seven inches and would have made an imposing NFL linebacker. Every time I see him in his office, I cringe. The standard academic office measures twelve feet by twelve feet, and, with the addition of an L-shaped desk, a couple of chairs, and a file cabinet, little space remains. Compounding this problem, Rye uses the most common academic filing system: stacks. Apart from a well-worn path between door and chair, every square inch of floor is occupied by a box or a stack of papers. He works like a caged bear, and the stacks of paper at his feet are like fermenting excrement left by some inattentive zookeeper.

His door was open, so I walked in. Rye was pounding on his computer keyboard. I waited about ten seconds before he looked up without saying anything.

"Dave?" I said.

He said glumly, "I gotta go to Iceland."

Iceland usually elicited more enthusiasm from him. "You don't sound too happy about it," I said.

Cracking his upper back as he stood up, he smiled, and like a man who has just made a momentous decision, he said with conviction, "I need to see some patients. Want to come?"

Rye specializes in sleep medicine, and while the prospect of talking to sleep-deprived patients sounded positively soporific, I was intrigued. He knew that my true love is research, and though I often saw Rye padding around the hospital corridors with his worn leather doctor bag and the trademark neurologist's reflex hammer poking obscenely out of it, I knew he wasn't asking me whether I wanted to see patients now. He was referring to his patients in Iceland.

Although Rye treated many types of sleep disorders, restless legs syndrome stoked his curiosity. Not quite a disease, RLS is termed a syndrome because its symptoms can vary from one patient to another. Its hallmark, though, is an irresistible urge, almost always more intense at night, to move the legs. The cause is unknown, but Rye was hot on the trail of RLS's possible genetic link to dopamine.

Close to the Arctic Circle, Iceland has extremes of day and night that affect its residents' moods in ways that are just beginning to be studied. More important from Rye's perspective, Icelanders are a small, homogeneous population ideally suited to serve as subjects in the search for genetic mutations in the dopamine system. About the only other thing I knew about Icelanders was that they rate the highest in the world in terms of life satisfaction.[1] Going to this wintry nation, apart from enabling Rye to pursue his interest in the genetics of sleep, seemed like a great way to learn what makes Icelanders the most satisfied people in the world.

I had no way of knowing that what I would find would have little to do with the comparatively prosaic forms of novelty I had, up to this point, pursued.

Without much thought, I called Rye's bluff. "Sure. When do you want to go?"

"Two weeks," he said. "Book your flight, and I'll take care of the rest."

## The Place of Greatest Torture

The flight to Reykjavík is unremarkable, except for the final fifteen minutes. After a night spent flying over the North Atlantic, the

final descent breaks through a low cloud ceiling; then a stark landscape of black lava and mossy green lurches out of the ocean to
meet the lumbering 757.

About an hour into the flight, Rye nudged me. He pointed to a
doughy middle-aged man across the aisle who had fallen asleep
with his tray table down, the remnants of his amber-colored mixed
drink sliding about. He was snoring softly.

After swallowing a sleeping pill, I was hoping to sleep myself,
and just as I was about to bury my head in a pillow against the window, Rye said, "Look at his foot."

The man's shoes were off, and his foot was sheathed in a navy
blue sock, whose threads were beginning to separate in the heel.

Rye said with excitement, "Watch this."

Nothing happened.

"Wait." Rye was counting out an adagio tempo like a symphony
conductor. "OK. Now!"

The man's big toe jerked upward. The movement was followed
immediately by a brief flexion of his ankle, knee, and hip. With a
staccato grunt, he shifted in his seat, never really waking up. The
whole sequence didn't last more than a couple of seconds and was
repeated every thirty seconds.

"Pretty cool, huh?" Rye said, rhetorically. "That guy has periodic limb movement disorder. PLMD. I bet he has restless legs
syndrome, too."

Restless legs syndrome was probably first described by the great
English physician Sir Thomas Willis in 1672. Willis wrote in
Latin, and it wasn't until thirteen years later that his description
was translated into English:

> Wherefore to some, when being a Bed they betake themselves
> to sleep, presently in the Arms and Leggs Leapings and Con-
> tractions of the Tendons, and so great a Restlessness and Toss-
> ing of their Members ensure, that the diseased are no more able
> to sleep, then if they were in a Place of the greatest Torture.[2]

Rye and other sleep researchers believe that RLS occurs far more commonly than first realized. While current estimates suggest that anywhere from 2 to 15 percent of the population is afflicted with RLS (which becomes more prevalent in older people and affects women about twice as often as men), Rye thought that the true incidence might be twice those numbers. RLS is the fourth leading cause of insomnia, and up to 20 percent of pregnant women experience its symptoms during pregnancy. Fortunately, few people suffer to the extent described by Willis. Most of the time, RLS is mild, like a vague ache in the calf. In moderate cases, RLS feels like bugs crawling under the skin; but when severe, it is a creeping, incessantly tugging, ache of the legs. Most patients report that their symptoms are worse at night and exacerbated by immobility, like sitting for long periods. In all cases, relief comes from getting up and moving around.[3]

PLMD is a more specific diagnosis than RLS. Almost 90 percent of patients with RLS also have PLMD. Although PLMD generally occurs in the legs, it can also be in the arms, and at least one case of pelvic PLMD has been reported.[4] As the slumbering, shoeless passenger demonstrated, PLMD is characterized by brief jerking movements of the limbs, usually the foot. Each movement lasts no more than a few seconds and typically occurs in sequences spaced 30 to 90 seconds apart. The movements often cause a partial awakening, which the patient doesn't usually remember.

Perhaps the most intriguing aspect of both RLS and PLMD is that they run in families. The fact that as many as 50 percent of patients report having a parent or a sibling with the disorder suggests a genetic cause of RLS. This pattern of inheritance is what drew Rye to Iceland several times each year. Icelanders, who keep better genealogical records than even the Mormon Church, may very well offer Rye the key to unlocking the riddle of RLS.

## Meet the Vikings

After landing, I cleared customs and found Rye standing outside the main terminal. It was about 60 degrees Fahrenheit, with a brisk ocean breeze putting a wet bite in the air. Rye was down to his shirt sleeves, smiling broadly and proclaiming, "Isn't this great?"

I wasn't so sure. Following Rye to Iceland to see RLS patients had seemed like a novel thing to do when he suggested it two weeks before, but standing outside the Reykjavík airport, trying to wake up, I already missed my family. Kathleen, although supportive, was not looking forward to a week of mind-numbing toddler conversation. Her parting words were "I love you," but with a whisper of seriousness she added, "And keep your hands off those Icelandic women."

For our caffeine fix, we stopped at Café Paris, in the heart of the capital, directly across from Parliament. Despite its tony name, the Paris was a typical Icelandic meeting place that was popular with tourists. The customers that morning also included local business executives and young mothers pushing baby carriages with one hand while sipping lattes with the other. It could have been any suburban Starbucks in the United States, except for the women.

After slumping into a seat by the window, I heard a deliciously feminine voice say, *"Góðan daginn"* [good morning]. In an effort to determine the source of this beautiful lilt, my head spun around so quickly that I almost snapped my neck. My cervical pirouette deposited my line of sight directly in front of a tawny midsection, a silver stud staring back at me from her navel, and a quick glance down confirmed that her legs went on forever. Naturally, if I was going to place my order, I had to look up. By forty-five degrees elevation, her flaxen tresses came into view, and, one notch higher, I gazed into eyes as blue as the Arctic sky, framed by cheekbones that could cut glass.

She returned with our breakfast, the aroma of freshly brewed coffee mixed pleasingly with her flowery perfume. She leaned gracefully over the table to place the cups in front of us. As she reached back to her serving tray, her hand brushed my arm. The cool whisper of skin on skin, lasting only milliseconds, was enough to trigger a cascade of autonomic reactions. Capillaries flushed open, and the hair on my arm stood erect. I could feel the warmth spreading upward toward my neck, then my face.

Quickly, I grabbed the coffee. The heat of the cup and the rising steam sufficiently overpowered any lingering warmth. Nobody noticed.

The ubiquity of blond hair and blue eyes in Icelandic women derives largely from Scandinavian, specifically Nordic, genes; however, Icelanders do not generally look like their distant Norwegian cousins. The Viking settlers of Iceland sailed from Norway in the ninth century. The harsh terrain of Iceland made farming difficult, so most of the economy relied on the sea. Although the cold waters of the North Atlantic and the Arctic Ocean provided a rich environment for fishing, the high winds and unpredictable weather at this latitude also made life at sea dangerous. Iceland lies roughly equidistant from Britain and Norway. The region now called Ireland, being the westernmost extension of the British Isles, was a favorite stopping point for the Vikings.

The Viking layovers in the land of the Celts were not always friendly. After weeks of fishing cold Atlantic waters, Viking men probably had more than cod on their minds. Celtic women, of course, looked different from their Nordic counterparts in Iceland. Dark-haired and wide-eyed, these exotic women must have made quite an impression on the lonely seafarers. The Vikings returned to Iceland with many Celtic women in tow, making them their wives and concubines. Perhaps because these stories have been recorded in the Sagas of Iceland, most Icelanders believe that they are about half Scandinavian and half Celtic.

Befitting an island nation a little smaller than the state of Ohio, Iceland has never been able to support a large population.

The current population is approximately 270,000, about half of whom now live in the capital, Reykjavík. Because of the strong Scandinavian tradition of recording births, almost every Icelander can trace his or her roots back at least eight generations, while some can trace their family tree to the earliest settlers.[5]


## deCODE

The completeness of the genealogies, coupled with the fact that all the residents live in basically the same environment, makes Iceland possibly the best place in the world to search for the genetic causes of diseases. The human genome is estimated to contain 20,000 to 25,000 genes,[6] so finding which ones might be responsible for a particular illness is a challenging problem. There are currently two broad approaches to the genetic basis of disease. One method, which assumes nothing about the arrangement of human genes, simply looks for recurring patterns in patients with a specific disorder. A kind of needle-in-the-haystack approach, it is called the genome-wide scan and depends heavily on sophisticated computer algorithms to identify patterns that occur more frequently than one would expect by chance, especially within a family. At the other extreme lies the mapping of the human genome, which has revealed a great deal about the approximate location of many genes. A number of geneticists believe that such mapping can hone the search for the causes of disease in exact regions of the genome.[7]

One of the staunchest advocates for genome-wide scanning is Kári Stefánsson, the CEO and founder of deCODE Genetics, headquartered in Reykjavík. Kári,[8] a native Icelander who traces his heritage to the original settlers, was a professor of neurology for many years at the University of Chicago, where Dave Rye received his medical training in the 1980s. It was in Chicago that Rye first experienced Kári, who has acquired, and I believe fostered, the aura of a modern Viking, right down to voluminous quotations of poetry and the metaphorical sword always drawn for a good battle. His six-foot, three-inch frame is all muscle, an effect augmented by his preference for collarless, tight-knit black shirts rather than the usual shirt and tie.

After our wake-up shot of caffeine, we drove to the inauspicious corporate headquarters of deCODE. Set back on a wide expanse of grassy meadow across from the University of Iceland campus, deCODE occupies a rectangular concrete building with three rows of windows and a tasteful, almost austere, wood-sided entrance. We were greeted politely by a man and a woman at the security desk in a vestibule that spanned the full three levels of the building. Behind them, a glass partition revealed a large common area in which employees were lining up for lunch. Rye pointed to the food queue and said, "Free lunch every day. Are you ready to try some Icelandic fish?"

I thought that eating might help to resynchronize my circadian rhythms, which were already jet-lagged. The jet lag was compounded by the fact that it was just two days after the summer solstice. At that time of year in Iceland, the sunlight has an ephemeral quality. It seems to come from everywhere, making ordinary objects glow. And during the solstice at Iceland's latitude, it was going to be daylight all the time. We sat down at one of the common tables with trays of fish soup, slabs of freshly baked whole grain bread, and a yogurt-like dish called *skyr* for dessert.

The common area is really an indoor courtyard opened up to the roof, which is basically one big skylight. On both sides of the common area, banks of windows revealed laboratories and offices. In one room, several white-coated technicians scurried about, placing and checking samples in several of the fifty-some DNA sequencers. In another room, flasks full of fluorescent red and green chemicals were arranged neatly above black lab countertops, themselves populated with centrifuges and banks of pipettes.

"What exactly," I asked, "are they doing at deCODE?"

"DeCODE," Rye began, "is using genome-wide scanning to search the Icelandic population for genetic markers of disease. At the first level, they use microsatellites."

Microsatellites are small bits of DNA that contain alternating sequences of base pairs. The string of repeats can be as short as two, or as long as thirty, or even more. The repeats tend to occur in parts of the genome that do not code for specific proteins—the so-called junk DNA—and vary in length from one person to another. Although the microsatellites do not function in the usual sense, they sit near genes that do, and can serve as markers for genes of interest. In practice, you take a sample of DNA, usually isolated from blood, amplified with polymerase chain reaction (PCR), and collect it into the bottom of a test tube using a centrifuge. This wad of material is mixed with synthetic DNA templates that match the microsatellites of interest and is amplified, once again, with PCR. The result is a collection of DNA fragments that can be sorted by size and measured by computer. The technique creates a genetic fingerprint, which, like true fingerprints, is unique to every person.

Rye continued, "The microsatellite patterns are correlated with the extensive family trees in Iceland. Almost everyone in Iceland can trace their genealogy back five generations. Some go back nine generations."

"How do they do that?" I asked.

"It's in the Book of Icelanders, and the Book of Settlements, and it's in the Sagas," Rye replied. "The Icelanders are obsessed with their origins."

"But that stuff is mythology," I objected. "How much of it is really true?"

"Kári tested it," Rye said.

"What are you talking about?"

"The guys at deCODE examined the DNA fingerprints on the

Y-chromosome of Icelandic men and compared them to their counterparts in other European countries."

"And?"

"The men look to be about 75 percent Norwegian and 25 percent Irish."

"So what?"

"They did another study on the women," Rye said. "They genotyped the mitochondrial DNA, which comes only from the mother, and found that the women did not have the same genetic ancestry as the men."[9]

"How can that be?"

"It's in the Sagas," Rye replied. "The Vikings raided Ireland and took the women."

"What do you do with this information?" I asked.

Rye looked annoyed. "Remember I told you that RLS runs in families?"

"Yes."

"DeCODE has access to all of the birth records in Iceland since records have been kept. That's almost two hundred years, ten generations, of family trees. I come here to examine patients with RLS, and I give them leg monitors to wear at night so I can measure how bad their RLS is. DeCODE takes this information and searches their database to see how these patients are related to each other. Everyone is related to everyone here."

Diseases with a genetic basis pepper some families more than others because the illnesses are passed from one generation to another. In the United States, immigration has left most families without good enough records to trace large family trees. So Rye came to Iceland. Once an extensive family tree is constructed, statistical tests can be run to see if patterns of disease occur randomly or follow lines of inheritance.

"Once we identify patients with RLS, we ask them to give blood for DNA analysis," Rye continued. "DeCODE then uses their microsatellite fingerprints to identify regions of the genome that might be carrying the genes that are responsible for the disease."

Microsatellites were great for quickly scanning the whole genome, but the chunks of DNA produced in the process were still so large that each one might contain several hundred genes. "But microsatellites don't let you identify genes," I interjected.

"That's right," Rye said. "Then we go in with SNPs."

*SNP*, pronounced *snip*, is the acronym for *single nucleotide polymorphism*, which refers to variations in single base pairs of DNA sequences. Increasingly, SNPs have become the geneticist's tool of choice for honing in on minute regions of the genome. Although SNPs are very specific, their sheer number approaches 500,000, so knowing which SNPs to focus on is paramount.

Not all geneticists agree with the genome-scanning approach. The major criticism is that genome scanning can pick up only diseases that follow simple patterns of inheritance. You inherit two copies of DNA, one from each parent. Because of variations between people, the maternal and paternal copies of each gene, the alleles, may not be identical. Through mutation or damage, some alleles may become defective, but since you have two copies of every gene, the odds are usually good that at least one copy will be fine, and therefore you suffer no ill effects unless you are unfortunate enough to inherit two bad copies. Tay-Sachs disease, one of the first genetic illnesses to be identified by family trees, is an example of an autosomal-recessive disorder (one that occurs only when both copies of the gene are defective). Sometimes one mutation is enough to cause illness. Huntington's disease is such an example.[10]

Although most diseases have at least a partial genetic basis, they are not caused by mutations in single genes. Almost all common illnesses, such as cancer, coronary artery disease, and Alzheimer's, occur because of alterations in several genes. If you search for several genes in a family tree, the number of possible combinations in which they can appear exceeds, quickly enough, the capacity of genome-wide scanning techniques to detect them.

"But RLS is unlikely to be caused by a single gene," I objected.

"Of course," Rye said. "We've already found that women have RLS two to three times as much as men. The younger they are when they have their first child also predicts the development of RLS, and iron deficiency makes it worse, too. Many factors go into the development of RLS, but if we can find one component, the genetic component, then we can target therapies toward that gene."

"And how do you treat RLS?"

"Dopamine," Rye answered. "L-dopa, the treatment for Parkinson's disease, works pretty well, but it has side effects. The newer $D_2$-agonists appear to work quite well and are far better tolerated."

Rye was referring to medications that activate a specific brain receptor for dopamine, the $D_2$-receptor. Unlike L-dopa, which increases the production of dopamine indiscriminately, drugs that activate a single receptor for dopamine target that part of the brain in which those receptors are concentrated. The highest concentration of $D_2$-receptors is found in my favorite region—the striatum. The striatum also happens to be the most iron-rich part of the brain, and I wondered whether this might have something to do with the link between iron deficiency and RLS—a double hit of low dopamine and low iron in the striatum.

"You know what causes dopamine to be released?" I asked rhetorically.

"Sex?"

"Yes," I said. "But more than sex, novelty causes dopamine to be released. Maybe there's not enough novelty in Iceland. You said how the Icelanders are obsessed with their past. Maybe if your patients increased the novelty in their lives, they would alleviate their RLS."

Rye pondered this for a moment and said, "Maybe they're already trying to do that, unconsciously. The link between young pregnancy and RLS might be a symptom of a type of itch for novelty. Girls who experiment sexually at a young age might be exhibiting symptoms of the itch for novelty, which appears as RLS when they get older."

"You're speculating," I said.

"Yes," Rye agreed. "But I can tell you that the best way of describing RLS is that it feels like claustrophobia. You just have to get up and do something. Anything."

"How do you know that?"

"Because," Rye answered, "I have it."

## Hidden People

To be useful in genetics, a family tree must contain more information than who is related to whom. By marking in the tree who has a particular illness, researchers can begin to identify patterns. If the genetics of the disease are complex—caused by more than one gene, for example—then the patterns can be difficult to see by casual inspection. Now, computers do the hard work and are able to search for patterns of disease inheritance that the naked eye might miss. After checking some family trees generated from the latest batch of RLS patients and discussing how many more patients would be needed for a definitive gene scan, Rye was finished with his business at deCODE. We headed back to our hotel and crashed for a few hours before meeting another of Rye's Icelandic friends.

·  ·  ·

Bodvar Thorisson typifies the admixture of Nordic and Gaelic ancestry. An air of serenity emanated from his chiseled Nordic features, but his riotously red hair, blown into wisps by the coastal breeze, betrayed his Irish heritage. Bodvar worked for the Icelandic company that manufactured the sleep-monitoring equipment that Rye used, like digital electroencephalograms and movement monitors for restless legs. A big fan of Bodvar's firm, Rye always went on some Icelandic adventure with him when he visited. This time, I tagged along for a trip to the southern coast in search of lobster and whale meat for dinner.

The three of us were headed out of Reykjavík in our host's well-equipped SUV, barely fifteen minutes after Bodvar had picked us up, when he pulled over to the side of the road. "Look," he said. "This is where I grew up."

Ironclad town houses with steeply pitched red and green corrugated roofs extended down one side of the road. Each house had a postage-stamp-size front yard. Pansies, generally a cold-weather flower in the eastern United States, reached full bloom in Iceland in the middle of summer, and their purple and white petals speckled many of the yards.

A freshly mowed grassy field stretched away from the other side of the road. A mound of rocks covered with moss bulged up from the side of the field.

Bodvar regarded the field and said sadly, "They mowed too close to the rocks."

"What do you mean?" I asked.

"Oh, nothing."

Rye momentarily stopped rummaging through the provisions of dried fish we had picked up and shot me a glance. "What's the big deal?" he asked.

Bodvar sat silently for a moment and then turned off the ignition. "Look at the road," he said.

I looked. It appeared to be an ordinary street. "What about it?"

Bodvar continued. "See how it curves around the rocks?"

I looked again and saw what I hadn't noticed before. Behind us, the road was dead straight. In front of us, the road continued straight for about one hundred yards and then jogged abruptly around the outcropping of rocks.

"The rocks are a special place," Bodvar explained. "You don't have a word in English for this. We call them *huldufólk*."

"What," I said. "The rocks?"

"No," Bodvar replied. "The people who live there. The closest translation is 'hidden people.'"

Neither Rye nor I knew what to say.

Bodvar went on. "The *huldufólk* are what you would call elves and trolls."

"But you don't really believe in that," Rye said. "Do you?"

Bodvar was getting irritated. "It's not a matter of belief—look at the road. The road curves around the rocks. *That* is reality. What more proof do you need?"

He had a point. But Rye was not going to let up. "Have you seen them?"

"No."

"Then how do you know they exist?"

"Because the road has been moved," Bodvar replied. "It is not just here, either. The pipeline carrying hot water from the geysers to Reykjavík has similar diversions. My brother is employed by the public works department, and they regularly consult experts in this matter to figure out where to build."

"Bodvar," I said. "You're a scientist."

"Yes."

"And this doesn't seem strange to you?"

"No." And with that, Bodvar started the car.

We drove on in awkward silence. After about ten minutes, Bodvar said finally, "If you really want to know about our culture, I can set up some places for you to visit."

"What kind of places?" I asked.

"Do you like stories?"

"Of course."

Bodvar said, "If you like stories, then you must find the pastor of the church in Reykholt. Reykholt is a special place in Icelandic literature. One of our most famous poets was executed there seven hundred years ago. The pastors of the Reykholt church have carried on the tradition of poetry, and only the most learned storyteller can become a pastor there. It is a very esteemed position. If you seek him out, he may be able to explain the origins of our religious beliefs."

"That would be great, but what about the hidden people?"

Bodvar said, "If you want to learn something about the *huldufólk*, then you must go to the Snaefellsnes Peninsula and climb to the top of the volcano."

Rye perked up and asked, "What's so great about the volcano?"

Bodvar smiled and said, "According to Jules Verne, that is the entrance to the center of the earth, but you will have to ask the people who live there. Some of them believe it is a place with special power."

"How so?" I asked.

Bodvar laughed and said, "You will have to see for yourself."

## God's Light

It was a little past six in the evening the next day when Rye and I pulled into the town of Reykholt, population 140. A light drizzle had fallen like a gray shroud over the town. There were no signs for the church, but within a few minutes we caught sight of a crimson steeple poking above a backdrop of concrete buildings.

Rye explained, "Bodvar said that there was a museum underneath the church and that we should ask for the priest there."

"Do you think that they're expecting us?"

We pulled into an empty gravel parking lot. The church, built on a hillside, was surprisingly large for such a small town. A glass walkway connected it to the rectory, and the compound sat atop the entrance to the museum. We walked up to the double doors and peered inside a dark antechamber. The lights had been dimmed, and the doors locked. The museum had closed at six, fifteen minutes before.

"What should we do now?" I asked. "I really have to take a piss."

"Let's take a walk around the church," Rye said. "Maybe we can find the priest."

"Pastor."

"Pastor, right."

The rain had dwindled to a light misting, and as we walked around the side of the church, we saw two men gesticulating at a flower bed. The man examining the ground wore blue coveralls, while the other, older gentleman sported a reddish Vandyke beard and was dressed in a tweed sport coat over a sweater vest; he leaned on a neatly coiled umbrella as they appeared to be debating the merits of a particular garden arrangement.

As we approached, they stopped talking in Icelandic and regarded us with diffidence. Rye undoubtedly looked like a giant, and, by comparison, I must have appeared to be a troll.

I stumbled over the trilled *r*'s of the unpronounceable phrase for "excuse me" in Icelandic, *fyrirge f ðu.*

The two men just stared at us.

Rye said, "We're looking for the priest."

"I'm he," said the older gentleman in English. "And who are you?"

"We're from the United States," Rye said. "We're doctors doing research here in Iceland. My name is Dave. I'm a neurologist, and this is my friend Greg, a psychiatrist."

"Yes? I am Geir."

"We heard that you were one of the most well-known story-tellers in Iceland," Rye said.

The pastor laughed. "Who told you that?"

"Bodvar Thorisson," Rye said. "Do you know him?"

This was not such a ridiculous question, since, as I had seen at deCODE, everyone was related to everyone else in some way.

"No," the pastor replied.

Unperturbed, Rye continued. "We've come a long way. Do you have any time to talk with us?"

The pastor pondered this request for a moment and said, "Well, we are having an organ recital tonight at the church. Perhaps, if you would like to come to the recital, we could talk afterward."

This seemed like a fair exchange. Besides, I thought, some classical music might be nice.

Rye looked down at his faded jeans and asked, "Do we need to change our clothes?"

"God doesn't care what you look like," the pastor said. "God sees your heart and your kidneys."

Exactly, I thought.

. . .

After the concert, Geir escorted us to the museum below the church. The three of us sat down over coffee in a hall adorned with ancient banners and examples of medieval Icelandic dress hung along the walls. Neither Rye nor I had specified what kind of story we were seeking, and I was curious as to how Geir would interpret our request. Bodvar's remarks about hidden people had already jarred my preconceptions about Icelandic society. I had not expected to find a culture as technologically advanced as Iceland's to coexist so tangibly with a belief system more than one thousand years old. If roads are moved to make way for hidden people, then, in a way, collective belief makes real the things you can't see. I was hoping that Geir could shed some light on this, because I sensed, even then, that the answer might have an impact on my quest for the biology of satisfaction. The archetypal experiences of living with elves and trolls and hidden people had been going on long enough to have become, potentially, insinuated into Icelandic DNA. It may sound crazy, but beliefs guide decisions, including reproductive ones, and fifty generations is more than enough time to nudge DNA patterns. Icelandic satisfaction appeared connected to the past—a sort of ongoing narrative—and it was beginning to look a little different from the American version, which is based predominately on the pursuit of happiness.

·  ·  ·

Pulling a slender horn-shaped container from his coat pocket, Geir deftly uncapped one end and tapped out a few grams of snuff onto the webbing between his thumb and index finger. He inhaled the powdery black substance in one smooth motion of hand to nose, with only a few grains clinging to his mustache.

"Shall we begin?" Geir asked.

We nodded anxiously.

"Poetry was extremely important in ancient times," Geir began. "And, as you surely know, this church we are in has special meaning in Icelandic history."

Geir referred to Snorri Sturluson (1179–1241), Iceland's most famous poet and the person primarily responsible for writing down old Norse mythology.[11] Much of what is known today about the Norse gods comes from Snorri's work. His genius lay not only in collecting the Viking myths but in the manner in which he recorded them. The Viking settlers brought with them from Norway the worship of heathen gods, but such pagan rituals were eventually stamped out by the spread of Christianity in the eleventh century. Thirteenth-century Iceland, when Snorri lived, was a time of upheaval. Many of the sagas, part historical and part epic accounts of blood feuds, were recorded during this period. By Snorri's time,

Christianity ruled, and although the heathen gods were not quite banished, public worship of them was outlawed. Born into an aristocratic family, Snorri eventually became rich, and with this wealth he was twice elected speaker of the Icelandic Parliament. But his political power did not arise solely from his money. As a child and young man, he had been schooled in the major languages and had become literate in the most revered form of Icelandic poetry, skaldic verse.

Skaldic verse is a form of fixed-meter poetry. The poems follow a rigid set of rules, not unlike Japanese haiku, and intensely employ metaphors, called kennings—typically, two-word phrases that signify a certain item. For example, "whale's-path" might mean "sea." Skaldic verse was most likely the preferred tool of the poets (skalds) that preceded Snorri. By his time, as the population became more literate and turned to various forms of prose for entertainment, the skaldic tradition, like many of the Viking customs, began to fade away.

Snorri's great contribution was to rejuvenate interest in this waning art form. Ingeniously, he crafted a book on poetics, and in order to make his subject more interesting, he used the stories of the ancient Norse gods for illustration. His work, known as the Prose (or Younger) Edda, was written as a manual for young poets,[12] elevating the art of poetry to the language of the heathen gods—an outrageous, almost blasphemous, undertaking in the Christian Middle Ages. But since the book was written as a manual, and the Nordic gods were used to illustrate its points, the author got away with it. Almost. For not holding up his end of a bargain to promote Norwegian interests in Iceland, he was hacked to death at the church of Reykholt by order of the Norwegian king Hakon Hakonarson.

"Snorri," Geir continued, "although a Christian, had a great respect for the ancient mythology. He loved the intricate personalities of the ancient gods, and the stories are not only entertaining, they are deeply wise. The stories tell us about the nature of man. About fear. About envy. About greed. And about fate.

"Snorri's Edda has been the source of material for many famous works of art. Wagner's *Ring*, of course, but most recently the work of Tolkien. Gandalf, for example, was the name of a dwarf in the Edda, but his appearance is exactly that of Odin, the all-father of the Norse gods, when he stole the sacred mead of poetry.

"Perhaps," Geir said, "if you are not too tired, we can discuss this story."

"What," I asked, "was the sacred mead?"

Geir pulled out his snuff container and inhaled another pinch. "Poetry was extremely valuable," he said. "You see, the kings depended on poets to celebrate their feats and tell about their victories. Without the poets, nobody would have known about these deeds, and so the poets were paid handsomely. To understand the sacred art of poetry, you must go back to very ancient times, when the Aesir invaded Scandinavia from Asia.

"The Aesir, Snorri says, were originally ordinary people, but the lands that they invaded were extremely prosperous. When they died, their families did not want to talk about their deaths. So, long after their deaths, people continued to celebrate the Aesir settlers, and even though they were not seen anymore, the people made them into gods. We know them today as gods like Thor and Odin.

"But the Aesir fought many long wars with the native Scandinavians, called the Vanir. The Aesir were warlike gods, but the Vanir were fertility gods."

"Do these gods have names, too?" I asked.

"Oh, yes," Geir said. "For example, Freyr was the god of fertility—the one with the great dick—and his sister, Freyia, was the goddess of love. She was driven around in a cart pulled by cats."

"Cats?" Rye asked.

"Cats," Geir reiterated. "And Freyr and Freyia, this brother and sister, seemed to have had some . . ." Geir's voice trailed off, and he made a rocking motion with both hands, implying an incestuous relationship between the two.

"The Aesir and the Vanir fought for a long time, but eventually both groups tired of fighting and made a truce," Geir said. "To secure this peace, they all went to a kettle and spat in it."

"I am confused," I interrupted. "You said the poetics were sacred. But these are heathen gods."

"Yes, but heathens have sacred things, too," Geir replied. "After the gods had spat in the kettle, they had this huge pot of spit. What were they to do with the spittle? So they took the spittle and created a man of it. But this man, whom they named Kvasir, did not work right. He simply visited people, and everywhere was received with great joy because he knew the answer to every question. He knew everything. You just asked him a question, and he answered. After all, he was created from the spittle of two nations and must have been very wise, but he had no soul. Once, when he was traveling, he came to the house of two evil dwarfs, who killed him with a heavy stone placed above the door to their house.

"The dwarfs took the body, drained it of its blood, mixed the blood with honey, and fermented it into the most magnificent mead. And anyone who drank this mead, made from the blood of Kvasir, became a poet. Now this mead was very valuable, so the dwarfs separated the mead into three huge kettles.

"Once, when the dwarfs were fishing, their boat capsized. They screamed out for help, and a giant, who was also fishing, came to their rescue, but in payment, the giant took the mead. The giant chose his daughter, Gunnlod, as guardian of this mead of poetry. Gunnlod is a beautiful name. It means 'the one who invites battle.' "

"Battle seems to be a big thing in Iceland," Rye said.

"Oh, yes, battle is closely associated with the cult of Odin," Geir explained, "Odin is obsessed with knowledge. He's like the CIA, the KGB, and the FBI all put together. He has to know everything. He sits on a throne, from which he can see into every corner of the world, but that is not enough for him."

Geir stared directly at me, and a shiver went down my spine. "He has two ravens, Hugin and Munin," Geir continued. "Hugin means 'the mind,' and Munin means 'memory.'" Geir paused and said with a hint of disdain, "Closely associated with your two cults."

We laughed nervously.

"The ravens fly out every morning to spy on the world, and they return every evening to sit on his shoulder and tell him everything that they have seen and heard, but this is not enough." Now Geir looked at Rye. "Odin has this ancient giant head that has been pre-served in a unique manner, so he can speak with it. He can converse with the giant head and ask it about ancient secrets. That is still not enough for him."

Geir turned to me and said, "He has ripped out one of his eyes, and it lies at the bottom of a well at the root of the tree of the world. From there, Odin's eye can see into the hidden mysteries of the universe. This is not enough. He experienced knowledge through pain. For nine nights and nine days, he hung in a tree by his neck with a spear through him."

I thought of Ariely's pain suit.

"And this," Geir continued, "was still not enough for him. He stooped so low in his craving for wisdom that he even had sexual transactions with men of his own. Just to hint at such conduct in ancient times was enough to cause death. Everything that Odin stands for is knowing, knowing, knowing."

Both Rye and I were transfixed.

Geir went on. "Odin could see where the mead of poetry was, and he decided that he had to have it. So he disguised himself and tricked Gunnlod into giving him the mead."

"How did he do that?" I asked warily.

"He seduced her," Geir answered. "For every night that he slept with her, Gunnlod gave him a drink from a kettle. Odin slept with her for three nights, and on each night he drank the contents of one of the kettles. And then he turned himself into a falcon and flew his way home, but Gunnlod's father, who was fishing at the time, saw the falcon and suspected what had happened. He turned himself into an eagle and chased after Odin.

"Odin, who was heavily laden with the mead, had a difficult time staying ahead of the eagle, and some of the mead fell out of his beak, and some of it he lost out of his ass. That portion spread all over the world, and you, probably as boys, tried to catch the rain-drops. Have you?"

Not knowing where this was going, I nodded.

"There is a possibility that one of these raindrops," Geir explained, "was not rain but mead, and if you have caught a drop of this mead, then you are a very bad poet but still able to make poetry. But the rest Odin contained and returned to his house, where he spat it up again. Odin preserves this sacred mead, and only true poets are allowed to drink from it."

We pondered this for a few moments while Geir reloaded his snuff.

Geir went on. "Everything that Odin stands for is knowledge. He is obsessed with knowing the future, too. He soon learns that at the end of the world, a great battle will be fought between the gods. So Odin begins recruiting an army of men. Men who die in battle serve under Odin, so naturally Odin incites war. The more men who die in battle, the more Odin gains for his army.

"So you see," Geir concluded, "how dangerous it is to be associated with the cult of Odin? You may gain knowledge, even produce beautiful poetry, but the price is high. To serve Odin is to incite battle."

I looked at the clock; it was two in the morning. Geir, who had been telling stories for almost four hours, showed no sign of stopping. There was no way that he could have known about my quest, but by telling the story of Odin and the sacred mead, perhaps he sensed my yearnings.

My uneasiness must have been apparent, because he concluded, "I think that that is enough stories for tonight."

The three of us walked out of the church into the brightening twilight. I thanked Geir for his time and apologized for keeping him up so late, especially since it was already Sunday morning, and he was to give a Mass in a few hours.

Geir shrugged off my apology, opened his arms wide to the sky, and said, "God did not create this beautiful light for men to sleep."

## The Golden Circle

Rye and I departed Reykholt late that morning for our next destination, the Snaefellsjökull Volcano. As we drove through the lush, treeless landscape, I thought more about the cult of Odin. I was part of this cult. Was not my ambition as a scientist the quest for knowledge? Don't all scientists aspire to discover something so profound that the world will remember their name? If I understood Geir's warning correctly, my little journey was flirting with danger—knowledge too powerful for mortals.

After driving for several hours, I still couldn't see the volcano. Heading northwest out of Reykholt, we had skirted several fjords, but for the last hour we had been heading due west onto the Snaefellsnes Peninsula. The Snaefellsnes holds special significance for Icelanders as a region rich in folklore. Jutting directly into the Atlantic Ocean as nearly the westernmost point of Iceland, the Snaefellsnes takes the brunt of the weather systems sweeping eastward. The farther we drove onto the peninsula, the worse the weather became. What started as a lightly misting fog became a windblown pelting of rain.

According to our topographic map, the volcano called Snaefells-jökull was situated at the tip of the peninsula and should have been directly in front of us. Instead, a gray bank of clouds condensed on the sheer cliffs that rose to our right. To the left, a sea of whitecaps churned in Faxaflói Bay. On a clear day, we should have been able to see fifty miles across the bay to Reykjavík. No such luck.

"How did Jules Verne get out here?" I asked rhetorically.

"He didn't," Rye replied. "He wrote *Journey to the Center of the Earth* without ever leaving Paris."

Part travelog, part coming-of-age story, Verne's narrative chronicled the adventure of the young teen, Axel, and his uncle, Professor Lidenbrock, as they journeyed to Iceland and then to the center of the earth. Lidenbrock, a geology professor, finds an old manuscript penned by a sixteenth-century alchemist who purports to have discovered a passage to the earthen interior. The cryptically encoded manuscript states:

> Descend into the crater of the Snaefellsjökul, over which the shadow of Scartaris falls before the kalends of July, bold traveller, and you will reach the center of the earth. I have done this. Arne Saknussemm.[13]

After an arduous trip from Hamburg, Germany, across the Norwegian Sea to Reykjavík, and then a 120-mile trek from Reykjavík to the Snaefellsnes, Axel and Lidenbrock hike up the volcano during the summer solstice ("before the kalends of July"). The tip of the volcanic crater casts a shadow on a passage to the center of the earth. With the help of Hans, their dutiful guide, Axel and his uncle make their way through the passage to their destination; ultimately, they emerge on the slopes of Mount Etna, in Sicily.

Since Verne's story appeared in 1864, thousands of tourists have ventured onto the slopes of the Snaefellsjökull in search of the passage to the center of the earth, but when Verne wrote *Journey*, the volcanic mountain had not yet been climbed. Although the slopes had been attempted by British climbers in the early 1800s, the English mountaineer Charles Forbes was the first to make a serious assault on the volcano, in 1860, only to be foiled by the treacherous crevasses splitting the glacier atop the cinder cone.[14] About forty years later, the Snaefellsjökull was scaled. At 4,744 feet, the mountain is not high, but the upper 2,000 feet are permanently encrusted by a shifting glacier, and its position on the tip of the Snaefellsnes Peninsula places the volcano more or less on its own in the middle of the Atlantic Ocean. The weather, particularly in winter, can rival the intensity of storms at 20,000 feet.

Fittingly, an ominous folklore shrouds the mountain in a mystique as thick as the ever-present cloud cover. Bárdar, the tragic hero of the eponymously named saga, reputably named the mountain. Bárdar was only half human, descended from trolls and giants. Unfortunately, his daughter, Helga, was pushed onto an ice floe by her cousins as they played on the banks of the Flaxaflói. Bárdar became enraged. With a boy in each hand, he carried his nephews up the mountain, tossed one off a cliff, breaking his neck, and tossed the other into a crevasse so deep that he was dead before he hit bottom.[15] In remorse, Bárdar eventually withdrew from society to live by himself in a cave on the mountain. Now one of the *huldufólk*, Bárdar is a benevolent guardian of the mountain, periodically helping travelers in trouble but also protecting the slopes against curious humans. Cloaked in a gray robe tied at the waist with walrus hide, Bárdar is said to patrol the mountain with a two-pronged walking staff and feather-shaped blades.

Helga, an attractive woman and the equal of men in everything she did, drifted all the way to Greenland, where she caught the eye of Erik the Red. Helga ended up with a business associate of Erik's, named Steggi, who, as it later turned out, already had a wife. Eventually Helga left Steggi and returned to Iceland, but she found no happiness. She roamed Iceland, living in caves. Like Rye's patients, Helga had difficulty sleeping, and to soothe herself, she played her harp late every night. She was perhaps the first documented case of RLS in Iceland.

As Rye and I drove further out on the Snaefellsnes Peninsula, I thought about Helga and her restless wanderings. I could almost hear her plaintive harp melodies in the wind blowing off the bay.

With the weather worsening, we pulled off the main road toward a small cluster of squat houses sitting on the bay. A sign announced HOTEL BREKKABAUER.

We pulled into a gravel drive and parked in front of a cedar building with a teal-blue corrugated roof. Planted directly in front of the building were twenty white posts, each about ten feet high, arranged in a perfect circle, approximately thirty feet in diameter, and bridged across their tops with horizontal members. A single pole, perhaps fifteen feet high, was positioned at the center of the circle.

"Stonehenge?" Rye said, pointing toward the annular colonnade.

"If it is," I replied, "it's a pretty poor copy."

We entered an airy vestibule. Beyond the inn's entrance, an inviting den looked out over the bay. Cushy sofas and big pillows were laid about casually in front of book-lined walls. New Age harp music floated down from an unidentifiable source.

A large young man with boyish features greeted us with decidedly non-Icelandic ebullience. "Hi! We've been expecting you," he said cheerily.

"You have?" I asked.

"Sure. You're from the sleep company, right? My name is Gulli."

Rye said, "We're from the United States, but Bodvar must have made the reservations."

He gestured to the mini-Stonehenge. "What is that?"

Gulli smiled and said, "Perhaps you better ask my parents. Will you be dining here? We cook only with organic ingredients. Besides, if you're really interested, I'm sure my parents will be happy to talk to you after dinner."

I was getting hungry. "Sounds good. We'd like that," I said.

Dinner consisted of squash soup, a salad of mixed greens, and braised lamb over potatoes. I had yet to have a bad meal of Icelandic lamb; rendered simply in a reduction of its juices, the lamb was deliciously tender and almost melted in my mouth.

Rye and I sipped herbal tea while we waited for Gulli's parents. The light shimmered off the bay as the summer sun skimmed the horizon behind limbus cloud formations. By now, it was about eleven o'clock at night, and just three days past the summer solstice. We debated whether the volcano would be visible tomorrow and whether we would be able to make the ascent. We could snowmobile up to the summit, but without clear weather, there would be nothing to see.

. . .

As we pondered the possibility of ascending the volcano under cloud cover, a nimble woman, about fifty years old, slid into a chair next to us. She had Nordic cheekbones, and grayish-blue round eyes set in a round face that suggested a strong Gaelic heritage.

"My name is Gudrun," she said, somewhat sternly and more Icelandically than Gulli. "My son says that you would like some information."

"Gudrun is a very famous name," I said.

She smiled and relaxed slightly. "You know of our history?"

"A little. Gudrun was the heroine of the Laxdaela Saga, which took place around here."[16]

"That's right," she said. "Gudrun was the most beautiful woman ever to have grown up in Iceland. She was also as smart as she was beautiful. If you visit her grave at Helgafell, you may have three wishes granted. But you must not tell anyone your wishes, and you must never look back."

"This area seems to have a lot of special power," I said.

"It does," Gudrun continued. "That is why my husband and I have created this place. You know of the Snaefellsjökull Volcano, but did you know that this is one of only seven places on the earth where the energy lines are in convergence?"

Rye and I gave each other puzzled looks.

Gudrun went on. "There are special places, usually associated with mountains, that have intense energy fields. In the United States you have Mount Shasta. Here, we are on a line connecting the Great Pyramid in Giza to the North Pole. It's called a ley-line.[17]

"Do you know about chakras?" she asked.

"You mean the Buddhist energy centers?" I said.

"Yes. The ley-lines open up the higher-level chakras. The one we are sitting on allows access to the very highest chakra."

Rye grunted.

Gudrun shot him a steely look. "You don't believe me? You haven't opened your eyes. When you return to Reykjavík, look up Erla Stefansdottir. She is the best-known seer in Iceland, and she can see the ley-lines. She is so well known that the public works department consults her on where to place the roads."

Rye's eyes widened, as I'm sure mine did, and he whispered to me, "Bodvar's brother works with her."

Pointing to the circular arrangement of posts, he asked Gudrun, "What is that?"

"A few years ago, we thought it would be nice to create a celebration of harmony. The circle signifies this."

"So it's not supposed to be like Stonehenge?" I asked.

"Oh, no," said Gudrun. "The circle symbolizes peace and unity."

"What about the volcano?" Rye asked.

Gudrun replied, "You really must go up it tomorrow. But only if it is clear. If it's clear, you can see all the way to Greenland."

"It doesn't look too promising," I said.

"You never know," Gudrun said. "The weather changes all the time. But if it's clear in the morning, you must go right away."

Although Geir surely would not have approved of Gudrun's pagan beliefs, the two did profess a similar philosophy. Geir had chosen a path of intellectual inquiry into Icelandic literature; as a Christian, he aligned himself naturally with Snorri's philosophy of respect, but not worship, of the heathen past. Although Gudrun gave no outward sign of worshipping the heathen gods, clearly she was closer to the pagan camp. But Geir and Gudrun were not so different from each other. In some form or another, everyone we had encountered in Iceland had found a way to maintain a reverence for their country—including the hidden people and the heathen gods.

## And Beauty Shall Reign Alone

I woke to sunlight streaming into my room. There were no clocks, and the constant light made it impossible to discern the time. I pulled back the curtains and was nearly blinded by what must have been the morning sun glaring off a brilliantly snowcapped volcano. Like a giant Hershey kiss dipped in white-blue icing, it seemed to summon me to reach out and touch it. I ran down the hall and pounded on Rye's door. "Dave! Wake up!"

I heard grunts and thuds as he padded to the door. He cracked it open.

"You look like shit," I said.

He rubbed his eyes and said, "I'm not getting much sleep in this light. What time is it, anyway?"

"I don't know. Look out your window."

He pulled back his blinds and blinked in the gleaming light. "Cool," he said. "Let's go."

Quickly, we suited up in what passed for our expedition clothing. Wearing a mishmash of denim and fleece, we jumped into the SUV, gunned the accelerator, and kicked up a trail of gravel as we headed off in search of a snowmobile.

About a mile down the road, in the village of Arnarstapi, we pulled up in front of a store with a hand-lettered sign advertising snowmobile tours.

After a brief exchange of funds, a thin young man named Ingvar shuttled us up to the snowline. During the twenty-minute drive over boulder-strewn roads, a dark gray bank of clouds began to condense over the bay. By the time we picked out some snowsuits and donned our helmets, the clouds were upon us. Visibility had dropped to one hundred feet.

I turned to Ingvar. "Is it even worth going up like this?"

Ingvar grinned and said, "Why not? It's always fun to snowmobile. Just follow me and stay on the track."

"Have you been up today?" I asked.

"No."

"How do you know that a new crevasse hasn't appeared overnight?"

Ingvar didn't answer. He just opened up the throttle and was off in a spray of glacial snow.

Ingvar was speeding up the mountain at about thirty miles an hour, and I had a hard time keeping up with him. The higher we went, the worse the visibility became, until finally I had to slow down just to follow his tracks. Several times the tracks crossed one-foot gaps in the ice. I just cranked up the throttle and crossed the openings as quickly as possible.

When I could barely see beyond the front of the snowmobile, I passed Ingvar, who had pulled off the track. He motioned me to stop. Rye pulled up behind me.

Ingvar said, "Here we are."

"Where?" Rye asked.

"The top."

I started to walk around, but after about twenty feet, I couldn't see anything.

"Careful," Ingvar called. "There's a windblown lip of snow over there. It's about one thousand feet down."

I thought about Bárdar's ill-fated nephews. I turned back toward the snowmobiles and was startled to see a lone figure striding up through the fog. As it got closer, I could see that it was a man on cross-country skis.

I heard a voice say, *"Guten tag!"*

As Rye chatted with the German skier, Ingvar and I pondered the fact that we had scaled the volcano, and the clouds magically began to dissipate. For a few brief moments, the mist evaporated to reveal two snow-encrusted basalt spires on opposite sides of us, each rising another hundred feet. Blue sky opened above.

I turned around and regarded the snow lip. The last wisp of cloud blew past the western spire, and the sun blazed down upon us. The full effect was of sitting at the center of a parabolic bowl, with the rays of the sun reflecting off the sides to concentrate on our location. The temperature instantly rose by ten degrees.

We were smack in the middle of the volcanic crater, which, except for the two spires, had filled in completely with glacial ice and snow. Below us to the east, a finger of black and green land stretched away to the horizon, calm waters on both sides. Islands dotted the fjords to the north. To the west, nothing but ocean.

Rye had lain down and was making a snow angel.

The German reached into his backpack and pulled out a small book. He read aloud:

> Where the glacier meets the sky, the land ceases to be earthly, and the earth becomes one with the heavens; no sorrows live there any more, and therefore joy is not necessary; beauty alone reigns there, beyond all demands.[18]

He was quoting *World Light,* by Halldór Laxness, the Nobel Prize–winning Icelandic writer. The words suffused me with a feeling of serenity, and a warmth grew outward from my belly. The crunchy ice below my feet began to soften, as if the crater floor were oozing, and my head soared and spun into the expansive vista. Weightless, I floated toward the sky, awash in beauty. Alone.

# 9

Sex, Love, and the
Crucible of Satisfaction

Satisfaction—that state of blessed contentment, nirvana, mystical enlightenment, peace, tranquillity, a sense of something beyond your existence—is ephemeral at best. You get snatches of these states, often when you least expect them. Everything I have encountered inside the lab and out in the world suggests that satisfaction is not the same as either pleasure or happiness, and that searching for happiness will not necessarily lead to satisfaction. If anything, the feeling of being satisfied that I have sought comes from hard work, grappling with uncertainty, and sometimes pain. Nor is satisfaction the opposite of pleasure; it is something entirely different—a feeling unto itself. But it is in the quest that you find satisfaction; within any search, you encounter novelty and your brain changes as a result. Novelty can take you far, but like everything, it, too, is subject to habituation, and the risks associated with pursuing novelty for its own sake may be substantial. How, for example, can you incorporate the sense of newness into a long-term relationship?

The mysteries of Iceland lingered with me for several weeks, leaving me desperate to capture a bit of that magic and bring it home. Standing atop the Snaefellsjökull Volcano, I felt the truth of Laxness's words: "beauty alone reigns there." Surely the endless supply of beauty in the world means that when mere physical pleasure fails to satisfy, an aesthetic solution, like a good book or a good movie, is there to take its place. Alas, what had seemed so right in Iceland had, nonetheless, faded rapidly at home in Atlanta. Rye had taken to carrying around some stones he'd collected from the volcano and, while knowing it was hopeless, I'd resorted to assembling pictures into a photo album.

The Icelanders' mythical bridge to the past—*huldufólk*, the Sagas—seemed to provide a cultural platform from which to experience a resolute satisfaction with life. The collective knowledge and enjoyment of Icelandic folklore provided a common language for daily transactions—like a 1,000-year-old running conversation. What appeared to many outsiders as a taciturn Icelandic temperament had, in fact, evolved as an efficient means of communication. Their pride provided many Icelanders with a basis for subtle communication, in which nuance was all that was needed. As they do between longtime lovers, single words often conveyed sentences.

What about the language of lovers? In many ways, communication in a long-term relationship resembles Icelandic shorthand. After you've spent years with another person, familiarity can be either the source of finely tuned conversation or the rock of predictability that breeds the proverbial contempt. When two people spend a significant amount of time together, they naturally create a running dialogue that, however unintended, provides a backdrop of predictability.

The experience I had in Iceland was sublime, but it was mine alone. Likewise, my journey in search of satisfaction had been fun and illuminating but ultimately selfish. Although ultramarathoners braving the Sierra Nevada was inspiring, and the mysteries of Ice-

land fed my spiritual cravings, my wish to bring the lessons of satisfaction into my home would inevitably lead to a confrontation with
the twin forces of predictability and novelty. As soon as my wife,
Kathleen, enters the picture, the equation of two people seeking
a way out of the rut of predictability becomes infinitely more
complex. Though each of us does our dance with novelty, sometimes together and sometimes alone, it is hard to deny that novelty
is inherently destabilizing to a relationship. That is why we experience the unexpected so pointedly in our brains. Despite the
potential for disaster, novelty's effects on sexual and emotional satisfaction are essential to the maintenance of any long-term relationship.

## The Battle of the Sexes

In a relationship, the first problem with novelty is that men and
women express their needs for it differently. On a crisp spring day
in the 1920s, President Calvin Coolidge and his wife were sched-
uled to tour an egg farm in the Midwest. Soon after their arrival,
the president and Mrs. Coolidge were taken on separate tours.
When Mrs. Coolidge passed the chicken pens, she paused to ask
the farmer if the rooster copulated more than once a day. "Dozens
of times" came the reply.

"Please tell that to the president," Mrs. Coolidge requested.

When the president passed the pens and was told about the
rooster, he asked, "Same hen every time?"

"Oh, no, Mr. President. A different one each time."

The president nodded slowly, then said, "Tell that to Mrs.
Coolidge."

Although the story is well known among students of sexual
behavior in animals, the conversation probably never occurred.[1]
The "Coolidge effect," which has a kernel of truth to it, arose as a

joke introducing a talk on animal behavior at a psychology conference in the 1950s. In most mammalian species, the male typically
copulates and ejaculates several times with a receptive female,
almost always fertile. Eventually the male's desire for sexual activity
tapers off, and he leaves the female alone. If the male is a human, he
usually rolls over and goes to sleep. Fatigue? No, a form of sexual
boredom. If a new, fertile female is placed in front of the male, he
will rise to the occasion and not only mate with her but also ejaculate. Henceforth, the Coolidge effect has become synonymous
with the male's ability to mate with a novel female.

It is tempting to extrapolate such behavior to humans, not so
much as an ex post facto justification for the philandering behavior
of men but because the story resonates with the sexual dilemmas of
many couples in long-term relationships. Donald Symons, an
anthropologist at the University of California at Santa Barbara,
went so far as to suggest that the human male has an innate drive
for sexual variety and the female does not.[2]

A contemporary version of the Coolidge effect, also a joke, reit-
erates the point more succinctly.

"What are the four needs of man?" a friend asked. Without
waiting for a reply, he answered, "Food, water, pussy, and new
pussy."

Like most men, I chuckled when I first heard the line. "But," I
countered, "what are the four needs of woman?"

Without missing a beat, he replied, "Food, water, sex, and cud-
dling."

Many people believe that men would like to have sex with a lot
of women, and women would like to settle down with one man
and raise children. If Symons is right, then both men and roosters
have an insatiable desire for sexual novelty, and women and hens
do not. But what if all of this is a myth? What if women have the
same desire for sexual novelty? Men and women may seek novelty
in different forms, but I have not encountered any fundamental

dissimilarities between the sexes in the desire for novelty, sexual or otherwise.

There is no reason to think that the pleasures of sex would be spared the fate of everything else on the hedonic treadmill. Familiarity leads to boredom, and the treadmill's incessant reduction of all pleasures poses a threat to the sexual glue that binds couples together. While novelty is a surefire way of creating great experiences, the belief that matrimonial harmony depends on stability, fidelity, and constancy stands in direct opposition to the idea. As in everything related to satisfaction, and perhaps everything related to relationships, the tension between what is predictable and safe versus what is novel and dangerous plays out constantly. The true nature of satisfaction lies in the way the tug-of-war is resolved.

The Coolidge effect and my friend's joke strike to the heart of a difference between men and women that is easily mistaken for an incontrovertible fact. The kernel of truth in the Coolidge effect is not in the president's desire for sexual novelty; it is in the president and his wife's joint desire to have satisfying sex. To figure out the puzzle of novelty, we must first examine the purpose of sex. The emergence of sexual reproduction, which requires two members of a species instead of one, represented a powerful strategy for the propagation of genes, which led to a form of competition between males and females. Today we call it the battle of the sexes.

## What Sex Is

The battle of the sexes is a complex interplay of cooperation and competition. To say that humans have sex simply because it feels good completely misses the point.[3] While men both compete and cooperate with one another, women do the same. In the battle for the best mates—the battle to propagate genes—you begin to decipher how the multilayered, multipartnered dance works. Not until you understand why sex feels good and why this dance is central to life can you comprehend the meaning of relationships between men and women. Once you do, you will begin to know how to incorporate novelty into the equation.[4]

Both men and women know that sex is better under some circumstances than others. Men generally equate sex with orgasm, and, notwithstanding the Coolidge effect, once a man has one, it's over. So men are easy to please sexually. If men are all looking for the easy way to pleasure, why are women any different? I would say they aren't necessarily different, but, yes, they are more complex.

The systematic exploration of the female sexual response began in earnest in the 1940s when the Indiana zoologist Alfred Kinsey polled both men and women about their sexual practices.[5] During his lifetime, his methods were criticized and largely discredited because those he interviewed were not randomly selected from the population at large. Prison inmates and prostitutes, for example, were overrepresented in his samples. Using face-to-face interviews, Kinsey and his colleagues reported startlingly high rates of many practices that were then considered taboo: masturbation, homosexuality, bisexuality, and infidelity. Moreover, the rates of marital infidelity that the researchers found—as high as 50 percent—not only shocked the nation but, in some sense, fueled the sexual revolution by revealing the ubiquity of the very acts that would soon lose their taboo.[6]

Twenty years later, at the height of the sexual revolution, Shere Hite, a nonscientist, followed up on Kinsey's work with her famous *The Hite Report*.[7] Though correcting for some of the problems that plagued Kinsey, Hite's investigation suffered from sampling biases of its own.[8] Between 1972 and 1974, Hite mailed out over 100,000 detailed questionnaires on female sexuality. Read today, *The Hite Report* packs a punch, because men have seemingly changed little in their attitude toward female sexuality. On the role of novelty, many women complained of the kissing-foreplay routine that served as a prelude to intercourse. Many women expressed disdain at the idea that men controlled women's orgasms and that, in fact, they were provided as a favor by men. In some respects, the situation today has improved. Many men are cognizant of a woman's desire for an orgasm; but even now, for men who care about such things, bringing a woman to orgasm is usually understood as another element of male pleasure.

Because cultural norms governing how men and women express their sexuality are not the same, double standards about what men and women should, or should not, do in bed abound. Cultural standards, not innate biological differences, I believe, are responsible for throttling human sexuality. The extent to which men and women pay attention to their partner's pleasure would appear to have implications for the degree of satisfaction that each can attain. Differences between cultures and between segments of a society are reflected in the variety of standards for sexual behavior that have been adopted; even within peer groups, the standards are constantly shifting. It may be that in the twenty-first century, we are moving toward an equality of sexual behavior. But until the convergence actually happens, the discrepancies between men's and women's sexual desires demand an exploration that must begin with biology and, ultimately, end with the brain's need for novelty.

## Sexual Selection

Evolution is fraught with mislabelings and misunderstandings. The best-known phrase, "survival of the fittest," wittily catches its essence: evolution as a process of adaptation to changes in the environment. But that is only half the process. Most people understand "survival of the fittest" to refer to natural selection through competition for survival; in other words, the individuals of a species best suited to a particular environment will survive, on average, better than those less suited. But survival is not enough. To pass on genes to the next generation, an individual must not just survive but reproduce, which, as we know, is not straightforward. Darwin recognized the distinction between evolution through survival selection and evolution through reproductive selection, which he termed sexual selection.[9] While natural selection operates on the relative fitness of individuals in their environment, sexual selection derives from the competition within a species for mates.

Geoffrey Miller, an evolutionary psychologist at the University of New Mexico, has argued that by the time Homo sapiens emerged on the planet 100,000 years ago, daily survival was no longer a significant factor in human evolution. The human population was small enough that there was little competition for natural resources, and humans had pretty much eliminated or learned to avoid the few remaining animals that could prey upon them. With the effects of natural selection slowed down, sexual selection gained the upper hand, leading to a runaway competition for access to the best mates.[10]

While natural selection operates through haphazard challenges set by the environment, sexual selection entails individual response, since selecting a mate is a conscious choice. So while our ancestors had no control over the last ice age or its effects on survival, they had numerous options in their choice of a mate. Precisely because sexual selection reflects choices, it has resulted in the evolution of all the traits that humans currently possess. If men today are obsessed with gadgets that showcase technological superiority, it is because our female ancestors found some antecedent of this preoccupation attractive, and they preferred to mate with males who displayed conspicuous know-how rather than with men who pursued other interests. Similarly, men today find attractive a female waist-to-hip ratio of 0.7 because our ancestors did so as well.[11] The key aspect of sexual selection is that different features evolve in males and females, and both sexes exhibit preferences among these traits.

While some people may possess intelligence or attractiveness or kindness, few individuals would score a 10 on all these characteristics, so a continuum exists in the population on any given dimension of fitness. In a process called fitness matching, humans tend to select mates who are like themselves. Walk down the street, and you will see fitness matching in action—most couples are well matched in physical appearance.

Sometimes a particular trait will be so appealing to the opposite sex that it will spur intense competition for mates exhibiting the best elements of this trait. The male peacock's tail, which serves no purpose other than to attract females, is an example of a runaway evolutionary process. Miller and others have suggested that the human characteristics of intelligence, language skill, creativity, and art are the result of runaway competitions for mates that exhibit these traits.

For humans, many of these traits would have signaled better survivability for their offspring, and that is why these traits became desirable. By the time hominids began to dominate the planet, 100,000 years ago, the absence of predators meant that mere physical strength was no longer necessary for survival. At that point, cerebral traits gave our ancestors the kind of critical advantages in predicting and planning for the future that spurred competition for intelligence.

Nobody would argue that, for our ancestors, intelligence conferred both a survival advantage and a sexual advantage. But unlike physical fitness, intellectual fitness is not visible. Female waist-to-hip ratios or jutting male jawlines do not indicate anything about an individual's intellect.[12] Without the benefit of SAT scores or advanced degrees, our ancestors would have had to rely on other manifestations of intelligence. Perhaps some produced works of art, composed music, or became the equivalent of Stone Age comedians. Still others would have displayed intelligence by solving problems such as how to catch prey or how to navigate. What these traits represent is the ability to adapt to shifting circumstances and to use the elements at hand to improve their lives—whether by creating tools of survival or of entertainment. In this way, sexual selection pushed humans toward both a desire for and an appreciation of novelty.

## Hidden Ovulation

With few exceptions, the female of most species gives clear signs when she is fertile, and that is the only time when male and female copulate. Not humans. As human survival became more assured, both men and women probably worried less about where their next meal was coming from and more about who was having sex with whom and how one could bed down a better mate. Men and women developed different strategies for the game of sexual competition. Because the woman ends up investing time and energy during pregnancy and child rearing, she would want the father of her children to be the best mate she could attract—hence the potent female strategy that conceals fertility. Hidden ovulation keeps the man guessing, and if he is serious about impregnating a woman, he has to hang around long enough to make sure she is fertile.

Nobody knows exactly how the battle of the sexes began, but in one scenario it starts with the distinctions between sperm and eggs. Sperm are abundant and easy for men to make, so if a man wants to pass on his genetic material, the best method is to have sex with as many women as possible. Thus he increases the odds of impregnating a woman, and he doesn't have to help raise the child when he could be busy impregnating other women. The fact that men confess to wanting to sleep with many women has been offered as teleological proof that men are fundamentally polygamous.[13]

Women, of course, would not have tolerated this situation, so they have evolved techniques to combat philandering. By concealing the time when they are fertile, women decrease the chances that a random act of sex will result in conception.[14] Hidden ovulation has become so efficient that even women don't know when they can conceive. If neither men nor women know when conception is likely to occur, then a man must have a lot more sex with a woman to conceive a child. In other words, the man must stay with one woman if she is to bear his child.

But don't take a woman's word for this. Look at the size of her man's testicles. Fertile female chimpanzees copulate up to fifty times a day with dozens of males. The males, who are competing to fertilize her, have evolved huge, four-ounce testicles to produce enough sperm. Gorillas, on the other hand, maintain harems, and the males don't need to compete sexually. Consequently, gorilla testicles are tiny. On a per weight basis, human testicles are intermediate in size between chimps and gorillas. Bigger testicles mean more sperm, and more sperm can flush out the previous paramour's deposit.[15] From today's moderately sized cojones, we can infer that not only were men moderately polygamous; so were women.

· · ·

Just how long does the man have to hang around? It wasn't until 1995 that this question could be answered with some certainty. In a massive study of fertility, Allen Wilcox, at the National Institute of Environmental Health Sciences, in Triangle Park, North Carolina, studied more than two hundred women trying to get pregnant.[16] Wilcox and his colleagues analyzed daily urine specimens for changes in several sex hormones. In the first half of the menstrual cycle, estrogen is much more abundant than progesterone, but on the day of ovulation, estrogen drops precipitously. By measuring the ratio of estrogen to progesterone, Wilcox could estimate the day of ovulation with a high degree of reliability. The women kept logs of when they had intercourse, and Wilcox subsequently computed the probability of conception relative to the day of ovulation. More than five days before ovulation, the probability of conception was essentially zero. Beginning at five days prior to ovulation, the probability rose from about 10 percent to a maximum of 33 percent on the day of ovulation itself. Surprisingly, the probability of conception dropped to zero within twenty-four hours after ovulation—strong refutation of the commonly held notion that conception can occur within a window on either side of ovulation. Wilcox's findings clearly demonstrated that intercourse must occur before, or at least coincident with, ovulation.

Wilcox's results addressed the probability of conception, but not every fertilized egg develops into a healthy baby. In Wilcox's study, two-thirds of known pregnancies resulted in live births. Using this information, we can compute how long a man must have sex with a woman to produce a baby. Even if the couple has sex every day, the odds of producing a baby in one menstrual cycle are only 25 percent. Having sex daily for four months increases the likelihood to 68 percent; six months of daily sex brings the figure to 82 percent; and after a full year, chances are 97 percent that a child will be produced.[17] Practically speaking, sex every other day results in probabilities only slightly lower. At the other extreme, the one-night, "wham, bam, thank-you ma'am" method has only a 3 percent chance of producing a child—pretty good odds for no-promises sex, but not so good for propagating genes.

The human proclivity to mate testifies to the fact that, in both men and women, sexual competition selected for the trait of enjoying sex—arguably, to increase the number of times people have sex. Prehistoric hominids, like all nonhuman animals, would have had sex to procreate. When reproduction got tangled up with pleasure, the act became compelling on its own. Because of hidden ovulation, hominids had to have plenty of sex to make babies, but they wouldn't have wasted their time having intercourse if it wasn't an adaptive behavior. Those who enjoyed sex would have copulated most often and been the most successful in propagating their genes. Hidden ovulation, which turned the mating ritual into a guessing game, may also have made sex more pleasurable, because it increased the need for frequent sexual activity to achieve fertility. In this environment, information becomes paramount. Women can never quite trust men, since it is their wont to deposit their sperm and leave, and men can never quite trust women, since it is difficult to determine if they have been impregnated. Indeed, hidden ovulation has clearly left its legacy. Without complete trust in the other sex, is it possible to attain satisfaction? The answer is, yes, but it depends on novelty.

## Who's Your Daddy?

While hidden ovulation protects women, it is a raw deal for men, and it has led to all sorts of unsavory behavior. Considering the physical and economic investment in a child, it behooves the man to know that he is, indeed, the father. Who can know what was going on nine months previously? Until the recent development of genetic testing, a man could never be sure of his paternity. The uncertainty might be expected to strengthen a man's commitment to a woman, if only to make sure that no other males impregnate her. The man who unwittingly raises another man's child not only fails to reproduce but has been duped into investing his resources to further someone else's genes. Perhaps it is for this reason that, historically, there has been less tolerance for female infidelity than for male infidelity.

David Buss, an evolutionary psychologist at the University of Texas, Austin, has suggested that male jealousy is a direct result of hidden ovulation.[18] In a study of 214 young married couples, Buss examined the prevalence of mate retention behaviors—in other words, the actions performed by men and by women to keep their partner from straying. Men's mate retention behaviors, which included resource display, submission and debasement, and intra-sexual threats, increased with the man's perception of his partner's potential for infidelity. Women, on the other hand, responded to the possibility of infidelity by enhancing their appearance and using verbal signals of possession.[19] To make matters worse, the greater the man's perception of his partner's attractiveness, the more likely he was to engage in mate retention tactics. While women enhance their appearance to retain their man, and men respond to a woman's increased attractiveness as a sign of her potential to stray, it doesn't take long before there's an escalation in the battle of the sexes. All of this, Buss argues, derives from the evolutionary adaptation that led to hidden ovulation.

Considered from the woman's point of view, there is another side to this story. Sarah Hrdy, an anthropologist at the University of California at Davis, has studied how often human adults kill children, and how infanticide is common in other primate societies, notably chimpanzees. Mating with many men, Hrdy says, can obscure the paternity of any child, while hidden ovulation works to conceal the identity of the father and, presumably, decreases the chance that a baby would be killed by a male.[20] A male who killed his child would be committing genetic suicide. In partial support of this theory, it has been found that women having sex with someone other than their primary partner tend to do so around the time of ovulation.[21] If female infidelity peaks around ovulation, it would certainly confuse paternity among a group of males.

Whether to keep men hanging around longer to support their children, or to obscure paternity in a bid for survival, hidden ovulation benefits women more than men. Even without knowing why it evolved, humans are left with its legacy: a good deal of sex. But like anything done repeatedly, sex is subject to habituation under the hedonic treadmill. Finding the clues to lessening the habituation requires digging deeper into the biology of human mating.

## Love Is in the Air

In the late 1960s, Martha McClintock, a young undergraduate at Wellesley College in Massachusetts, upset the scientific establishment by demonstrating the effects of human pheromones. While only a junior, McClintock was shrewd enough to follow her intuition about the synchronization of women's menstrual cycles, which up until then had remained a folk tale. With the encouragement of her faculty advisor, McClintock enlisted the help of 135 women in her dormitory. The women recorded their menstrual cycles throughout one academic year, noting such pertinent factors as which other women they spent the most time with and the frequency of their dates with men. Over the course of the year, McClintock found that women's menstrual cycles gradually came into synchrony. Moreover, women with three or more days per week of exposure to men had a significantly shorter cycle than women with less male contact.[22] Though it would take her twenty years to prove it, McClintock hypothesized that chemical signals passed between individuals and that these signals mediated changes in menstrual cycles.[23]

The discovery of pheromones and their effects on sexual function has shown that humans need not rely exclusively on conscious actions during the mating game. The term *pheromone* is derived from the Greek words *pherein*, meaning "carry," and *hormon*, meaning "excite." The term was introduced in 1959 to describe a class of chemical compounds, transmitted between animals, which evoke behavioral responses. Of course, basic life-forms such as bacteria communicate chemically, but until pheromones were discovered, most scientists had presumed that chemical signaling had been replaced in higher animals by more sophisticated forms of communication.

Human pheromone production comes almost entirely from sweat glands in the skin and from secretions in specific parts of the body, notably the underarms and the genitals. Most of the time you can't detect their presence, because they have no scent, but in high-enough concentrations you know what these chemicals smell like—body odor. Human body odor results from a complex inter-action between bacteria and chemicals secreted by the body. It's the bacteria living on the skin that lend body odor its distinctive aroma. Humans emit a surprisingly high amount of pheromones, far more than any other primate (which is ironic, given the presumptions that pheromones were holdovers from earlier life-forms). Men and women, despite all their sophisticated language and writing, con-tinue to engage in chemical warfare.

Until the 1990s, it had been difficult to demonstrate how human pheromones exert their effects. The fundamental question is whether pheromones have a main line to the brain or work indi-rectly on other organs. In humans, the most extensively studied pheromones derive from the sex hormones. Men emit derivatives of testosterone, called the 16-androstenes, in quantities almost five to twenty times that of women.[24] One form, androstenol, has a musk-like scent, but the bacteria inhabiting male skin metabolize androstenol in such a way that it changes into the more-pungent-smelling androstenone in about twenty minutes. Brain imaging has shown that these compounds ultimately exert their effects on the hypothalamus of the female recipient, near the same regions that control ovulation.[25]

McClintock collected her samples from the underarms of one group of women, and rubbed the samples under the noses of another group of women, priming them more intensely than nor-mal. She demonstrated that secretions obtained before ovulation sped the recipients' cycle, while those secretions obtained at ovula-tion lengthened the cycle. With one pheromone shortening and the other lengthening menstrual cycles, the result would be a syn-chronization between women. Synchronization would seem to negate any benefit of hidden ovulation, because even if men didn't know when the women were ovulating, they could be sure that women were ovulating at the same time.[26]

It's not clear how important menstrual synchronization was in prehistoric times. Robert Bonsall, a colleague at Emory University and an early researcher of female pheromones in the 1970s,[27] pointed out that regularity of menstrual cycles may occur only when a woman is well nourished. In prehistoric times, cycles would likely have been far more irregular, and so pheromonal signaling probably evolved for other reasons. As McClintock noted, contact with men shortened the menstrual cycle. Because most cycle variability comes in the time before ovulation, contact with men must speed up ovulation. From a man's perspective, this, too, would partially negate the effect of hidden ovulation. Even if he didn't know when a woman was ovulating, he could, by spending time with her, at least speed up the process—a sort of chemical counteroffensive. This may, in fact, be consensual, because if a woman is spending time with a man she likes, it would make sense to become fertile more quickly so that he can father her child.

Pheromonal modulation of fertility is just one aspect of the battle of the sexes. The all-important orgasm is another.

## The Big O

Orgasm looms large in any discussion of sex, but what exactly does orgasm have to do with sexual satisfaction? The *Kama Sutra*, a well-worn starting point for sexual research, provides a wealth of detail on this point. Though almost a thousand years old, the Hindu work contains prescient observations about the nature of sex and love. The condensed form (sutra) was meant for easy memorization, but it contains much more meaning than is apparent on first, casual reading.[28] Although the work describes the mechanics of sex fairly well, it also makes the point that satisfaction derives from more than the mere physical act. Kama—meaning love or eroticism—should be pursued, in fact, as only one of three aims in life; wealth and virtue are the other two. Satisfaction occurs when all three are in balance.

In the 1990s, researchers at the University of Chicago set out to determine what, exactly, Americans were doing sexually and how their behavior was related to satisfaction. The investigation, called the National Health and Social Life Survey, or NHSLS,[29] was an effort to correct the sampling biases inherent in previous surveys by Kinsey, Hite, and others. Between 1988 and 1994, the researchers, using true random sampling of the population, selected 3,432 people across the country, a group that represented an accurate cross-section of American adults. Because of their persistence and forthrightness, the investigators obtained response rates of 80 percent, far more than in any previous survey. As in the earlier studies, the NHSLS consisted of a lengthy questionnaire on all sorts of practices, including frequency of sex and of orgasm, type of sex, and masturbation. In addition, the NHSLS researchers included questions about happiness and satisfaction. Although not specifically defined in the questionnaire, the satisfaction questions may be interpreted much as I did those in Chapter 2. Because it is comprehensive, and because it represents an objective view of what Americans do sexually, and what they think about what they do, the NHSLS data provide one of the best sources to ferret out information on the relationship between sex and satisfaction.

Not surprisingly, the relationship between orgasm and satisfaction is complex. Approximately 75 percent of men but only 25 percent of women reported having an orgasm every time they had sex. When the survey expanded the group to include those who usually have an orgasm, the figures rose to 90 percent and 75 percent, respectively. Regardless, women have significantly fewer orgasms than men. The story gets more interesting when the percentages are broken down by type of relationship. Married couples mirrored the overall average, but short-term relationships, defined as lasting less than a month, increased the percentages of "always orgasming," to 81 percent for men and a substantial 43 percent for women. This increase in orgasms, especially in women, suggests a potent novelty effect at work.

But orgasms alone do not make for a satisfying sexual experience. Although the data were not subdivided according to the frequency of orgasm, the percentages of people who were extremely physically satisfied were 51 percent of married men and 40 percent of married women, but these percentages plummeted to 16 percent of both men and women in short-term relationships. Emotional satisfaction yielded similar findings.[30] As for overall happiness, the happiest half of people tended to be married and having sex at least two times a week, with the woman always having an orgasm.[31]

Using frequency of orgasm as a metric of either satisfaction or happiness seems a rather blunt approach. As any adult knows, all orgasms are not created equal, and as the NHSLS demonstrated, for both men and women, having an orgasm ceases, in itself, to be sufficient for satisfaction. The best example of this point, taken from the study, is that married women, who orgasmed less often than single women, reported higher rates of satisfaction.

The seemingly inordinate fascination with female orgasm may arise because science and sexology have been, until recently, a predominately male field, or because the male orgasm is out there for all to see, and the woman's is more mysterious (to men at least). I think that the fascination has more to do with the greater complexity of female sexuality. Geoffrey Miller, the evolutionary psychologist, has argued persuasively that female orgasm, precisely because it is so fickle, may have evolved as a rating system of sorts. If men have an orgasm 75–90 percent of the time, and women 30–75 percent, this disparity indicates that women have more complex requirements for attaining the Big O than do men. Invariably, women point to the psychological dimension of these requirements, citing the need for physical, mental, and emotional arousal. The extent to which all three dimensions—as well as others—come into alignment correlates significantly with the woman's attraction to her partner. Some scientists have argued that physical pleasure serves to bond couples, a sort of operant conditioning view of sexuality.[32] This perspective seems rather mechanistic, in light of the fact that both men and women can pleasure themselves much more easily. Something else must account for the difference in satisfaction between intercourse and masturbation. The NHSLS data strongly suggest that sexual satisfaction derives from the trust and mutual respect that tend to be found in long-term relationships, especially marriage.[33]

The link between sexual satisfaction and marriage, while reassuring, is also puzzling, because it flies in the face of the Coolidge effect and those who would suggest that humans are fundamentally not monogamous. Alternatively, the NHSLS data can be seen as anomalous in that the findings represent an American, and not a universal, view of sex, love, and marriage. Pondering this question, I realized that more than scientific curiosity was at stake.

• • •

The relationship among orgasm, marriage, and satisfaction may derive from the role of the female orgasm in facilitating conception. From an evolutionary perspective, this conclusion makes great sense. If a woman is really attracted to a man, he has the qualities that she desires. Perhaps it is physical attraction, or perhaps it is what he says or does. The specific traits don't matter, but the likelihood of achieving orgasm goes way up when the male meets all the woman's criteria. The woman doesn't have to be consciously aware that her standards have been met, and the process may work even better if it happens subconsciously. Some call the phenomenon romance, others call it passion, but women are invariably more aware than men are of the difference between mediocre sex and great sex.

The possibility that female orgasm can facilitate conception by mechanical means has been investigated by several researchers. The St. Louis gynecologist William Masters and his psychologist wife, Virginia Johnson, investigated this possibility in the 1960s by injecting dye into a woman's vagina and x-raying her after orgasm to see if the muscular contractions associated with orgasm helped transport the dye up into the uterus. As you might imagine, it was a messy, imprecise measurement, and the results were ambiguous. In the end, Masters and Johnson concluded that orgasm probably did not facilitate conception.[34] More recently, R. Robin Baker and Mark Bellis, of Manchester University, tried to measure the concentration of sperm in the vaginal "flowback" after sex and came to the opposite conclusion, that female orgasm did enhance sperm retention; they dubbed their findings the upsuck theory.[35]

It is more likely that orgasm subtly alters a woman's hormonal state. A group in Germany monitored changes in the major sex hormones as women masturbated to orgasm.[36] Two hormones, prolactin and oxytocin, increased markedly. Prolactin stimulates lactation, and oxytocin stimulates, among other things, uterine contractions. The German group also detected a slight increase in luteinizing hormone (LH) after orgasm. LH is found in low concentrations in a woman's bloodstream. As I described in Chapter 4, LH is synthesized in a tiny region of the hypothalamus, and right before ovulation the hypothalamus starts to pump it out. The release starts as small spurts but quickly grows into a pulsatile outflow, which occurs approximately midway in the menstrual cycle and is known as the LH surge. The surge in LH circulates through the blood to the ovaries, where it triggers a change in the balance of estrogen and progesterone production; the complete process culminates in the release of an egg into the fallopian tubes.

McClintock's findings on menstrual synchronization demonstrated that pheromones can shift the onset of ovulation by a few days, and Wilcox showed that ovulation must occur after sex to result in conception. It is entirely possible, therefore, that within a window of forty-eight hours around the time of ovulation, orgasm can cause enough of an increase in LH to trigger the surge, in essence serving up the egg for the waiting sperm. If this conclusion is correct, you can see why the complexity of female orgasm is an asset: it serves as a gatekeeper for potential mates and a powerful mechanism of sexual selection.

Mental state clearly influences both the ability to have an orgasm and the intensity of the climax itself. The role of the mind in sexual satisfaction, especially in women, may have evolved as a way to select the best potential fathers of their children. And similar factors may well operate in the male, perhaps increasing sperm production or motility when he is in the embrace of a particularly appealing female. Either way, evolutionary pressures on sexual selection have resulted in orgasm being a type of overall score for mate fitness.

Under the brutal reduction of the hedonic treadmill, the waning of orgasms, both in quantity and quality, would seem to have dire consequences for long-term relationships, but the NHSLS data tend to contradict this theory. The most satisfying sex occurs in marriage—the bastion of predictability. Indeed, marriage can be understood to enhance overall life satisfaction, in part because sex improves in the context of a relationship. But since more than 50 percent of marriages end in divorce, researchers do not know whether the couples that stay together just happen to be the most compatible, and therefore most satisfied sexually, or whether marriage itself confers the benefit of overall satisfaction. It is probably a little of both, but regardless of what causes and affects compatibility, the passion-enhancing effects of novelty diminish rapidly, so that without conscious effort, both the male and the female libido run the risk of atrophying or going astray. If either the quality or the quantity of orgasms diminishes, dissatisfaction creeps in. Although anyone might resist libidinous impulses, most individuals in long-term relationships ultimately face the fidelity dilemma, which is the need for sexual novelty.

## Sexual Dilemmas

Imagine that you and an accomplice have robbed a bank and are subsequently apprehended. Following standard police procedure, you are held in separate cells and interrogated separately. In an effort to strengthen the state's case, the prosecutor offers you a deal. If neither of you talks, there will be no testimony, and both of you will be convicted of a lesser charge and probably do about a year in prison. If you confess and your partner does not, the prosecutor will use your confession against your accomplice and drop all charges against you. Likewise, if your partner confesses and you remain silent, the accomplice will go free and you will end up in prison for twenty years. Finally, if you both confess, the prosecutor can avoid a lengthy trial and, in exchange, will settle for a plea bargain for both of you of ten years, with eligibility for parole in three. To make it simpler, if you confess, you may go free or you may get three years. If you keep quiet, you might get a year or you might do twenty. What would you do?

This is the prisoner's dilemma. It is described as such because there is no single preferred solution. The best course of action depends on what your partner does, but you won't find out until you make a move.

The prisoner's dilemma was a game invented by Rand scientists in the 1950s, but it remains paradigmatic of any interaction between two people in which one's gains don't necessarily equal the other's losses. The game has been used to model political conflict, military strategy, and social choices. In many ways, the battle of the sexes is a prisoner's dilemma. The daily choices that partners in a committed relationship make provide fertile ground for games of all types. Who does the dishes? Who handles the finances? Do you see a movie or go to the symphony? When having sex, who's on top? My point is not to trivialize the dilemmas that couples face; any interaction between two people is a game, one whose rules are mutually decided and which invites negotiation.

In a brain imaging study of the prisoner's dilemma, Jim Rilling, a postdoctoral student in my department, found that parts of the striatum were activated when people cooperate. Given the close relationship of the striatum with reward and action, he naturally concluded that social cooperation is rewarding to the human brain.[37] But it was not the act of cooperation alone that activated the striatum; it was *mutual* cooperation. By design, mutual cooperation does not always result in the best outcome for each participant, not only because cooperation entails risk but also because it depends on making yourself vulnerable, which, in turn, creates opportunities for betrayal. Whether it is a romantic relationship or a business deal, cooperation means uncertainty. When you do cooperate, and the act is reciprocated, the novelty of this outcome is picked up by the striatum. Perhaps that is the reason mutually reciprocated acts feel so good. The fact that cooperation doesn't always happen is exactly why it is so satisfying.

Most people, of course, do not like being betrayed; therefore, they do not cheat on their significant other. Still, infidelity persists. It would be a denial of the obvious not to recognize that people are tempted to copulate outside marriage. For evidence, you need only look at common sexual fantasies. But even in the area of imaginary sex, you will encounter the misconception that such thoughts are predominately held by men; the NHSLS showed that women also fantasize about partners other than their own.[38]

Fantasies of sex with other people do not necessarily lead to infidelity. NHSLS data are quite clear on this: 85 percent of women and 75 percent of men report being faithful for the duration of their marriages.[39] It is safe to assume that, at one time or another, most people hold fantasies about someone other than their spouse; but because most couples are faithful to each other, fantasy, in and of itself, does not lead to infidelity. Marital infidelity is limited by a number of factors: social stigma, financial constraints (e.g., the cost of getting caught and getting a divorce), concern for children, and one's moral structure. Is it fair to consider fidelity as the classic prisoner's dilemma, in which potentially greater rewards can be reaped for one party but only at the expense of the other? Unless a calculated decision is made that the other person is also cheating, I don't think so.

But this nice, even comforting, explanation glosses over a paradox. While most couples report being happy, the NHSLS found significant sexual dissatisfaction. Despite the rates of orgasm previously mentioned, both men and women reported being "extremely physically satisfied" or "extremely emotionally satisfied" less than half the time.[40] Although marriage improved these rates to about 50 percent, the majority of married men and women reported that sex could be better. Maybe their dissatisfaction stems from the memory of hot sex early in the relationship, or from bombardment of the media's images of perfect human specimens. Or maybe sexual dissatisfaction, either at a particular time or throughout a relationship, is inevitable in any long-term bond. How many times can you have sex with one person before you get bored?

Sex is subject to the hedonic treadmill; indeed, some degree of boredom seems bound to occur. If the proverbial seven-year itch is a predictable consequence of married life, what can you do?[41] The most obvious solution is to seek gratification outside marriage, but here you run into the prisoner's dilemma. While the adulterous partner experiences pleasure, the other partner loses out—even if he or she doesn't know it. Mutual defection, the equivalent of an open marriage, could bring some measure of satisfaction to both participants. Strip clubs and Internet pornography provide easy access for those seeking novelty without physical contact. Serial monogamy without the commitment of marriage is yet another possibility.

All these options, which at times may seem appealing, do not hold much promise for long-term satisfaction. Whatever the reason, most people do not want to risk losing a solid relationship by breaking their vows.

## The Sexual Crucible

Marriage begins with vows of eternal fidelity, in sickness and in health. Nobody says anything about boredom or routine. But what happens after the initial passion fades? Do long-term relationships always result in the diminution of sexual satisfaction? The NHSLS results seemed to contradict themselves in reports of marriages that were described as happy overall but that included fewer earth-moving orgasms than passionate short-term flings. There must be a reservoir of unmet needs among even the most satisfied adults—married couples.

I have found only one practical, thoughtful approach to the problem of predictability—and the looming threat of novelty—in long-term relationships. Dubbed the "sexual crucible" by its creator, David Schnarch, a marital and sex therapist in Colorado, it requires couples to confront challenges to their relationship, sexual or nonsexual, in the context of sex. Schnarch argues that the bedroom is the crucible, for it is where difficulties are crystallized into the personal, concrete manner in which people relate to each other most intimately.[42] As couples become dependent on each other and behavior falls into patterns, their routines present a formidable obstacle to satisfaction, sexual or otherwise. In Schnarch's view, routinization is a natural process, one that is reflected most powerfully in the bedroom. Routine by itself is not the problem; rather, Schnarch identifies the unfortunate consequence of routine: the human tendency to forget that the other person is an individual. Unless something unexpected and even unwelcome happens, you assume that your partner has the same thoughts as you do. When partners fail to differentiate from each other, sex becomes routine, almost like having intercourse with yourself.

Differentiation is the ability to maintain a sense of self when emotionally and physically close to another person, and it is at the core of the sexual crucible.[43] It sounds simple, but differentiating takes work. The longer that two people are together, the more experiences they have in common, the more their boundaries blur. As Schnarch points out, there is nothing wrong with the situation; it is the natural evolution of any relationship, and like many aspects of the battle of the sexes, what is natural is not necessarily optimal, and what comes naturally is often the most difficult to change.

The predictability of behavior can make both spouses feel as if the other doesn't really know them. For marital harmony to happen, each partner must make concessions to the other, but what begins as a compromise willingly forged between two people can become expected or even compulsory. If the relationship becomes the primary identity for both spouses, then each has necessarily forfeited some personal identity to a process Schnarch calls fusion. When couples are fused emotionally, the partners lose a critical dimension of their individuality, and eventually one spouse begins to become isolated. How the pattern plays out in a relationship is unique to each couple. Sometimes resentment may occur simultaneously, making both feel lonely. I believe that many couples mistakenly confuse the loss of individuality with its consequences: petty fighting, alcoholism, and infidelity.

Isolation in a relationship, even if it falls short of the critical degree just described, can occur across many dimensions, but its manifestation in sex is the most concrete. It is easy to turn off the lights, close one's eyes, and be transported into a fantasy world while going through the mechanics of sex. For many couples, this type of sex is perfectly adequate. But every so often, you catch a glimpse of what really, really good sex is like. Perhaps it is the shadow of this memory that makes fantasy, with or without a partner, mediocre by comparison. Fortunately, a means for momentarily stepping off the hedonic treadmill exists; though it is frightening, it is vital for the attainment of satisfaction.

For differentiation to take place, the two partners must, in a cooperative effort, reaffirm their individuality. But after they have spent years together, true individuality may not be readily apparent. If a couple survives the process and continues to differentiate, then, says Schnarch, the relationship will be richer on all levels. Everything that I have learned about the brain supports this idea. Predictability degrades all that is pleasurable, especially with regard to the dopamine system, and what better way to inject novelty into a relationship than to have both partners change? This does, however, entail risks. In the process of individuation, one person might be transformed into somebody the other doesn't like.

How to change? There is no simple formula, but Schnarch targets intimacy, especially sexual intimacy, as the place to start. Real intimacy, he says, is achieved through conflict, self-validation, and unilateral disclosure. I believe that conflict is a sign that novel forces are at work. If you are not feeling a little anxiety—a little cortisol—then nothing has altered. Self-validation means not only keeping sight of your identity but also doing things to comfort yourself when you experience the inevitable anxiety that comes from differentiation from your spouse.

Before you enter the sexual crucible, it is critical to confront yourself—that is, to acknowledge your own desires and the obstacles that stand in the way of achieving them. Your partner cannot be counted on to confront himself or herself, nor be expected to change. Differentiation begins with the individual. Disclosure is perhaps the most difficult step. Although you cannot transform another person, honest disclosure can make your partner see you in a new light. Schnarch advocates the most literal form of seeing each other: having sex with open eyes, from foreplay right through orgasm.

In the sexual crucible, disclosure means asserting what you want—whether it is being touched in a certain way or being spanked with a riding crop—no matter how odd the request. With disclosure comes consequences, and one of these is, ironically, the willingness to forgo sex, the ultimate consequence. No more mercy sex, or simple acquiescence to the other's desire. If you admit that you want to have sex with someone else, then you should be prepared for your partner to give the go-ahead, knowing that the permission may also represent your partner's intention to do the same. The ultimate question, which every couple—conversant with the sexual crucible or not—faces eventually can be asked just in time, before the relationship ceases to exist.

·  ·  ·

If sex isn't exactly the crucible as Schnarch defines it, it comes close—a fact I realized when I could no longer hide behind science. At this point in my life, I realized that the driving force behind this book could not be described solely as a philosophical quest for satisfaction. No matter how hard I tried—in an attempt to outwit predictability—to explain the hedonic treadmill, I still understood my own marriage as the only meaningful testing ground on which I could prove the viability of sustaining satisfying experiences. If I— that is, my wife, Kathleen, and I—couldn't create satisfaction in the Venn diagram of our two lives, then I'd have to declare the hedonic treadmill the winner.

My personal search for satisfaction had taken a toll on our marriage. As is so often the case, the job of child rearing fell to Kathleen. Our children were becoming little people with their own personalities. While mostly endearing, the preschool years, as any parent knows, can be difficult for parents unaccustomed to the way three- and four-year-olds think. Although Kathleen had the choice of putting her career on hold to raise our children, she regretted, at times, that the decision brought with it few sources of adult stimulation. As I jetted around to one place or another, and, at home, was constantly absorbed in what I found, I made the classic mistake of taking my wife for granted.

Perhaps, just as selfishly, I was specifically concerned about sex. After fifteen years of marriage and two children, our sex life had become routine. I began to worry that in my search for satisfying experiences, I might be tempted by someone else. And in my absences, perhaps Kathleen might be similarly led astray. Fortunately I stumbled upon Schnarch's sexual crucible, which he set up to confront just such a scenario. Schnarch wasn't being melodramatic when he used the word *crucible*. When I broached the subject with Kathleen, she immediately assumed that my dissatisfaction meant that we were headed for divorce.

. . .

The particulars of our transformation were specific to us, but since we are not so different from other couples in long-term relationships, with kids or not, there emerged some generalities worth sharing. My crucible, our crucible, began with a conversation. We had both read Schnarch's book, and it was time to lay bare our true desires.

For the first time in maybe ten years, I looked at Kathleen and experienced a tingle of excitement as I had on our first date. After so long together, I thought that I knew her and her effect on me. Even so, I had no idea what she was thinking.

Waiting for her to speak, I became acutely aware of every gulp of saliva, which seemed to be in short supply. Kathleen's face looked pale, and a slight flush rose up her neck. The cocktail of anxiety, giddiness, and uncertainty was making my head spin and my fingers tingle. And yet this tension was charged with eroticism. Simultaneously, I hated and cherished the feeling of anxiety because I knew it meant something was happening. Would she view me as a freak? Did she think I was ready to toss out our marriage? What about the children? This torrent of fear and insecurity is familiar to anyone who has ventured into the dating scene, but now, married, I knew that the risk that came with airing them was far greater. If either of us said or did something that alienated the other, we were gambling everything we had invested in each other—whose value is the very reason these conversations are so rarely begun.

I wanted to ask Kathleen what she was thinking, but doing so would have been chicken on my part. There was no risk in asking what she thought. No, I had to face my prisoner's dilemma and go first, putting my neuroses out there for her to judge.

"I think we're stuck in a rut," I said.

She didn't look at me for several seconds. "I suppose," she said finally. "But what do you expect?" She pointed out the obvious: fifteen years and two children later, our sex life had fizzled. It wasn't even the frequency; it was the predictability.

"Listen," I continued. "There are things I haven't told you."

"Like what?"

"Things that I would like to do."

Now, she looked straight at me. "What, like have sex with someone else?"

This was a difficult question. And why did she ask it? Maybe she was testing the waters. To answer tactfully when denying my own desires would be folly, and a repudiation of everything Schnarch's effort stands for. Since the crucible is about self-revelation, I had to choose honesty. "Yes," I said. "I think about it."

Because she was expecting a sugar-coated denial, I think my answer rang true.

She pondered my admission, then added, "Me, too."

Her answer was a relief, as if she had opened a door between each of us and our secret desires. I was aroused.

"Well," I said. "What do you want to do about it?"

"I don't know."

"Do *you* want to screw someone else?"

"Like who?" she asked.

"I don't know. How about that guy at the hardware store?"

Kathleen laughed at the absurdity of it.

I couldn't believe we were talking like this. It didn't feel as though our marriage was dissolving. The intense anxiety continued, even as we revealed our secret desires. We sat there, husband and wife, talking about sex like two gossipy friends, one revelation begetting another, until after an hour of disclosures, I had pretty much laid bare all my fantasies. Not one was rejected, and Kathleen's imagination went even beyond mine. I saw her then not as the mother of my children but as the sensual woman I met over fifteen years ago.

We made love that night, with the lights on and eyes open, as Schnarch suggests, and what I saw surprised me. I saw deep satisfaction in Kathleen, and within her I saw my reflection. The feeling was not unlike our first time—tense and awkward—but now with a familiarity that smoothed out the rough spots and took us deeper into emotion. Was it dopamine? Cortisol? I think it was probably both, not unlike the cocktail of transcendence I saw in the ultramarathoners. Whatever it was, it is not the type of thing science could deconstruct anytime soon.

## What Is Love?

Our willingness to enter the sexual crucible led to something deeper, something outside sex. The cycle of self-revelation and experimentation, which we undertook to sharpen our individuality, sparked a shared passion that had been absent for many years. The sexual abandonment that we enjoyed was a direct consequence of passing through the anxiety of revealing our true desires, only to find acceptance on the other side. No source of novelty can exceed that created between two people who truly, deeply trust each other. The freedom and trust to do novel things in a natural way makes sex creative and complex.

In the weeks that followed, I found myself thinking about that evening. Entering the crucible changed our relationship, but something of a whole other order happened that night, a perceptual shift approximating a spiritual one, a mystery accentuated by the carnal nature of the circumstances. I was not ever going to see God, but abandonment to the physical realm opened a window onto the place where many people find Him: somewhere or something else, different from this world.

Kathleen had her own epiphany weeks later. Late one night, she turned to me and said, "I feel different."

"How so?"

"I don't know exactly. But it's like I've tapped into a source of power that I didn't have before. Just letting go, really letting go, surprises me. I didn't know that I could do it. Even the little annoyances during the day don't bother me as much."

I can scarcely believe all of this myself. Anyone telling me that there was a sexual experience beyond imagination I would have considered crazy. Even my experience could be dismissed as anomalous, but now my partner in crime was confirming that what we enjoyed wasn't just some sort of mutual pornographic delusion. Together we had agreed to create novelty in the intricacies of our relationship, and the novelty has proved far more satisfying than anything I have encountered to date. It is boundless.

# Epilogue

First you experience. Then you share.

These are the words of Francis Mallmann, the Argentine chef I visited in the Hamptons, and in them lies a great truth: experience—and hence satisfaction—are personal affairs. Even activities undertaken with others are experienced alone, and differently, so that at the end of the day, we are left with our own perceptions and our own memories. The meal two people share, even if their servings are identical, is experienced uniquely. Five hundred people, each solving the same crossword, have a different experience of completing it, even if they arrive at the same answers.

Satisfying experiences are no different. At the outset, I said that the essence of a satisfying experience can be found in your brain. Although some details remain to be worked out, novel experiences—because they release dopamine and cortisol—are the surest route to satisfaction. But even this prescription is not enough. Presciently, Francis's great bit of wisdom is in the commandment to share. Here is the place humans differ from every other animal; because we have language, experience need not remain locked inside us. What we can express, no matter how crudely, we can share. Imagine how lonely a chimpanzee must be, with a lifetime of experience locked up in an almost-human brain.

Every experience in our lives is part of a larger narrative; the act of telling a story not only transmits some small bit of one person's experience to another person, linking individual narratives, it also solidifies that experience in the memory of the storyteller. You could say that sharing makes things real. And even if we each have our personal versions of satisfaction—like a good meal— satisfaction is an experience best shared collectively, and reciprocally, with others. Above all else, the most important thing I have learned—and would like to leave with you—is that satisfaction is an emotion within everyone's grasp.

Throughout this book, I have alluded to the fickle nature of pleasure, which I have taken great pains to distinguish from satisfaction. True, pleasure feels good, but its transience leaves in its wake a relative normality that, by comparison, often feels like a void—one screaming to be filled with more and more pleasure. The end result of this process is, of course, what Phil Brickman called the hedonic treadmill. A life without pleasure would be dismal indeed, but, more often than not, the pursuit of pleasure for its own sake leads to its opposite—misery—and does not satisfy the brain.

Seeking satisfaction is distinct from chasing pleasure. Satisfaction is an emotion that captures the uniquely human need to impart meaning to one's activities. When you are satisfied, you have found meaning, which I think we'd all agree is more enduring than pleasure or even happiness.

Satisfaction differs critically from both pleasure and happiness by its inclusion of the dimension of action. While you might find pleasure by happenstance—winning the lottery, possessing the genes for a sunny temperament, or having the luck not to live in poverty—satisfaction can arise only by the conscious decision to do something. And this makes all the difference in the world, because it is only your own actions for which you may take responsibility and credit.

The route to satisfaction I have described in this book flows through novelty. When you do something you've never done before, the novelty releases dopamine, which gooses the action system of your brain. Although you might not always be aware of this process, you certainly know the feeling of satisfaction that ensues. Hopefully, I have given you a sense of the biology behind this process and the variety of ways in which people tap into it. But however you find satisfaction, your brain changes in the process, and with it the world you live in and how you see it. I saw brains change when Compay Segundo knocked out a syncopated harmony in novel riffs; I saw brains change during the solution of crossword puzzles packed with puns; and, finally, I saw the brains (and other body parts) of ultramarathoners change with the grit and determination required to run one hundred miles across the Sierra Nevada. I felt my own brain change, too, as I cooked a meal with Francis, looked for hidden people, and found intimacy—again.

# NOTES

—— • ——

## Chapter 1: The Slave in the Brain

1. Saleem M. Nicola, D. James Surmeier, and Robert C. Malenka, "Dopaminergic Modulation of Neuronal Excitablity in the Striatum and Nucleus Accumbens," *Annual Review of Neuroscience* 23 (2000):185–215.

2. Wolfram Schultz, Paul Apicella, Eugenio Scarnati, and Tomas Ljungberg, "Neuronal Activity in Monkey Ventral Striatum Related to the Expectation of Reward," *Journal of Neuroscience* 12 (1992):4595–610.

3. The ethics board, or Institutional Review Board (IRB), a committee composed of professors and community members, reviews all human research at a university. The IRB evaluates potential risks and benefits of each experiment, but the federal guidelines have become increasingly complex, and both researchers' and IRBs' suffer under greater federal oversight. Sex research is particularly difficult, since Congress has pulled funding from many research projects aimed at understanding the human sexual response.

4. Gregory S. Berns, Samuel M. McClure, Giuseppe Pagnoni, and P. Read Montague, "Predictability Modulates Human Brain Response to Reward," *Journal of Neuroscience* 21 (2001):2793–98.

5. Kent C. Berridge and Terry E. Robinson, "What Is the Role of Dopamine in Reward: Hedonic Impact, Reward Learning, or Incentive Salience?" *Brain Research Review* 28 (1998):309–69.

6. Henry D. Thoreau, *Walden* (Princeton: Princeton University Press, 1854/1973); Epicurus, *The Essential Epicurus*, trans. Eugene O'Connor (Amherst: Prometheus Books, 1993).

7. Claude E. Shannon and Warren Weaver, *The Mathematical Theory of Communication* (Urbana: University of Illinois Press, 1949/1963). The information content, *I*, of a single event, *x*, is given by the equation $I = -\log_2 P[x]$, where $P[x]$ is the probability of occurrence of $x$. To first order, $I$ can be approximated by $1/P[x]$.

8. C. Robert Cloninger, "Neurogenetic Adaptive Mechanisms in Alcoholism," *Science* 236 (1987):410–16; Jonathan Benjamin, Lin Li, Chavis Patterson, Benjamin D. Greenberg, Dennis L. Murphy, and Dean H. Hamer, "Population and Familial Association Between the D4 Dopamine Receptor Gene and Measures of Novelty Seeking," *Nature Genetics* 12 (1996):81–84; Richard P. Ebstein, Olga Novick, Roberto Umansky, Beatrice Priel, Yamima Osher, Darren Blaine, Estelle R. Bennett, Lubov Nemanov, Miri Katz, and Robert H. Belmaker, "Dopamine D4 Receptor (D4DR) Exon III Polymorphism Associated with the Human Personality Trait of Novelty Seeking," *Nature Genetics* 12 (1996):78–80.

## Chapter 2: For the Love of Money

1. Colin F. Camerer, George F. Loewenstein, and Drazen Prelec, "Neuroeconomics: How Neuroscience Can Inform Economics," *Journal of Economic Literature* 43 (2005); Paul W. Glimcher, *Decisions, Uncertainty, and the Brain: The Science of Neuroeconomics* (Cambridge: MIT Press, 2003); Paul W. Glimcher and Aldo Rustichini, "Neuroeconomics: The Consilience of Brain and Decision," *Science* 306 (2004):447–52.

2. Philip Brickman, Dan Coates, and Ronnie Janoff-Bulman, "Lottery Winners and Accident Victims: Is Happiness Relative?" *Journal of Personality and Social Psychology* 36 (1978):917–27.

3. Philip Brickman and Donald T. Campbell, "Hedonic Relativism and Planning the Good Society," in *Adaptation Level Theory: A Symposium*, ed. M. H. Appley (New York: Academic Press, 1971).

4. Jonathan Gardner and Andrew Oswald, "Does Money Buy Happiness?: A Longitudinal Study Using Data on Windfalls," in *Warwick University*, working paper (Coventry: 2001).

5. David G. Blanchflower and Andrew J. Oswald, "Money, Sex, and Happiness: An Empirical Study," in *NBER Working Paper Series* (Cambridge, Mass.: 2004).

6. Ed Diener and Robert Biswars-Diener, "Will Money Increase Subjective Well-Being?" *Social Indicators Research* 57 (2002):119–69.

7. Caridad is not her real name. I gave her an alias to protect her identity in Cuba.

8. Sonja Lyubomirsky and Heidi S. Lepper, "A Measure of Subjective Happiness: Preliminary Reliability and Construct Validation," *Social Indicators Research* 46 (1999):137–55.

9. Ed Diener, Robert A. Emmons, Randy J. Larsen, and Sharon Griffin, "The Satisfaction with Life Scale," *Journal of Personality Assessment* 49 (1985):71–75.

10. Because such assessments are influenced by one's current mood, I think that the added element of cognitive appraisal makes the SWLS a slightly more reliable measurement of satisfaction than of happiness. For an accessible explanation of the different ways of assessing happiness and satisfaction, see Martin E. P. Seligman, *Authentic Happiness: Using the New Positive Psychology to Realize Your Potential for Lasting Fulfillment* (New York: Free Press, 2002).

11. The top five countries were Iceland, Sweden, Australia, Denmark, and Canada. The bottom five were East Germany, the Soviet Union, China, Cameroon, and the Dominican Republic. Other curiosities: Belgium was nineteenth, but France was thirty-first, followed by Spain, Portugal, and Italy. So much for the European ideal. See Ed Diener, Marissa Diener, and Carol Diener, "Factors Predicting the Subjective Well-Being of Nations," *Journal of Personality and Social Psychology* 69 (1995):851–64.

12. The correlation, $r^2$, between income and well-being ranges from 0.12 to 0.24, and thus the percentage of variance, $r$, ranges from about 1 to 5 percent. See Diener and Biswars-Diener, "Will Money Increase Subjective Well-Being?" Table I.

13. The idea of conspicuous consumption originated with Thorstein Veblen, but for a more modern interpretation, see Michael Marmot, *The Status Syndrome: How Social Standing Affects Our Health and Longevity* (New York: Times Books, 2004).

14. Jeremy Bentham, *The Principles of Morals and Legislation* (Amherst: Prometheus Books, 1780/1988).

15. The probability of winning, $p$, is 1 in 100 million, or $10^{-8}$, and the value of the jackpot, $V$, is $100 million. Expected value, $E[V]=p^*V$, or $1.

16. Daniel Bernoulli, "Exposition of a New Theory on the Measurement of Risk," *Econometrica* 22, (1738/1954):23–36. For a particularly lucid summary of Bernoulli's ideas, see Glimcher, *Decisions, Uncertainty, and the Brain: The Science of Neuroeconomics.*

17. John von Neumann and Oskar Morgenstern, *The Theory of Games and Economic Behavior*, 2nd ed. (Princeton: Princeton University Press, 1947).

18. The importance of differentiating between objective and subjective risk was not fully appreciated until Leonard Savage formulated a theory of statistics based on subjective probability. Savage, *The Foundations of Statistics* (New York: Dover Publications, 1954/1972).

19. Not everyone agrees with this; see Barry Schwartz, *The Paradox of Choice: Why More Is Less* (New York: HarperCollins, 2004).

20. The British epidemiologist Michael Marmot has compiled an impressive array of data showing that increased autonomy increases life expectancy. Marmot, *The Status Syndrome: How Social Standing Affects Our Health and Longevity.*

21. Actually, Bernoulli said that money had diminishing *marginal* utility. *Marginal* is another word for *derivative*. In plain language, the difference in utility

between $100 and $110 is less than the difference in utility between $10 and $20, although the change in amount is $10 in both cases.

22. Daniel Kahneman and Amos Tversky, "Prospect Theory: An Analysis of Decision Under Risk," *Econometrica* 47 (1979):263–91. Prospect theory has become a pillar of economic theory, and Kahneman was awarded the Nobel Prize in 2002 for his work on the subject (Tversky died in 1996). Researchers still do not understand, however, why people behave the way they do.

23. Daniel Read and George Loewenstein, "Diversification Bias: Explaining the Discrepancy in Variety Seeking Between Combined and Separated Choices," *Journal of Experimental Psychology: Applied* 1 (1995):34–49.

24. Thomas Gilovich and Victoria Husted Medvec, "The Experience of Regret: What, When, and Why," *Psychological Review* 102 (1995):379–95; Daniel Kahneman and Dale T. Miller, "Norm Theory: Comparing Reality to Its Alternatives," *Psychological Review* 93 (1985):136–53.

25. Brian Knutson, Grace W. Fong, Shannon M. Bennett, Charles M. Adams, and Daniel Hommer, "A Region of Mesial Prefrontal Cortex Tracks Monetarily Rewarding Outcomes: Characterization with Rapid Event-Related fMRI," *Neuro-Image* 18 (2003):263–72; Brian Knutson, Charles M. Adams, Grace W. Fong, and Daniel Hommer, "Anticipation of Increasing Monetary Reward Selectively Recruits Nucleus Accumbens," *Journal of Neuroscience* 21 (2001):1–5.

26. Peter Redgrave, Tony A. Prescott, and Kevin Gurney, "Is the Short-Latency Dopamine Response Too Short to Signal Reward Error?" *Trends in Neuroscience* 22 (1999):146–51; J. C. Horvitz, "Mesolimbocortical and Nigrostriatal Dopamine Responses to Salient Non-Reward Events," *Neuroscience* 96 (2000): 651–56.

27. Caroline F. Zink, Giuseppe Pagnoni, Megan E. Martin-Skurski, Jonathan C. Chappelow, and Gregory S. Berns, "Human Striatal Responses to Monetary Reward Depend on Saliency," *Neuron* 42 (2004):509–17.

28. Max Weber, *The Protestant Ethic and the "Spirit" of Capitalism and Other Writings*, trans. Peter Baehr and Gordon C. Wells (New York: Penguin Books, 1905/2002).

29. A few economists have viewed work as a positive. See Tibor Scitovsky, *The Joyless Economy: The Psychology of Human Satisfaction*, 3rd ed. (New York: Oxford University Press, 1992); Robert E. Lane, "Work as 'Disutility' and Money as 'Happiness': Cultural Origins of a Basic Market Error," *Journal of Socio-Economics* 21 (1992):43–64.

30. Brooks Carder and Kenneth Berkowitz, "Rats' Preference for Earned in Comparison with Free Food," *Science* 167 (1970):1273–74.

31. The story of the Buena Vista Social Club is beautifully captured, along with the group's music, in Wim Wenders's 1999 film of the same name.

## Chapter 3: Puzzling Gratifications

1. The *New York Times* crossword puzzle increases in difficulty each day from Monday, when it is easiest, to Saturday, the most difficult. The Sunday puzzle, while larger than those in the dailies, is generally considered a little easier than Saturday's.

2. The answer was probably *a raincloud*. See Tony Augarde, *The Oxford Guide to Word Games*, 2nd ed. (Oxford: Oxford University Press, 2003).

3. The answer is *man*.

4. Lowell Edmunds, *The Sphinx in the Oedipus Legend*, vol. 127, *Beiträge zur klassischen Philologie* (Meisenheim: Verlag Anton Hain, 1981).

5. Henry Ernest Dudeney, "Mrs. Timpkins's Age," *The Strand Magazine* (1911). The answer is *18*.

6. Will Shortz, "Early American Word Puzzles, Part I," *Word Ways: The Journal of Recreational Linguistics* 7 (1974):131–38.

7. Coral Amende, *The Crossword Obsession: The History and Lore of the World's Most Popular Pastime* (New York: Berkley Books, 2001).

8. I am indebted to George Loewenstein's excellent review on the history and psychology of curiosity: Loewenstein, "The Psychology of Curiosity: A Review and Reinterpretation," *Psychological Bulletin* 116 (1994):75–98.

9. Saint Augustine, *The Confessions of St. Augustine*, trans. Edward B. Pusey (New York: P. F. Collier & Son, 1909), Book 10.

10. Bentham, *The Principles of Morals and Legislation*, p. 34.

11. Michael Kubovy, "On the Pleasures of the Mind," in *Well-Being: The Foundations of Hedonic Psychology*, ed. Daniel Kahneman, Ed Diener, and Norbert Schwarz (New York: Russell Sage Foundation, 1999). Berlyne amassed a sizable corpus of data to make his case, having people view images of varying complexity and collecting their ratings of pleasantness, or having subjects listen to clips of music of varying complexity.

12. Mihaly Csikszentmihalyi, *Flow: The Psychology of Optimal Experience* (New York: Harper Perennial, 1990).

13. Loewenstein, "The Psychology of Curiosity: A Review and Reinterpretation."

14. Robert W. Weisberg, "Prolegomena to Theories of Insight in Problem Solving: A Taxonomy of Problems," in *The Nature of Insight*, ed. Robert J. Sternberg and Janet E. Davidson (Cambridge: MIT Press, 1995).

15. Wolfgang Köhler, *The Task of Gestalt Psychology* (Princeton: Princeton University Press, 1969). For a review of the psychology of problem solving, see Janet E. Davidson, "Insights About Insightful Problem-Solving," in *The Psychology of Problem Solving*, ed. Janet E. Davidson and Robert J. Sternberg (Cambridge: Cambridge University Press, 2003).

16. Köhler's favorite rube was a chimp named Rana, meaning "frog" in Spanish, a moniker acquired from her clumsy, froglike movements. See Köhler,

*The Task of Gestalt Psychology;* Wolfgang Köhler, *The Mentality of Apes* (New York: Harcourt Brace, 1925).

17. Weisberg, "Prolegomena to Theories of Insight in Problem Solving: A Taxonomy of Problems."

18. Henry Ernest Dudeney, *536 Puzzles & Curious Problems,* ed. Martin Gardner (New York: Charles Scribner's Sons, 1967), puzzle 533. Dudeney did not actually write this puzzle. It is attributed to Philip Boswood Ballard, who constructed intelligence tests in the early twentieth century.

19. Graham Wallas, *The Art of Thought* (New York: Harcourt Brace, 1926). Wallas didn't call it by this name; see Colleen M. Seifert, David E. Meyer, Natalie Davidson, Andrea L. Patalano, and Ilan Yaniv, "Demystification of Cognitive Insight: Opportunistic Assimilation and the Prepared-Mind Perspective," in *The Nature of Insight,* ed. Robert J. Sternberg and Janet E. Davidson (Cambridge: MIT Press, 1995).

20. The answer is *sextant.*

21. Seifert, Meyer, Davidson, Patalano, and Yaniv, "Demystification of Cognitive Insight: Opportunistic Assimilation and the Prepared-Mind Perspective."

22. J. Allan Hobson and Edward F. Pace-Schott, "The Cognitive Neuroscience of Sleep: Neuronal Systems, Consciousness and Learning," *Nature Reviews Neuroscience* 3 (2002):679–93.

23. Magdalena J. Fosse, Roar Fosse, J. Allan Hobson, and Robert Stickgold, "Dreaming and Episodic Memory: A Functional Dissociation?" *Journal of Cognitive Neuroscience* 15 (2003):1–9.

24. Avi Karni, David Tanne, Barton S. Rubenstein, Jean J. M. Askenasy, and Dov Sagi, "Dependence on REM Sleep of Overnight Improvement of a Perceptual Skill," *Science* 265 (1994):679–82.

25. Steffen Gais, Werner Plihal, Ullrich Wagner, and Jan Born, "Early Sleep Triggers Memory for Early Visual Discrimination Skills," *Nature Neuroscience* 3 (2000):1335–39; R. Stickgold, J. A. Hobson, R. Fosse, and M. Fosse, "Sleep, Learning, and Dreams: Off-Line Memory Reprocessing," *Science* 294 (2001):1052–57.

26. Matthew A. Wilson and Bruce L. McNaughton, "Reactivation of Hippocampal Ensemble Memories During Sleep," *Science* 265 (1994):676–79.

27. Jerome M. Siegel, "The REM Sleep–Memory Consolidation Hypothesis," *Science* 294 (2001):1058–63.

28. Matthew P. Walker, Conor Liston, J. Allan Hobson, and Robert Stickgold, "Cognitive Flexibility Across the Sleep-Wake Cycle: REM-Sleep Enhancement of Anagram Problem Solving," *Cognitive Brain Research* 14 (2002):317–24.

29. Frank Schneider, Raquel E. Gur, Abass Alavi, Martin E. P. Seligman, Lyn H. Mozley, Robin J. Smith, P. D. Mozley, and Ruben C. Gur, "Cerebral Blood Flow Changes in Limbic Regions Induced by Unsolvable Anagram Tasks," *American Journal of Psychiatry* 153 (1996):206–12.

30. Jing Luo and Kazuhisa Niki, "Function of Hippocampus in 'Insight' of Problem Solving," *Hippocampus* 13 (2003):316–23.

31. Another fMRI study, with 18 volunteers, has also found hippocampal activation associated with insight. See Mark Jung-Beeman, Edward M. Bowden, Jason Haberman, Jennifer L. Frymiare, Stella Arambel-Liu, Richard Greenblatt, Paul J. Reber, and John Kounios, "Neural Activity When People Solve Verbal Problems with Insight," *PLoS Biology* 2 (2004):E97.

32. Thomas Hobbes, *Leviathan*, World Classics ed. (Oxford: Oxford University Press, 1651/1998); Sigmund Freud, *The Joke and Its Relation to the Unconscious*, trans. Joyce Crick (New York: Penguin Books, 1905/2003); Henri Bergson, *Laughter: An Essay on the Meaning of the Comic*, trans. Cloudesley Brereton and Fred Rothwell (Los Angeles: Green Integer, 1900/1999).

33. V. Goel and R. J. Dolan, "The Functional Anatomy of Humor: Segregating Cognitive and Affective Components," *Nature Neuroscience* 4 (2001):237–38.

34. Dean Mobbs, Michael D. Greicius, Eiman Abdel-Azim, Vinod Menon, and Allan L. Reiss, "Humor Modulates the Mesolimbic Reward Centers," *Neuron* 40 (2003):1041–48; Gregory S. Berns, "Something Funny Happened to Reward," *Trends in Cognitive Sciences* 8 (2004):193–94.

## Chapter 4: The Sushi Problem

1. Gray Kunz and Peter Kaminsky, *The Elements of Taste* (Boston: Little, Brown, 2001).

2. Bernd Lindemann, "Receptors and Transduction in Taste," *Nature* 413 (2001):219–25; Peter Mombaerts, "Genes and Ligands for Odorant, Vomeronasal and Taste Receptors," *Nature Reviews Neuroscience* 5 (2004):263–78.

3. Mombaerts, "Genes and Ligands for Odorant, Vomeronasal and Taste Receptors."

4. Peter Kaminsky, *The Fly Fisherman's Guide to the Meaning of Life: What a Lifetime on the Water Has Taught Me About Love, Work, Food, Sex, and Getting Up Early* (New York: Rodale Press, 2002).

5. Richard J. Herrnstein, "Relative and Absolute Strength of Response as a Function of Frequency of Reinforcement," *Journal of the Experimental Analysis of Behavior* 4 (1961):267–72; Peter A. de Villiers and Richard J. Herrnstein, "Toward a Law of Response Strength," *Psychological Bulletin* 83 (1976):1131–53.

6. The average nectar in the blue flowers is, of course, 2 µl. The average nectar in the yellow flowers is the probability of hitting a flower with nectar (1/3) times the amount of nectar in those flowers (6 µl), which also equals 2 µl.

7. Leslie A. Real, "Animal Choice Behavior and the Evolution of Cognitive Architecture," *Science* 253 (1991):980–86.

8. For a description of the computer game and the correlation with imaging data, see P. Read Montague and Gregory S. Berns, "Neural Economics and the Biological Substrates of Valuation," *Neuron* 36 (2002):265–84.

9. Unpublished data from Read Montague.

10. Harold McGee, *On Food and Cooking: The Science and Lore of the Kitchen* (New York: Scribner, 1984), p. 406.

11. Emiliano Macaluso, Chris D. Frith, and Jon Driver, "Modulation of Human Visual Cortex by Crossmodal Spatial Attention," *Science* 289 (2000): 1206–08.

12. Andro Zangaladze, Charles M. Epstein, Scott T. Grafton, and K. Sathian, "Involvement of Visual Cortex in Tactile Discrimination of Orientation," *Nature* 401 (1999):587–90.

13. S. Baron-Cohen, L. Burt, F. Smith-Laittan, J. Harrison, and P. Bolton, "Synaesthesia: Prevalence and Familiality," *Perception* 25 (1996):1073–79.

14. Richard E. Cytowic, *Synesthesia: A Union of the Senses* (New York: Springer-Verlag, 1989); Richard E. Cytowic, *The Man Who Tasted Shapes: A Bizarre Medical Mystery Offers Revolutionary Insights into Emotions, Reasoning, and Consciousness* (New York: G. P. Putnam's Sons, 1993).

15. V. S. Ramachandran and E. M. Hubbard, "Psychophysical Investigations into the Neural Basis of Synaesthesia," *Proceedings of the Royal Society, London, Series B* 268 (2001):979–83.

16. Anina N. Rich and Jason B. Mattingly, "Anomalous Perception in Synaesthesia: A Cognitive Neuroscience Perspective," *Nature Reviews Neuroscience* 3 (2002):43–52.

17. E. Paulesu, J. Harrison, S. Baron-Cohen, J. D. Watson, L. Goldstein, J. Heather, R. S. Frackowiak, and C. D. Frith, "The Physiology of Coloured Hearing: A Pet Activation Study of Colour-Word Synaesthesia," *Brain* 118 (1995):661–76; J. A. Nunn, L. J. Gregory, M. Brammer, S.C.R. Williams, D. M. Parslow, M. J. Morgan, R. G. Morris, E. T. Bullmore, S. Baron-Cohen, and J. A. Gray, "Functional Magnetic Resonance Imaging of Synesthesia: Activation of V4/V8 by Spoken Words," *Nature Neuroscience* 5 (2002):371–75.

18. Peter G. Grossenbacher and Christopher T. Lovelace, "Mechanisms of Synesthesia: Cognitive and Physiological Constraints," *Trends in Cognitive Sciences* 5 (2001):36–41.

19. Jorge Louis Borges, "El enemigo generoso," in *Selected Poems* (New York: Viking, 1999).

20. Robert Desnos, "J'ai tant rêvé de toi," in *Domaine Public* (Paris: Librairie Gallimard, 1953).

21. Robert Graves, "In Broken Images," in *Poems 1929* (London: Seizin Press, 1929).

22. J. A. Brillat-Savarin, *The Physiology of Taste, or Meditations on Transcendental Gastronomy* (New York: Dover Publications, 1825/1960).

23. Julia A. Chester and Christopher L. Cunningham, "GABAA Receptor Modulation of the Rewarding and Aversive Effects of Alcohol," *Alcohol* 26 (2002):131–43. Rats do not generally like alcohol, but through generations of selectively breeding rats who are not averse to it, an "alcoholism" trait can be

brought out, with the final offspring actually showing a preference for alcohol over water.

24. Of course, some of this may have been familiarity. Salty foods are often paired with alcoholic beverages. See S. J. Caton, M. Ball, A. Ahern, and M. M. Hetherington, "Dose-Dependent Effects of Alcohol on Appetite and Food Intake," *Physiology & Behavior* 81 (2004):51–58.

25. Dana M. Small, Robert J. Zatorre, Alain Dagher, Alan C. Evans, and Marilyn Jones-Gotman, "Changes in Brain Activity Related to Eating Chocolate: From Pleasure to Aversion," *Brain* 124 (2001):1720–33.

26. Louis Petit de Bachaumont, "Secret Memoirs for the History of the Republic," quoted in Sophie D. Coe and Michael D. Coe, *The True History of Chocolate* (London: Thames & Hudson, 1996).

27. Peter J. Havel, "Peripheral Signals Conveying Metabolic Information to the Brain: Short-Term and Long-Term Regulation of Food Intake and Energy Homeostasis," *Experimental Biology and Medicine* 226 (2001):963–77.

28. Paolo Prolo, Ma-Li Wong, and Julio Licinio, "Leptin," *International Journal of Biochemistry & Cell Biology* 30 (1998):1285–90.

29. Julio Licinio, Andre B. Negrao, Christos Mantzoros, Virginia Kaklamani, Ma-Li Wong, Peter B. Bongiorno, Abeda Mulla, et al., "Synchronicity of Frequently Sampled, 24-H Concentrations of Circulating Leptin, Luteinizing Hormone, and Estradiol in Healthy Women," *Proceedings of the National Academy of Sciences, USA* 95 (1998):2541–46.

## Chapter 5: The Electric Pleasuredome

1. Alan W. Scheflin and Edward M. Opton, Jr., *The Mind Manipulators* (New York: Paddington Press, 1978).

2. Ibid.

3. Perhaps the most vivid description of Greystone is that found in Allen Ginsberg's epic poem *Howl*:

. . . Pilgrim State's Rockland's and Greystone's foetid halls, bickering with the echoes of the soul, rocking and rolling in the midnight solitude-bench dolmen-realms of love, dream of life a nightmare, bodies turned to stone as heavy as the moon. . . .

4. Robert G. Heath, *Exploring the Mind-Brain Relationship* (Baton Rouge: Moran Printing, 1996).

5. Arnold J. Mandell, "Psychosurgery—1954" (unpublished ms. 1972).

6. Heath's exact definition of the septal area: "The caudal border of this region is formed by the anterior commissure; the rostral extent is the tip of the anterior horn of the lateral ventricle. It extends medially to the midline space separating

the hemispheres. The dorsal extent is the septum pellucidum and the base of the lateral ventricles. It extends ventrally to the base of the brain and laterally about 5 mm from the midline. The region includes the following structures: nucleus accumbens, ventromedial aspect of the head of the caudate nucleus, the nucleus basalis Meynert, septal nuclei proper, nucleus of the diagonal band of Broca, subcallosal gyrus, rostrum of the corpus callosum, olfactory tubercle, subcallosal fasciculus, and various olfactory pathways." See Heath, *Exploring the Mind-Brain Relationship*.

7. Fundamental to operant learning theory is the recognition of three components of learning: a discriminating stimulus, a response, and a reinforcer or punisher.

8. J. Olds and P. Milner, "Positive Reinforcement Produced by Electrical Stimulation of Septal Area and Other Regions of Rat Brain," *Journal of Comparative Physiology and Psychology* 47 (1954):419–27.

9. In the midline of the brain, between the two cerebral hemispheres, the ventricles are separated by a thin structure, called the septum. The hypothalamus, which is closely linked to the production of many hormones, lies just beneath the septum. It was these regions that Olds and others stimulated.

10. Heath, *Exploring the Mind-Brain Relationship*.

11. Ibid.

12. Robert G. Heath, "Pleasure and Brain Activity in Man: Deep and Surface Electroencephalograms During Orgasm," *Journal of Nervous and Mental Disease* 154 (1972):3–18.

13. In Heath's published articles and in his documentation, he diagnosed patient B-19 as schizophrenic, but that label, prior to the 1970s, could mean almost anything. It wasn't until after this time that psychiatrists codified the symptomatology that defined major mental disorders.

14. It was the publicity stemming from this episode that for the first time, affected Heath's career. Before he died in 1995, Heath catalogued all the data that he had amassed but left specific instructions that the cases of two patients, including the one he showed in 1952, should not be viewed by nonscientists. In fact, these films have, from time to time, been viewed by nonscientists. For similar descriptions, see Judith Hooper and Dick Teresi, *The Three-Pound Universe* (New York: Macmillan, 1986).

15. Scheflin and Opton, *The Mind Manipulators*.

16. The original form of electroconvulsive treatment (ECT) was performed without anesthesia and was called "unmodified." The well-known scene in *One Flew over the Cuckoo's Nest* is a graphic portrayal of unmodified ECT. Current medical practice uses anesthesia to render the patient unconscious prior to inducing a seizure. Insulin shock therapy was the predecessor to ECT. Injecting insulin caused a patient's blood sugar to plummet, which resulted in a seizure. The rationale for inducing seizures remains empirical, but ECT is still the most effective treatment for severe depression. Why it works is still the subject of debate.

## Chapter 6: It Hurts So Good

1. Ronald Melzack and Patrick D. Wall, "Pain Mechanisms: A New Theory," *Science* 150 (1965):921–79; James C. Craig and Gary B. Rollman, "Somesthesis," *Annual Review of Psychology* 50 (1999):305–31.

2. Harold Merskey and Nikolai Bodguk, *Classification of Chronic Pain: Descriptions of Chronic Pain Syndromes and Definitions of Pain Terms*, 2nd ed. (Seattle: IASP Press, 1994).

3. L. R. Watkins and S. F. Maier, "The Pain of Being Sick: Implications of Immune-to-Brain Communication for Understanding Pain," *Annual Review of Psychology* 51 (2000):29–57.

4. Robert M. Sapolsky, "Why Stress Is Bad for Your Brain," *Science* 273 (1996):749–50.

5. Francine du Plessix Gray, *At Home with the Marquis de Sade: A Life* (New York: Penguin Books, 1998).

6. Ibid., p. 64. A cat-o'-nine tails is a whip with multiple tassels, classically nine, and each tassel is about one to two feet long. Usually the tassels are made of leather or rope, but as Sade describes, they can be any material.

7. Leopold von Sacher-Masoch, *Venus in Furs*, trans. Fernanda Savage (1870/1921; reprint, Project Gutenberg).

8. The terminology of the contemporary SM scene can be confusing. As subtypes of SM, we find dominance (doms) and submission (subs) or just DS, which is sometimes called master/slave; we also find bondage and discipline (BD) as a subtype of SM. The acronym BDSM refers to both forms of SM. You also hear of tops and bottoms, sometimes as synonyms for doms and subs. A top is sometimes said to provide the beatings for a masochist, who is actually in control. For further explanation, see Philip Miller and Molly Devon, *Screw the Roses, Send Me the Thorns: The Romance and Sexual Sorcery of Sadomasochism* (Fairfield, Conn.: Mystic Rose Books, 1995).

9. Von Sacher-Masoch, *Venus in Furs*.

10. Leopold von Sacher-Masoch, *Venus in Furs*, trans. Aude Willm (New York: Zone Books, 1870/1989).

11. Dossie Easton and Janet W. Hardy, *The New Topping Book* (Emeryville, Calif.: Greenery Press, 2003); Dossie Easton and Janet W. Hardy, *The New Bottoming Book* (Emeryville, Calif.: Greenery Press, 2001). More vividly, see Pauline Réage, *Story of O*, trans. Sabine d'Estrée (New York: Ballantine Books, 1954/1965).

12. Richard von Krafft-Ebing, *Psychopathia Sexualis: A Medico-Forensic Study*, trans. Harry E. Wedeck, first unexpurgated ed. in English (New York: G. P. Putnam's Sons, 1886/1965).

13. Ibid., p. 127.

14. Sigmund Freud, *Beyond the Pleasure Principle*, trans. James Strachey, standard ed. (New York: W. W. Norton, 1961).

15. Antonio R. Damasio, *Descartes' Error: Emotion, Reason, and the Human Brain* (New York: Putnam, 1994).

16. David Julius and Allan I. Basbaum, "Molecular Mechanisms of Nociception," *Nature* 413 (2001):203–10.

17. Henry Head and Gordon Holmes, "Sensory Disturbances from Cerebral Lesions," *Brain* 34 (1911):102–254; Rolf-Detlef Treede, Daniel R. Kenshalo, Richard H. Gracely, and Anthony K. P. Jones, "The Cortical Representation of Pain," *Pain* 79 (1999):105–11.

18. M. C. Bushnell, G. H. Duncan, R. K. Hofbauer, B. Ha, J.-I. Chen, and B. Carrier, "Pain Perception: Is There a Role for Primary Somatosensory Cortex?" *Proceedings of the National Academy of Sciences, USA* 96 (1999):7705–09.

19. Donald D. Price, "Psychological and Neural Mechanisms of the Affective Dimension of Pain," *Science* 288 (2000):1769–72.

20. Ronald Melzack and Joel Katz, "Pain Measurement in Persons in Pain," in *Textbook of Pain*, ed. Patrick D. Wall and Ronald Melzack (London: Churchill Livingstone, 1994).

21. Price, "Psychological and Neural Mechanisms of the Affective Dimension of Pain"; Howard L. Fields, "Pain: An Unpleasant Topic," *Pain* Supplement 6 (1999):S61–S69; Richard H. Gracely, "Studies of Pain in Normal Man," in *Textbook of Pain*, ed. Patrick D. Wall and Ronald Melzack (London: Churchill Livingstone, 1994).

22. Subtle psychological differences between actual control, perceived control, and self-efficacy (confidence in one's ability) may mediate different aspects of the pain response—e.g., pain threshold and pain tolerance. See Mark D. Litt, "Self-Efficacy and Perceived Control: Cognitive Mediators of Pain Tolerance," *Journal of Personality and Social Psychology* 54 (1988):149–60; Sharon L. Baker and Irving Kirsch, "Cognitive Mediators of Pain Perception and Tolerance," *Journal of Personality and Social Psychology* 61 (1991):504–10; Albert Bandura, Delia Cioffi, C. Barr Taylor, and Mary E. Brouillard, "Perceived Self-Efficacy in Coping with Cognitive Stressors and Opioid Activation," *Journal of Personality and Social Psychology* 55 (1988):479–88.

23. Madelon A. Visintainer, Joseph R. Volpicelli, and Martin E. P. Seligman, "Tumor Rejection in Rats After Inescapable or Escapable Shock," *Science* 216 (1982):437–39.

24. Sondra T. Bland, Carin Twining, Linda R. Watkins, and Steven F. Maier, "Stressor Controllability Modulates Stress-Induced Serotonin but Not Dopamine Efflux in the Nucleus Accumbens Shell," *Synapse* 49 (2003):206–08; Simona Cabib and Stefano Puglisi-Allegra, "Opposite Responses of Mesolimbic Dopamine System to Controllable and Uncontrollable Aversive Experiences," *Journal of Neuroscience* 14 (1994):3333–40.

25. Robert W. Gear, K. O. Aley, and Jon D. Levine, "Pain-Induced Analgesia Mediated by Mesolimbic Reward Circuits," *Journal of Neuroscience* 19 (1999):

7175–81; Nadege Altier and Jane Stewart, "The Role of Dopamine in the Nucleus Accumbens in Analgesia," *Life Sciences* 65 (1999):2269–87.

26. N. Hagelberg, I. K. Martikainen, H. Mansikka, S. Hinkka, K. Nagren, J. Hietala, H. Scheinin, and A. Pertovaara, "Dopamine D2 Receptor Binding in the Human Brain Is Associated with the Response to Painful Stimulation and Pain Modulatory Capacity," *Pain* 99 (2002):273–79.

27. Lino Becerra, Hans C. Breiter, Roy Wise, R. Gilberto Gonzalez, and David Borsook, "Reward Circuitry Activation by Noxious Thermal Stimuli," *Neuron* 32 (2001):927–46.

28. Jimmy Jensen, Anthony R. McIntosh, Adrian P. Crawley, David J. Mikulis, Gary Remington, and Shitij Kapur, "Direct Activation of the Ventral Striatum in Anticipation of Aversive Stimuli," *Neuron* 40 (2003):1251–57.

29. Hugo Besedovsky, Adriana del Rey, Ernst Sorkin, and Charles A. Dinarello, "Immunoregulatory Feedback Between Interleukin-1 and Glucocorticoid Hormones," *Science* 233 (1986):652–54.

30. E. Ron de Kloet, Melly S. Oitzl, and Marian Joëls, "Stress and Cognition: Are Corticosteroids Good or Bad Guys?" *Trends in Neurosciences* 22 (1999): 422–26.

31. Pier Vincenzo Piazza and Michel Le Moal, "The Role of Stress in Drug Self-Administration," *Trends in Pharmacologic Science* 19 (1998):67–74; Michela Marinelli and Pier Vincenzo Piazza, "Interaction Between Glucocorticoid Hormones, Stress and Psychostimulant Drugs," *European Journal of Neuroscience* 16 (2002):387–94. The effect of cortisol blockers on humans is not as clear as in rats. When ketoconazole was tried as a treatment for heroin addicts, it actually increased their use of cocaine. But to prevent adrenal insufficiency in these patients, they were also given hydrocortisone, the synthetic form of cortisol, which probably negated the effect of the ketoconazole. See T. R. Kosten, A. Oliveto, K. A. Sevarino, K. Gonsai, and A. Feingold, "Ketoconazole Increases Cocaine and Opioid Use in Methadone Maintained Patients," *Drug and Alcohol Dependence* 66 (2002):173–80. Currently, there are no published reports on the use of RU-486 as a treatment for drug abuse in humans.

32. Dexamethasone, however, does not get into the brain easily and would not be expected to have significant mood-altering effects on its own, except at high doses.

33. Werner Plihal, Rosemarie Krug, Reinhard Pietrowsky, Horst L. Fehm, and Jan Born, "Corticosteroid Receptor Mediated Effects on Mood in Humans," *Psychoneuroendocrinology* 21 (1996):515–23; Sonia J. Lupien, Charles W. Wilkinson, Sophie Brière, Catherine Ménard, N. M. K. Ng Ying Kin, and N. P. V. Nair, "The Modulatory Effects of Corticosteroids on Cognition: Studies in Young Human Populations," *Psychoneuroendocrinology* 27 (2002):401–16; Heather C. Abercrombie, Ned H. Kalin, Marchell E. Thurow, Melissa A. Rosenkranz, and Richard J. Davidson, "Cortisol Variation in Humans Affects Memory for

Emotionally Laden and Neutral Information," *Behavioral Neuroscience* 117 (2003):505–16.

34. Bernard P. Schimmer and Keith L. Parker, "Adrenocorticotropic Hormone; Adrenocortical Steroids and Their Synthetic Analogs; Inhibitors of the Synthesis and Actions of Adrenocortical Hormones," in *Goodman & Gilman's The Pharmacological Basis of Therapeutics*, ed. Joel G. Hardman and Lee E. Limbird (New York: McGraw-Hill, 2001).

## Chapter 7: Running High

1. Although the measurement of salivary cortisol is not difficult, its relationship to cortisol in the bloodstream is complex. The concentration of cortisol in the saliva parallels the concentration of free cortisol in the blood, but variable percentages of cortisol in the blood are bound to proteins, effectively locking up to half the cortisol. Moreover, unless the saliva is frozen, enzymes may degrade cortisol, giving a low measurement. The half-life of a chemical in the body is the amount of time it takes for its concentration to drop by half and is determined by a variety of factors, including whether it is fat- or water-soluble and the rate at which the liver and kidneys break it down. See C. Kirschbaum and D. H. Hellhammer, "Salivary Cortisol in Psychobiological Research: An Overview," *Neuropsychobiology* 22 (1989):150–69.

2. Csikszentmihaly, *Flow: The Psychology of Optimal Experience*.

3. Hal V. Hall, *The Western States Trail Guide* (Auburn: Auburn Printers, 1998).

4. Daniel P. Davis, John S. Videen, Allen Marino, Gary M. Vilke, James V. Dunford, Steven P. Van Camp, and Lewis G. Maharam, "Exercise-Induced Hyponatremia in Marathon Runners: A Two-Year Experience," *Journal of Emergency Medicine* 21 (2001):47–57; J. Carlos Ayus, Joseph Varon, and Allen I. Arieff, "Hyponatremia, Cerebral Edema, and Noncardiogenic Pulmonary Edema in Marathon Runners," *Annals of Internal Medicine* 132 (2000):711–14. Although the overconsumption of water contributes to hyponatremia, females seem to be more predisposed than males, and the use of analgesics like ibuprofen also increases the risk of developing hyponatremia.

5. Mark R. Rosenzweig and Edward L. Bennett, "Psychobiology of Plasticity: Effects of Training and Experience on Brain and Behavior," *Behavioural Brain Research* 78 (1996):57–65.

6. James E. Black, Krystyna R. Isaacs, Brenda J. Anderson, Adriana A. Alcantara, and William T. Greenough, "Learning Causes Synaptogenesis, Whereas Motor Activity Causes Angiogenesis, in Cerebellar Cortex of Adult Rats," *Proceedings of the National Academy of Sciences, USA* 87 (1990):5568–72.

7. James D. Churchill, Roberto Galvez, Stanley Colcombe, Rodney A. Swain, Arthur F. Kramer, and William T. Greenough, "Exercise, Experience and the Aging Brain," *Neurobiology of Aging* 23 (2002):941–55.

8. G. Kempermann, H. G. Kuhn, and F. H. Gage, "More Hippocampal Neurons in Adult Mice Living in an Enriched Environment," *Nature* 386 (1997): 493–95.

9. Not everyone agrees that the BrdU technique proves the existence of adult neurogenesis. The main criticism is that although BrdU indicates DNA synthesis, it does not necessarily indicate cell division. BrdU-labeled cells could, for example, be repairing themselves. And even if the labeled cells were new neurons, nobody knew if these neurons functioned. For both sides of the neurogenesis argument, see Pasko Rakic, "Adult Neurogenesis in Mammals: An Identity Crisis," *Journal of Neuroscience* 22 (2002):614–18; and Elizabeth Gould and Charles G. Gross, "Neurogenesis in Adult Mammals: Some Progress and Problems," *Journal of Neuroscience* 22 (2002):619–23.

10. Henriette van Praag, Brian R. Christie, Terrence J. Sejnowski, and Fred H. Gage, "Running Enhances Neurogenesis, Learning, and Long-Term Potentiation in Mice," *Proceedings of the National Academy of Sciences, USA* 96 (1999): 13427–31.

11. J. D. Bremner, P. Randall, T. M. Scott, R. A. Bronen, J. P. Seibyl, S. M. Southwick, R. C. Delaney, G. McCarthy, D. S. Charney, and R. B. Innis, "MRI-Based Measurement of Hippocampal Volume in Patients with Combat-Related Posttraumatic Stress Disorder," *American Journal of Psychiatry* 152 (1995):973–81.

12. Sapolsky, "Why Stress Is Bad for Your Brain."

13. Churchill, Galvez, Colcombe, Swain, Kramer, and Greenough, "Exercise, Experience and the Aging Brain"; Carl W. Cotman and Nicole C. Berchtold, "Exercise: A Behavioral Intervention to Enhance Brain Health and Plasticity," *Trends in Neurosciences* 25 (2002):295–301.

14. Kenji Hashimoto, Eiji Shimizu, and Masaomi Iyo, "Critical Role of Brain-Derived Neurotrophic Factor in Mood Disorders," *Brain Research Reviews* 45 (2004):104–14.

15. Amanda D. Smith and Michael J. Zigmond, "Can the Brain Be Protected Through Exercise?: Lessons from an Animal Model of Parkinsonism," *Experimental Neurology* 184 (2003):31–39.

16. P. E. Di Prampero, C. Capelli, P. Pagliaro, G. Antonutto, M. Girardis, P. Zamparo, and R. G. Soule, "Energetics of Best Performances in Middle-Distance Running," *Journal of Applied Physiology* 74 (1993):2318–24.

17. The total metabolic cost is not highly dependent on the runner's pace. Running faster requires more kcals/min, but since the distance is covered in less time, the total energy *per mile* remains approximately constant.

18. Jeffrey F. Horowitz, "Fatty Acid Mobilization from Adipose Tissue During Exercise," *Trends in Endocrinology and Metabolism* 14 (2003):386–92.

19. In addition to carbohydrates and fats, proteins can be metabolized for energy, but they are not a major source of energy except under starvation conditions.

20. Ronald J. Maughan and Louise M. Burke, *Sports Nutrition: Handbook of Sports Medicine* (Oxford, UK: Blackwell Science, 2002). The quadriceps contain

the bulk of usable glycogen, which at moderate intensity can be consumed in two to four hours.

21. H. Maurice Goodman, *Basic Medical Endocrinology*, 3rd ed. (San Diego: Academic Press, 2003).

22. Theodore B. VanItallie and Thomas H. Nufert, "Ketones: Metabolism's Ugly Duckling," *Nutrition Reviews* 61 (2003):327–41; Lori Laffel, "Ketone Bodies: A Review of Physiology, Pathophysiology and Application of Monitoring to Diabetes," *Diabetes/Metabolism Research and Reviews* 15 (1999):412–26.

23. Steen G. Hasselbach, Peter L. Madsen, Lars P. Hageman, Karsten S. Olsen, Niels Justesen, Soren Holm, and Olaf B. Paulson, "Changes in Cerebral Blood Flow and Carbohydrate Metabolism During Acute Hyperketonemia," *American Journal of Physiology (Endocrinology and Metabolism)* 270 (1996):E746–E51. Subsequent studies with MRI confirmed that the availability of ketones determines what the brain uses for fuel, but the mechanism that regulates the relative use of glucose and ketones remains unknown.

24. J. W. Pan, F. W. Telang, J. H. Lee, R. A. de Graaf, D. L. Rothman, D. T. Stein, and H. P. Hetherington, "Measurement of B-Hydroxybutyrate in Acute Hyperketonemia in the Human Brain," *Journal of Neurochemistry* 79 (2001):539–44.

25. W. G. Lennox, "Ketogenic Diet in the Treatment of Epilepsy," *New England Journal of Medicine* 199 (1928):74–75.

26. R. S. El-Mallakh and M. E. Paskitti, "The Ketogenic Diet May Have Mood-Stabilizing Properties," *Medical Hypotheses* 57 (2001):724–26.

27. Amanda E. Greene, Mariana T. Todorova, and Thomas N. Seyfried, "Perspectives on the Metabolic Management of Epilepsy Through Dietary Reduction of Glucose and Elevation of Ketone Bodies," *Journal of Neurochemistry* 86 (2003):529–37.

28. Yoshiro Kashiwaya, Takao Takeshima, Nozomi Mori, Kenji Nakashimi, Kieran Clarke, and Richard L. Veech, "D-B-Hydroxybutyrate Protects Neurons in Models of Alzheimer's and Parkinson's Disease," *Proceedings of the National Academy of Sciences, USA* 97 (2000):5440–44.

29. Allan Rechtschaffen, Marcia A. Gilliland, Bernard M. Bergmann, and Jacqueline B. Winter, "Physiological Correlates of Prolonged Sleep Deprivation in Rats," *Science* 221 (1983):182–84.

30. L. J. West, H. H. Janszen, B. K. Lester, and F. S. Cornelisoon, "The Psychosis of Sleep Deprivation," *Annals of the New York Academy of Sciences* 96 (1962):66–70.

31. Harvey Babkoff, Helen C. Sing, David R. Thorne, Sander G. Genser, and Frederick W. Hegge, "Perceptual Distortions and Hallucinations Reported During the Course of Sleep Deprivation," *Perceptual and Motor Skills* 68 (1989):787–98.

32. Anna Wirz-Justice and Rutger H. Van den Hoofdakker, "Sleep Deprivation in Depression: What Do We Know, Where Do We Go?" *Biological Psychiatry* 46 (1999):445–53.

33. D. Ebert, H. Feistel, W. Kaschka, A. Barocka, and A. Pirner, "Single Photon Emission Computerized Tomography Assessment of Cerebral Dopamine D2 Receptor Blockade in Depression Before and After Sleep Deprivation—Preliminary Results," *Biological Psychiatry* 35 (1994):880–85; Karen J. Maloney, Lynda Mainville, and Barbara E. Jones, "C-Fos Expression in Dopaminergic and GABAergic Neurons of the Ventral Mesencephalic Tegmentum After Paradoxical Sleep Deprivation and Recovery," *European Journal of Neuroscience* 15 (2002): 774–78; Monica Levy Anderson, Magda Bignotto, and Sergio Tufik, "Facilitation of Ejaculation After Methamphetamine Administration in Paradoxical Sleep Deprived Rats," *Brain Research* 978 (2003):31–37.

34. The origins of this quotation are obscure, but it is sometimes attributed to Aeschylus. Versions of it are always used to open the modern Olympic Games.

35. Arnold J. Mandell, "The Second Second Wind," *Psychiatric Annals* 9 (1979):57–64.

36. Candace B. Pert and Solomon H. Snyder, "Opiate Receptor: Demonstration in Nervous Tissue," *Science* 179 (1973):1011–14; Avram Goldstein, "Opioid Peptides (Endorphins) in Pituitary and Brain," *Science* 193 (1976):1081–86.

37. For example, H. C. Heitkamp, K. Schmid, and K. Scheib, "Beta-Endorphin and Adrenocorticotropic Hormone Production During Marathon and Incremental Exercise," *European Journal of Applied Physiology and Occupational Physiology* 66 (1993):269–74; L. Schwarz and W. Kindermann, "Changes in Beta-Endorphin Levels in Response to Aerobic and Anaerobic Exercise," *Sports Medicine* 13 (1992):25–36; L. Schwarz and W. Kindermann, "Beta-Endorphin, Catecholamines, and Cortisol During Exhaustive Endurance Exercise," *International Journal of Sports Medicine* 10 (1989):324–8; P.-E. Fournier, J. Stalder, B. Mermillod, and A. Chantraine, "Effects of a 110 Kilometers Ultra-Marathon Race on Plasma Hormone Levels," *International Journal of Sports Medicine* 18 (1997):252–56.

38. For a review of the endogenous opioid system, see Howard B. Gutstein and Huda Akil, "Opioid Analgesics," in *Goodman & Gilman's The Pharmacological Basis of Therapeutics*, ed. Joel G. Hardman and Lee E. Limbird (New York: McGraw-Hill, 2001).

39. Nina Balthasar, Roberto Coppari, Julie McMinn, Shun M. Liu, Charlotte E. Lee, Vinsee Tang, Christopher D. Kenny, et al., "Leptin Receptor Signaling in POMC Neurons Is Required for Normal Body Weight Homeostasis," *Neuron* 42 (2004):983–91.

40. Heinz Harbach, Kornelia Hell, Christian Gramsch, Norbert Katz, Gunter Hempelmann, and Hansjörg Teschemacher, "Beta-Endorphin (1–31) in the Plasma of Male Volunteers Undergoing Physical Exercise," *Psychoneuroendocrinology* 25 (2000):551–62.

41. Mandell, "The Second Second Wind."

## Chapter 8: Iceland: The Experience

1. Diener, Diener, and Diener, "Factors Predicting the Subjective Well-Being of Nations."

2. T. Willis, "Instructions for Curing the Watching-Evil." In *London Practice of Physik*, 1685, cited in Juliane Winkelmann, "Restless Legs Syndrome," *Archives of Neurology* 56 (1999):1526–27.

3. K. P. Parker and D. B. Rye, "Restless Legs Syndrome and Periodic Limb Movement Disorder," *Nursing Clinics of North America* 37 (2002):655–73.

4. C. Lombardi, F. Provini, R. Vetrugno, G. Plazzi, E. Lugaresi, and P. Montagna, "Pelvic Movements as Rhythmic Motor Manifestation Associated with Restless Legs Syndrome," *Movement Disorders* 18 ( 2003):110–113.

5. Icelandic genealogy begins with two major documents, *Íslendingabók* (Book of Icelanders) and *Landnámabók* (Book of Settlements), both probably written between the eleventh and twelfth centuries. *Landnámabók* mentions 3,500 people by name, more than 400 of whom were original settlers. The Sagas of Iceland provide another type of historical documentation, but they are generally a mixture of fact and fiction.

6. International Human Genome Sequencing Consortium, "Finishing the Euchromatic Sequence of the Human Genome," *Nature* 431 (2004):931–45.

7. For opposing views of genome-wide scan versus specific gene loci mapping, see Jeffrey R. Gulcher, Augustine Kong, and Kári Stefánsson, "The Role of Linkage Studies for Common Diseases," *Current Opinion in Genetics and Development* 11 (2001):264–67; and Neil J. Risch, "Searching for Genetic Determinants in the New Millennium," *Nature* 405 (2000):847–56.

8. I use the Icelandic tradition of referring to people by their first name. The surname reflects who a person's father was—e.g., *Stefánsson* and *Stefansdottir* indicate the son and daughter of Stefan, respectively. Surnames are almost never used in Icelandic common speech, and customary titles of respect like *Mister* and *Doctor* are not used either.

9. A. Helgason, S. Sigurðardottir, J. R. Gulcher, R. Ward, and K. Stefánsson, "MtDNA and the Origin of the Icelanders: Deciphering Signals of Recent Population History," *American Journal of Human Genetics* 66 (2000):999–1016; A. Helgason, S. Sigurðardottir, J. Nicholson, B. Sykes, E. W. Hill, D. G. Bradley, V. Bosnes, J. R. Gulcher, R. Ward, and K. Stefánsson, "Estimating Scandinavian and Gaelic Ancestry in the Male Settlers of Iceland," *American Journal of Human Genetics* 67 (2000):697–717.

10. Huntington's disease is not really caused by a defective gene. It is caused by an expansion of junk DNA adjacent to a gene called huntington, whose function is not fully known.

11. Snorri lived about two hundred years after the Age of Settlements in Iceland.

12. The Prose Edda is distinguished from the Poetic (or Elder) Edda, which is a much older collection of verse, compiled over the previous centuries from a variety of sources. The Elder Edda was a major source of Snorri's material, but Snorri also drew upon oral tradition. See Snorri Sturluson, *Edda*, trans. Anthony Faulkes (London: Everyman, 1987). For translations of the Poetic Edda, see *The Poetic Edda*, trans. Carolyne Larrington (Oxford: Oxford University Press, 1996); Anonymous, *The Poetic Edda*, trans. Lee M. Hollander (Austin: University of Texas Press, 2003).

13. Jules Verne, *Journey to the Centre of the Earth*, trans. Robert Baldick (London: Penguin Books, 1965).

14. David Roberts and Jon Krakauer, *Iceland: Land of the Sagas* (New York: Villard Books, 1990).

15. *Bárdar Saga*, trans. Jon Skaptason and Phillip Pulsiano (New York: Garland Publishing, 1984).

16. "The Saga of the People of Laxardal," in *The Sagas of Icelanders: A Selection* (New York: Penguin Books, 1997).

17. Much of this material also appears in Gudrun's self-published pamphlet; see Gudrun G. Bergmann, *The Mystique of Snaefellsjökull* (Olafsvik: Leidarljos, 1999).

18. Halldór Laxness, *World Light*, trans. Magnus Magnusson (Madison: University of Wisconsin Press, 1969).


## Chapter 9: Sex, Love, and the Crucible of Satisfaction

1. G. Bermant, "Sexual Behavior: Hard Times with the Coolidge Effect," in *Psychological Research: The Inside Story*, ed. Michael H. Siegel and H. Philip Zeigler (New York: Harper & Row, 1976).

2. This argument is based heavily on the differences in sexual behavior between homosexual men and homosexual women. Symons suggests that the behavior of homosexuals offers the perfect test case of what men and women would do sexually if they were unconstrained by the contingencies of the other sex. Homosexual men, Symons points out, invariably have many sexual partners, often onetime encounters, whereas homosexual women do not. This sexual dimorphism exists in heterosexuals, but it is throttled by sexual selection and the need to modify behavior if one is to reproduce. See Donald Symons, *The Evolution of Human Sexuality* (New York: Oxford University Press, 1979).

3. It has been suggested that sexual motivation can be understood as an entirely mechanistic response. See Anders Agmo, "Sexual Motivation—An Inquiry into Events Determining the Occurrence of Sexual Behavior," *Behavioural Brain Research* 105 (1999):129–50.

4. Jared Diamond, *Why Is Sex Fun?: The Evolution of Human Sexuality* (New York: Basic Books, 1997).

5. Alfred C. Kinsey, Wardell B. Pomeroy, and Clyde E. Martin, *Sexual Behavior in the Human Male* (Philadelphia: W. B. Saunders, 1948); Alfred C. Kinsey, Wardell B. Pomeroy, Clyde E. Martin, and Paul H. Gebhard, *Sexual Behavior in the Human Female* (Philadelphia: W. B. Saunders, 1953).

6. Kinsey's overestimate of the prevalence of many sexual practices stemmed from the fact that the people who volunteered for his study tended to be the most sexually active and experimental individuals.

7. Shere Hite, *The Hite Report: A Nationwide Study of Female Sexuality* (New York: Dell, 1976).

8. Only 3 percent responded to Hite's questionnaire, raising the question of whether those women who responded were an accurate representation of the female population.

9. Charles Darwin, *The Descent of Man, and Selection in Relation to Sex* (Princeton: Princeton University Press, 1981).

10. Geoffrey Miller, *The Mating Mind: How Sexual Choice Shaped the Evolution of Human Nature* (New York: Anchor Books, 2001).

11. David M. Buss, "Sex Differences in Human Mate Preferences: Evolutionary Hypotheses Tested in 37 Cultures," *Behavioral and Brain Sciences* 12 (1989): 1–49.

12. Actually, physical traits can become markers for other, hidden, traits if people with one consistently mate with the other. For example, if tall people mate with smart people, then the result will be that height is an indicator of intelligence.

13. In a massive survey of 16,288 people across the world, psychologists found that men consistently desired about three times as many partners in any given time period as did women. See David P. Schmitt, "Universal Sex Differences in the Desire for Sexual Variety: Tests from 52 Nations, 6 Continents, and 13 Islands," *Journal of Personality and Social Psychology* 85 (2003):85–104.

14. Symons, *The Evolution of Human Sexuality*.

15. Miller, *The Mating Mind: How Sexual Choice Shaped the Evolution of Human Nature*.

16. Joseph B. Stanford, George L. White, and Harry Hatasaka, "Timing Intercourse to Achieve Pregnancy: Current Evidence," *Obstetrics & Gynecology* 100 (2002):1333–41; Allen J. Wilcox, Clarice R. Weinberg, and Donna D. Baird, "Timing of Sexual Intercourse in Relation to Ovulation—Effects on the Probability of Conception, Survival of the Pregnancy, and Sex of the Baby," *New England Journal of Medicine* 333 (1995):1517–21.

17. If the probability of viable pregnancy in a single menstrual cycle is 0.25 for daily sex, then the probability of *not* becoming pregnant is 0.75. After $n$ months of daily sex, the probability of still not being pregnant is $0.75^n$, and so the probability of having a viable pregnancy is $1 - 0.75^n$.

18. David M. Buss, *The Dangerous Passion: Why Jealousy Is as Necessary as Love and Sex* (New York: Free Press, 2000).

19. David M. Buss and Todd K. Shackelford, "From Vigilance to Violence: Mate Retention Tactics in Married Couples," *Journal of Personality and Social Psychology* 72 (1997):346–61. Buss's study focused on young couples, in their prime reproductive years, for whom issues of reproduction might be most salient; the extent to which these tactics played out in older couples was not addressed.

20. Sarah Blaffer Hrdy, *Mother Nature: A History of Mothers, Infants, and Natural Selection* (New York: Pantheon, 1999).

21. In a study of 2,708 females, 13.8 percent of 145 extra-pair copulations (EPC) occurred during the ovulatory phase of the menstrual cycle and were preceded in most cases by intra-pair copulations (IPC). EPCs were rarely followed by IPCs. See James V. Kohl, Michaela Atzmueller, Bernhard Fink, and Karl Grammer, "Human Pheromones: Integrating Neuroendocrinology and Ethology," *Neuroendocrinology Letters* 22 (2001):309–21.; M. A. Bellis and R. R. Baker, "Do Females Promote Sperm Competition?: Data for Humans," *Animal Behavior* 40 (1991):991–99.

22. Martha McClintock, "Menstrual Synchrony and Suppression," *Nature* 229 (1971):244–45.

23. Kathleen Stern and Martha McClintock, "Regulation of Ovulation by Human Pheromones," *Nature* 392 (1998):177–79.

24. D. B. Gower and B. A. Ruparelia, "Olfaction in Humans with Special Reference to Odorous 16-Androstenes: Their Occurrence, Perception and Possible Social, Psychological and Sexual Impact," *Journal of Endocrinology* 137 (1993):167–87; Ivanka Savic, Hans Berglund, Balazs Gulyas, and Per Roland, "Smelling of Odorous Sex Hormone-Like Compounds Causes Sex-Differentiated Hypothalamic Activation in Humans," *Neuron* 31 (2001):661–68; Kohl, Atzmueller, Fink, and Grammer, "Human Pheromones: Integrating Neuroendocrinology and Ethology."

25. Savic, Berglund, Gulyas, and Roland, "Smelling of Odorous Sex Hormone-Like Compounds Causes Sex-Differentiated Hypothalamic Activation in Humans."

26. Theories abound for why menstrual synchronization exists. A variant of the "sex-for-meat" theory suggests that women synchronized menstruation to organize a sex strike, forcing men to go out hunting. See Chris Knight, *Blood Relations: Menstruation and the Origin of Culture* (New Haven: Yale University Press, 1991). Another theory posits that synchronization forced each man to pair up with one woman, because if all the women were fertile at the same time, there would be no way he could mate with all of them. See Leonard Shlain, *Sex, Time, and Power: How Women's Sexuality Shaped Human Evolution* (New York: Viking, 2003).

27. Richard T. Michael, Robert W. Bonsall, and Patricia Warner, "Human Vaginal Secretions: Volatile Fatty Acid Content," *Science* 186 (1974):1217–19.

28. Alain Danielou, *The Complete Kama Sutra: The First Unabridged Modern Translation of the Classic Indian Text by Vatsyayana*, trans. Alain Danielou (Rochester, Vermont: Park Street Press, 1994).

29. Edward O. Laumann, John H. Gagnon, Robert T. Michael, and Stuart Michaels, *The Social Organization of Sexuality: Sexual Practices in the United States* (Chicago: University of Chicago Press, 1994).

30. Ibid., Table 3.8B.

31. Ibid., Table 10.4. We can infer that some people report being happy despite not having an orgasm; however, the NHSLS data were not analyzed in this manner, so we do not know what percentage these people represent.

32. Agmo, "Sexual Motivation—An Inquiry into Events Determining the Occurrence of Sexual Behavior."

33. Laumann, Gagnon, Michael, and Michaels, *The Social Organization of Sexuality: Sexual Practices in the United States*, Table 10.5.

34. William H. Masters and Virginia E. Johnson, *Human Sexual Response* (Boston: Little, Brown, 1966).

35. Their methods relied on the collection of flowback after sex, which—although they claimed it was easily done—I found to be problematic. Of 127 flowback samples, 93 came from one couple, a 44-year-old male and 24-year-old female, so their conclusions are necessarily drawn predominately from this couple, separated in age by twenty years. See R. Robin Baker and Mark A. Bellis, "Human Sperm Competition: Ejaculate by Males and the Function of Masturbation," *Animal Behavior* 46 (1993):861–85; R. Robin Baker and Mark A. Bellis, "Human Sperm Competition: Ejaculate Manipulation by Females and a Function for the Female Orgasm," *Animal Behavior* 46 (1993):887–909.

36. Michael S. Exton, Anne Bindert, Tillman Kruger, Friedmann Scheller, Uwe Hartmann, and Manfred Schedlowski, "Cardiovascular and Endocrine Alterations After Masturbation-Induced Orgasm in Women," *Psychosomatic Medicine* 61 (1999):280–89.

37. J. K. Rilling, D. A. Gutman, T. R. Zeh, G. Pagnoni, G. S. Berns, and C. D. Kilts, "A Neural Basis for Social Cooperation," *Neuron* 35 (2002):395–405.

38. Laumann, Gagnon, Michael, and Michaels, *The Social Organization of Sexuality: Sexual Practices in the United States*; Robert T. Michael, John H. Gagnon, Edward O. Laumann, and Gina Kolata, *Sex in America: A Definitive Survey* (New York: Warner Books, 1994).

39. The prevalence of male infidelity, however, increases with the duration of marriage, implying a constant rate of infidelity of about 1 percent per year.

40. Laumann, Gagnon, Michael, and Michaels, *The Social Organization of Sexuality: Sexual Practices in the United States*, Table 3.7.

41. The "seven-year itch," although an invention by the playright George Axelrod for his play of the same name, has a kernel of truth. Seven years is probably about the average half-life of enamoration with one's partner for a variety of reasons. Helen Fisher believes the half-life of a relationship to be even shorter,

about four years. See Helen E. Fisher, *Anatomy of Love: The Natural History of Monogamy, Adultery, and Divorce* (New York: W. W. Norton, 1992).

42. David Schnarch, *Passionate Marriage: Love, Sex, and Intimacy in Emotionally Committed Relationships* (New York: Henry Holt and Company, 1997); David M. Schnarch, *Constructing the Sexual Crucible: An Integration of Sexual and Marital Therapy* (New York: W. W. Norton, 1991).

43. Schnarch, *Passionate Marriage: Love, Sex, and Intimacy in Emotionally Committed Relationships.*

# ACKNOWLEDGMENTS

——•——

I am grateful to the many people who appear in this book for sharing their thoughts and allowing me to write about them in a highly personal way. Read Montague, my longtime friend and collaborator, deserves special thanks; without his penchant for pancakes, none of this might have happened. Dan Winstead, at Tulane, was very generous in allowing me to see the Heath films. Arnold Mandell freely shared an unpublished manuscript he had written about his years with Heath; the material helped fill in many blanks. My trip to Cuba was made possible thanks to the efforts of Mark Rasenick to bring together U.S. and Cuban scientists. Special thanks to Dan Ariely for sharing his bodysuit and his own experience with pain. Ragan Petrie and Janice Anderson went out on a limb to meet with me in the first place, which I am sure must have seemed like some crackpot idea, but they showed me something special indeed. Behind the scenes, thanks to all the volunteers at the Western States Run, particularly Greg Soderlund—the race director—and Heidi Ryan and the Shadowcase Running Club for staffing the Highway 49 aid station.

Peter Kaminsky, who I'm sure must curse the day he sent me an e-mail about the effects of food on the brain, not only shared his thoughts with me but introduced me to the world of professional chefs and offered writing suggestions early on. To Francis Mallmann: blame Peter for sending me your way. Francis's hospitality and willingness to open his home to a complete stranger strikes me as a rarity these days and something to be admired.

In Iceland, Bodvar Thorisson took my questions in stride, but without his knowledge of contemporary Icelandic culture I would never have known to seek out Geir Wegge, who is truly a modern-day Homer. I am also grateful to Gudlauger and Gudrun Bergmann, owners of the Hotel Brekkabauer, for introducing me to another side of Icelandic culture. And without Dave Rye's unflagging enthusiasm for the country, I wouldn't have made the trip in the first place, which was unforgettable, to say the least. Dave also read many drafts of the manuscript and provided helpful suggestions.

None of this would have been possible without the support and patience of my parents—Michael and Roberta Berns—and colleagues at Emory that anyone working at a university should hope for. Chuck Raison, Andy Miller, Lucile Capuron, Clint Kilts, Mike Owens, Robert Bonsall, Jay Weiss, Krish Sathian, and Steve Levey all listened patiently, read drafts, and suffered my endless blabbering about "the book." That they still speak to me says volumes about their patience. The chairman of my department, Charles Nemeroff, encouraged me in this project of potentially dubious academic value when I probably should have been doing something else, and I will always be grateful for that. The experiments that started me down this path would not have been done were it not for the dedication and talent of the people in my lab—Megan Martin-Skurski, Giuseppe Pagnoni, Cary Zink, and Jonathan Chappelow. Most of this research was made possible by funding from the

National Institute on Drug Abuse and the continuing support of Steven Grant, David Shurtleff, and Joe Frascella. Outside of Emory, my fellow neuroeconomists—Hans Breiter, Colin Camerer, Jonathan Cohen, Randy Gallistel, Paul Glimcher, Brian Knutson, George Loewenstein, Kevin McCabe, Drazen Prelec, and Aldo Rustichini— have changed the way I think about motivation and decision making, and they listened patiently to me as I explained my problems with sushi.

My literary agent, Susan Arellano, along with Susan Rabiner, believed in the potential of this project before it even was a project and, despite my complete naïveté about book publishing, guided me through the process with professionalism and tough love. Vanessa Mobley was the one who believed in it enough to bring me into the fold of Henry Holt and Company, and apart from editing the book, acted as writing therapist, coach, and friend.

In the end, the final thanks and apologies are due my family, and especially my wife, Kathleen. My obsession with novelty has dragged us all through the crucible, and even though none asked for it, we have all changed.

# INDEX

———•———

## About the Author

GREGORY S. BERNS, M.D., Ph.D., is an associate professor of psychiatry and behavioral sciences at Emory University. In the last four years alone, Berns has been profiled twice in the Science section of the *New York Times*, and his research has been featured in media as diverse as *O! The Oprah Magazine, Forbes, Nature, Money, New Scientist, Psychology Today, Self, Reader's Digest,* the *International Herald Tribune*, CNN, NPR, and the BBC. He lives in Atlanta, Georgia, with his wife and children.